The Jacksonian Conservatism of Rufus P. Ranney

Ohio University Press Series on Law, Society, and Politics in the Midwest

SERIES EDITORS: PAUL FINKELMAN AND L. DIANE BARNES

The History of Ohio Law, edited by Michael Les Benedict and John F. Winkler

Frontiers of Freedom: Cincinnati's Black Community, 1802–1868, by Nikki M. Taylor

A Place of Recourse: A History of the U.S. District Court for the Southern District of Ohio, 1803–2003, by Roberta Sue Alexander

The Black Laws: Race and the Legal Process in Early Ohio, by Stephen Middleton

The History of Indiana Law, edited by David J. Bodenhamer and Hon. Randall T. Shepard

The History of Michigan Law, edited by Paul Finkelman and Martin J. Hershock

The Fairer Death: Executing Women in Ohio, by Victor L. Streib

The Rescue of Joshua Glover: A Fugitive Slave, the Constitution, and the Coming of the Civil War, by H. Robert Baker

The History of Nebraska Law, edited by Alan G. Gless

American Pogrom: The East St. Louis Race Riot and Black Politics, by Charles L. Lumpkins

No Winners Here Tonight: Race, Politics, and Geography in One of the Country's Busiest Death Penalty States, by Andrew Welsh-Huggins

Democracy in Session: A History of the Ohio General Assembly, by David M. Gold

The Dred Scott *Case: Historical and Contemporary Perspectives on Race and Law,* edited by David Thomas Konig, Paul Finkelman, and Christopher Alan Bracey

The Jury in Lincoln's America, by Stacy Pratt McDermott

Degrees of Allegiance: Harassment and Loyalty in Missouri's German-American Community during World War I, by Petra DeWitt

Justice and Legal Change on the Shores of Lake Erie: A History of the United States District Court for the Northern District of Ohio, edited by Paul Finkelman and Roberta Sue Alexander

The Life and Death of Gus Reed: A Story of Race and Justice in Illinois during the Civil War and Reconstruction, by Thomas Bahde

Surveillance and Spies in the Civil War: Exposing Confederate Conspiracies in America's Heartland, by Stephen E. Towne

The Jacksonian Conservatism of Rufus P. Ranney: The Politics and Jurisprudence of a Northern Democrat from the Age of Jackson to the Gilded Age, by David M. Gold

DAVID M. GOLD

The Jacksonian Conservatism of Rufus P. Ranney

THE POLITICS AND JURISPRUDENCE OF A NORTHERN DEMOCRAT FROM THE AGE OF JACKSON TO THE GILDED AGE

Ohio University Press ~ Athens

Ohio University Press, Athens, Ohio 45701
ohioswallow.com

Cover image and frontispiece courtesy of the Ohio History Connection.

Printed in the United States of America
Ohio University Press books are printed on acid-free paper ∞ ™

27 26 25 24 23 22 21 20 19 18 17   5 4 3 2 1

Library of Congress Cataloging-in-Publication Data
Names: Gold, David M., 1950– author.
Title: The Jacksonian conservatism of Rufus P. Ranney : the politics and jurisprudence of a northern Democrat from the Age of Jackson to the Gilded Age / David M. Gold.
Description: Athens : Ohio University Press, 2016. | Series: Ohio University Press series on law, society, and politics in the Midwest | Includes bibliographical references and index.
Identifiers: LCCN 2016048996| ISBN 9780821422342 (hc : alk. paper) | ISBN 9780821445792 (pdf)
Subjects: LCSH: Judges—Ohio—Biography. | Ranney, R. P. (Rufus Percival), 1813–1891.
Classification: LCC KF373.R36 G65 2016 | DDC 347.771/035092 [B] —dc23
LC record available at https://lccn.loc.gov/2016048996

CONTENTS

ACKNOWLEDGMENTS

Professional historians usually have lots of help in thinking about, researching, and writing their books. In formal acknowledgments they customarily thank fellow professors, graduate assistants, support staff, funding entities, and others who aided them.

They also absolve everyone but themselves from any responsibility for the defects that nevertheless mar their work. As an independent scholar who held a full-time, nonacademic job while working on this book, I had no funding, little research assistance, and few contacts in the academic world. Consequently, I have few people to thank and no one to blame (even if I were inclined to spread the fault around) for what appears in the following pages. However, I would be remiss if I did not express my gratitude to several individuals. Christian Samito and Austin Allen read the entire manuscript and made valuable suggestions for its improvement. Once the book is in print, I will probably regret not having taken all of them. Michael Les Benedict read and offered thoughtful insights on an early version of the introduction—the sort of thing he has been doing for me since my graduate school days of the 1970s. John Ashworth and John Brooke, neither of whom had any idea who I was, kindly consented to read small portions of the manuscript and assured me that I was not completely off base. Last but not least, Anya Berg, having graciously agreed to rummage through a collection of semi-organized papers at a distant university, sent me useful information that I would not otherwise have obtained. My heartfelt thanks to them all.

Introduction

WHEN RUFUS P. RANNEY turned old enough to vote, Andrew Jackson, the scourge of corporations, occupied the White House, while Jackson's nemesis, the old Federalist John Marshall, presided over the United States Supreme Court. Ranney extolled Jackson as the greatest man of his time; as a good Jacksonian, Ranney sought to keep business corporations under legislative and judicial control. Today Ranney lies buried in the same cemetery as his former client, the oil tycoon John D. Rockefeller. His statue flanks the north entrance of the Cuyahoga County Courthouse in Cleveland; on the other side of the doorway sits a bronze John Marshall. For as long as he remained active in public life, Ranney adhered to the Jacksonian creed of his youth. That he became Rockefeller's favorite lawyer and Marshall's perpetual companion tells us something about both the nature of both Jacksonian Democracy and the evolution of nineteenth-century American conservatism.

After Ranney died in 1891, a distinguished Cleveland attorney remembered him as "a great advocate, a great lawyer, a great judge and a great man." Ranney had been an important figure in Ohio since 1850. A three-time Democratic candidate for Congress in the 1840s, he came to statewide prominence as an outspoken delegate to Ohio's midcentury constitutional convention and then as a judge of the state supreme court. He was the Democratic candidate for governor on the eve of the Civil War, engaging in a series of debates with Republican William Dennison that captivated audiences across the Buckeye State. During the war Ranney stirred up controversy among otherwise like-minded Democrats by recruiting troops for the Union cause. After the war he chaired state Democratic conventions, represented his state party at national conventions, and presided over the Democratic counterpart to the reformist Liberal Republican movement. Ranney also became one of Ohio's leading corporate attorneys, representing Standard Oil and possibly creating the first industrial trust. He was a founder of the Ohio State Bar Association and the Case School of Applied Science, serving as first president of the former and first board chairman of the latter. When Ranney died eulogists ranked him "with the great American lawyers and jurists." Historian James Ford Rhodes called Ranney "a profound jurist" whose decisions on state constitutional law, "for sound doctrine, clearness of thought and expression, are probably not surpassed in the court records of any State."[1]

The importance of nineteenth-century state judges in the development of American common and constitutional law is undeniable; the dearth of biographies of such significant figures might therefore be justification enough for a book on Ranney.[2] But Ranney has the additional merit, from a historian's perspective, of having been a Jacksonian Democrat. Scholars have published works on Roger B. Taney and other Jacksonians who served on the United States Supreme Court before the Civil War; but the Court's jurisdiction, limited to federal issues and such diversity cases as happened to come the Court's way, restricted the scope of the justices' jurisprudence. Antebellum state judges, who plowed a much bigger field, remain a rarely studied breed. It is especially hard to think of full-length works on state judges who were Democrats in the Age of Jackson, even when that age is extended into the 1850s. Ranney's participation in the Ohio constitutional convention of 1850–51, where Democrats and Whigs fought over fundamental ideological issues, together with his immediately subsequent service on the Ohio Supreme Court, offer an opportunity to examine constitutional and common law as developed by a Democratic state judge at the end of the Jacksonian era.

Ranney's jurisprudence can be best understood within the context of Jacksonian Democracy. Historians disagree over the nature of that political phenomenon. One scholar, taking note of interpretations based on class conflict, nostalgia for Jeffersonian republicanism, ethnicity and religion, and so on, concludes that "it is futile to apply such phrases as '*the* age of Jackson,' '*the* Jacksonian persuasion,' or '*the* concept of Jacksonian democracy.'" Another student of Jacksonian politics points out that Democrats occupied a spectrum "which encompassed a wide range of social thought and theory ranging from the anti-capitalist protest of the radicals to the entrepreneurial commercialism of the conservatives." Still, it is fair to say that the chief components of Jacksonian Democracy, whatever the reasons for their being, were majority rule by the "producing classes" of independent farmers and artisans; opposition to "associated wealth," especially in the form of banking corporations with special privileges; equal rights, at least for white men; states' rights; limited government; popular participation in government; and territorial expansion for the benefit of native-born and immigrant whites.[3]

"[T]he first principle of our system," proclaimed Andrew Jackson, is "that the majority is to govern." The will of the majority became the guiding principle of the Democratic Party. The great party organizer, Jackson's vice president and close political ally Martin Van Buren, believed that the party's purpose was to make "every aspect of government . . . directly responsible to the majority will of the people." A Democratic newspaper declared itself "ready to be advised and instructed by the party—the people themselves—we will always *obey the voice of the majority.*" "The democratic theory," intoned the *New York Evening Post,* "is that the people's voice is the supreme law."[4]

Majority rule had a concomitant: political equality. By definition, a majority could not be a wealthy, privileged elite. Some historians reject the term "Jacksonian Democracy" because Jacksonian equality did not extend to women, blacks, and Indians. Furthermore, even "white male democracy"—that is, universal white male suffrage—came about naturally and largely before Jackson took office.[5] But Jackson went beyond suffrage to insist that being of the lower classes did not preclude one from holding public office—"no one man has any more intrinsic right to official station than another," he avowed—or deprive one of the right to the equal solicitude of government. As military governor of Florida in 1821, Jackson declared that "just laws can make no distinction of privilege between the rich and the poor. . . . In general, the great can protect themselves, but the poor and humble require the arm and shield of the law." As president he announced that "the humble members of society, the farmers, mechanics, and laborers," had the same rights under the law as the rich and powerful.

Moreover, Jackson had "great confidence in the virtue of a great majority of the people" and believed that they could be trusted to do the right thing. According to Robert V. Remini, this political and social egalitarianism—the obligation of government to treat all classes the same and to protect the weak from abuse by the rich and powerful—was "the fundamental doctrine of Jacksonian Democracy."[6]

Jacksonians linked equality to limited government. With political power too apt to be abused for the benefit of the wealthy, Jacksonians generally believed that government should be confined to a few essential tasks and otherwise leave people alone. "We want," said an Ohio Democratic congressman, "a plain, a simple, a frugal government." Limited government could be ensured by frequent elections, rotation in office, checks and balances among the three branches of government, the right of the people to instruct their representatives, and strict construction of the powers delegated to the government by the people.[7]

The concept of limited government would make Jacksonian Democracy a constitutional as well as a political movement. Although Jackson feared that too much governmental power at any level could endanger the liberties of the people, he worried primarily about the accretion of power at the federal level. "Consolidation," warned Jackson, would constrict the states' ability "to manage their own concerns in their own way" and thereby imperil the "Liberty of the people."[8] For Jackson, states' rights bolstered the principle of majority rule by keeping the federal government out of entanglements with privately owned internal improvement projects and by leaving "the great mass of legislation" to the state governments, which were closer to the people.[9]

The limited-government, states'-rights ideology of the Democratic Party has been called "functionally proslavery" because it promised to prevent a potential antislavery northern majority from using the federal government to confine or abolish slavery.[10] But the idea of limited government had wider application; even within the states, it sometimes collided with the principle of majority rule. Jackson claimed to have learned his political creed "in the old republican school." In 1829, though, the Old Republican John Randolph scorned "King Numbers" and railed against the "deadly principle" "that a bare majority may oppress, harass, and plunder the minority at pleasure." Virgil Maxcy, Jackson's solicitor of the Treasury, observed in 1833 that a majority was no more exempt than individuals from natural human selfishness. "The majority therefore will oppress and throw an undue share of the burthens of government upon the minority, or promote its own interest at the expense of the minority," said Maxcy, "unless there be interposed, for the protection of the latter, some check upon this selfish principle." Bills of rights were classic examples of such checks, shielding individual rights from legislative action, "however large the majority." Democratic journalist William Leggett, too radical for party regulars, complained in 1837 that despotism had come to mean not only autocratic rule by a single individual but also the tyranny of "the majority of a community, combined under strict party organization, and ruling the minority with dictatorial and imperious sway."[11]

The conflict between majority rule and minority rights came to a head in the state constitutional conventions of the mid-nineteenth century. After Ohio and other states, as a result of their heavy involvement in internal improvement schemes, got hammered by the depression of the late 1830s and 1840s, many Democrats sought strict constitutional controls on the taxing and spending powers of state and local governments, even to the point of prohibiting the creation of public debt approved by the electorate. "Sir, I am not afraid to trust the people," declared one Democrat. "But I will not give my consent that a majority shall tax and virtually rob a minority." The clash between majority rule and minority rights meant that Jacksonian Democrats would leave an ambiguous legacy for jurists and politicians to consult in the postbellum period and for historians to interpret thereafter.[12]

Ranney, as a constitution-maker and judge, viewed issues involving popular government, equality, and limited government through a Jacksonian lens. He strictly construed the state and federal constitutions to safeguard the sovereignty of the states and the rights of the people. In shaping the common law, he enhanced the power of the jury, made corporations liable for injuries to employees and third parties, and protected society's underdogs. Scholarly discussions of Jacksonian jurisprudence tend to focus on a handful of United States Supreme Court cases; but Ranney's opinions, taken as a whole, point to the existence of a broader approach to judicial decision-making that reflected Jacksonian political values.

I do not mean to imply that Ranney or any other judge consciously formulated doctrine or rendered decisions on partisan grounds. Democratic judges sometimes disagreed with each other, and Whig judges often concurred with their Democratic colleagues. When a delegate to Ohio's constitutional convention insinuated that some judges were tools of "the money power," Peter Hitchcock, the state's distinguished chief justice, retorted:

> When I took my seat upon the bench, Mr. Chairman, I took an oath . . . that I would administer justice without respect to persons, and do equal justice to poor and rich; that I would faithfully and impartially discharge and perform all the duties incumbent upon me as a judge of the supreme court, to the best of my ability, understanding, and *agreeably to the constitution and law of this State*. . . . [S]hall I sacrifice that oath in order to meet the wishes of a political cabal or a political party?

Joseph Swan, also of the Ohio Supreme Court, would forfeit his judicial career a few years later by casting a key vote against his own political preference.[13] Still, however conscientious judges might have been about deciding cases on the basis of law rather than politics, the same values underlay their approach to both.

Ranney made his greatest mark where politics and law met: at the constitutional convention and in judicial decisions on Ohio's new constitution. His thinking at this junction reveals the continuing impact of Jacksonian ideology beyond the time when the Age of Jackson supposedly ended and new issues replaced the old ones that had traditionally distinguished Democrats from Whigs. Ranney went into the convention with a reputation as a Radical Democrat, but there was a conservative strain to his thought that became clearer as he steadfastly adhered to Democratic principles through the intensification of the sectional crisis in the 1850s and the eruption of civil war. ("Radical" with a capital *R* generally refers to the dominant wing of the Democratic Party during the Jacksonian period or, later on, to the most antislavery Republicans. When used with a lowercase *r*, "radical" is a more generic adjective.)

To call Ranney a conservative is to raise the perplexing question of the nature of conservatism in nineteenth-century America. Clinton Rossiter called *conservatism* "one of the most confusing words in the glossary of political thought." "The conservative movement," wrote Russell Kirk, "can accommodate a considerable diversity of views on a good many subjects, there being no Test Act or Thirty-Nine Articles of the conservative creed." Perhaps that explains why historians have characterized all the major parties of Ranney's time—Whig, Democratic, and Republican—as conservative.[14]

In the sprawling, brawling, decentralized American democracy of the 1830s and 1840s, no political party could hope to succeed by forcing a creed on its adherents, although Martin Van Buren tried to create a disciplined Democratic Party that would unite behind policies adopted, at least theoretically, by the majority of its members. After Van Buren's accession to the presidency and the shock of the Panic of 1837, Democrats split into Conservative and Radical camps. The Conservatives often cooperated with the Whigs, and some eventually joined the Whig Party. Van Buren, meanwhile, moved the Democratic Party in a Radical direction. Although there were true radicals in America who sought large-scale social or political changes, Van Buren was not by nature one of them. But as party differences sharpened after the Panic and as Democratic leaders insisted upon party loyalty in battles over the administration's economic policies, mainstream democracy came to be characterized by Radical attitudes—extreme hostility toward banks and their paper money, deep suspicion of governmental power that too easily became the tool of corporations and "aristocrats," a belief that "power is always stealing from the many to the few" (the motto of the *United States Telegraph* and other Democratic newspapers). In the battle for the soul of the Democratic Party, the Van Burenites crushed the Conservatives. Jacksonian Democracy came to be Radical Democracy.

Conservatives (with a small "c") found their political home among the Whigs. The *American Review,* the Whigs' intellectual organ from 1845 to 1852, gloried in the conservative label. The distinctive conservative principles of the Whig Party, wrote the *Review,* were "its steady and habitual submission to law—its deference for vested rights—and abhorrence of all violent and disorderly attempts to alter or overthrow existing institutions." Whigs, as true conservatives, were not averse to change, but they insisted upon "the intelligent and seasonable combination of Order and Improvement." The conservative party, according to the *Review,* "venerates the wisdom of experience and loves the virtue and purity, the customs and associations of the past, and feels its connection with the race, and would not strike boldly out of the track, or forsake the direction or quicken the prudent pace at which the world has arrived at its present position." In contrast, "Young America," the exuberant young Democrats who wanted to create a new American culture and fulfill America's "manifest destiny" to spread freedom across the continent, "despises the old-womanish maxims of the Past . . . would set the world upon wholly new feet, and at once reduce an ideal theory . . . to practice, at any cost and in the face of any difficulties. There is a law and order, a slow and sure, a distrustful and cautious party—a conservative, a Whig party; and there is a radical, innovating, hopeful, boastful, improvident and go-ahead party—a Democratic, a Loco-Foco party!"[15]

Jacksonian Democrats gladly conceded the conservative designation to the Whigs, calling themselves the party "of movement, of progress, of reform." After listing a host of reforms accomplished in the United States and England—the extension of suffrage, moderation of the penal laws, abolition of imprisonment for debt, establishment of asylums for the handicapped, restriction of monopolies, and so on—the *United States Magazine and Democratic Review* declared them all to be "the legitimate fruits" of American Democratic and English liberal principles. Some antebellum northern Democrats were Burkean conservatives who believed in "the importance of community, the sanctity of established institutions, the authority of existing arrangements, and the necessity of public policies that harmonized with local customs." But while the Democratic Party was broad enough to accommodate admirers of Edmund Burke, Burkean conservatism appealed more to Whigs than to Democrats.[16]

It is true that even in Jackson's day many Democrats revered the wisdom of the past. When Orestes Brownson, in his Radical Democratic phase, called for a society in which every man worked for himself in his own shop or on his own farm, he was looking back to "Jefferson's vision of a self-sufficient yeomanry" while "articulat[ing] an implicit ideal of Democratic theory and policy." But Jefferson was not a conservative. Russell Kirk observed that Jefferson's doctrines "always were more radical than his practice"; but the doctrines were the stuff to which Jacksonian Democrats appealed. No one who derived the equality of men from universal reason, believed in a "wall of separation" between church and state, saw Shays's Rebellion as a salutary "refreshing" of the "tree of liberty," and sympathized with the French Revolution could have qualified as a conservative.[17]

It similarly seems a stretch to regard the Jacksonians of Ranney's time as conservative for seeking to "restore" the Jeffersonian radicalism that had flourished in their own lifetimes. Andrew Jackson's leading biographer, Robert V. Remini, described Jackson as a "conservative, cautious man" with "a conservative philosophy of government."[18] That is not how Jackson's contemporaries saw him. Jackson's National Republican and Whig opponents thought of the president and his followers as revolutionaries. A Boston newspaper equated Jacksonianism with Jacobinism. "Its Alpha is ANARCHY and its Omega is DESPOTISM," the paper howled. Henry Clay warned about Jackson, "We are in the midst of a revolution, hitherto bloodless, but rapidly tending towards a total change of the pure republican character of the Government." Seven years later, with Jackson's chosen successor in the White House, New York Whigs were still crying, "We are in the midst of a revolution! Your Federal Government . . . is undergoing a change fatal to its republican character."[19] Even allowing for rhetorical excess, it is clear that Jackson's enemies attributed his failings to radicalism, not conservatism.

Jackson did not think of himself as a conservative. When a question involving Conservative Democrats arose, he declared his detestation of conservatism in general as well as the political faction. Conservatives, Jackson asserted, think "the people unfit to govern themselves."[20] After Jackson's death, a writer for the *Democratic Review* defined radicalism as "that which is constantly *modifying, changing, reforming,* and *improving* the institutions of society," as opposed to conservatism, which was stuck in the past. The author hailed Jefferson and Jackson as the "champions of Radicalism."[21]

Ranney admired Andrew Jackson and his principles. Ranney believed in equality among (white) men, popular government, a government without the power to direct either economic or moral life; he attacked corporate privilege, favored hard money, and sympathized with the legal codification movement. Although advocacy of small government today tends to get people tagged as conservatives, in the 1840s it was a hallmark of Radical Democracy. And no one who approved of Jackson's populism and egalitarianism could have passed as a conservative at that time. The Whigs who knew Ranney in 1850 certainly did not regard him as one. They called him radical, even "destructive." Recalling Ranney's role at the constitutional convention, a Republican paper in 1859 said that he "took an active part in favor of the most radical views."[22]

But soon after the convention, mainstream Democrats, including Ranney, began to think of themselves as conservatives. Before then both Whigs and Democrats had often invoked the past, but for different reasons. For Whigs, the past was a teacher, a guide, and a constraint. "Our American liberty," intoned Daniel Webster, "has an ancestry, a pedigree, a history." Edward Everett asserted that the Founding Fathers had built the "temple of freedom" on "history and tradition," digging the foundation "deep down to the eternal rock" so that the temple might be expanded on that foundation in the future. For Democrats, the past was a launching pad for future progress. The *Democratic Review* warned against an undue appeal to "the wisdom of our fathers" and a fear of "untried experiments." The American Revolution, said the *Review,* was the boldest of experiments, "the germ from which has sprung the revolution of the world." Despite occasional bumps in the road, Democrats in the 1850s could look back on a steady march of progress against conservatism. The Revolutionary generation had overthrown monarchical government. Jefferson had routed the Federalists,

Jackson and his successors the National Republicans and Whigs. The demise of property qualifications for voting, followed by high voter turnout in boisterous political campaigns, and the change from the appointive to the elective method of choosing major public officers, spoke to the advance of government by "the people."[23]

In the 1850s, though, the "go-ahead party" perceived a new threat, not from conservatives but from radical abolitionists and the new Republican Party. Democrats thought they saw American institutions under assault by a "revolutionary and agrarian" party filled with fanatics and determined to use its numerical majority to discard hard-won political compromises, run roughshod over the Constitution, and create a powerful central government. They complained of the "revolutionary movements" of the "black republicans." The old Whig Rufus Choate, who supported the Democrat Buchanan for president in 1856, disdained the Republicans' "revolutionary banner." The state party convention that nominated Ranney for governor called upon the people of Ohio to rebuke "the wanton, factious, revolutionary designs of the leaders of the self-styled Republican party." Believing themselves charged by history with preserving American liberty, Democrats adopted the mantle of conservatism and wore it through political upheavals, civil war, and industrialization. Men such as Ranney remained devoted to the Jeffersonian tradition of strict construction of the government's constitutional powers, to states' rights, and to a government close to the people. Ranney went from radical to conservative without changing his principles or his party.[24]

It was Ranney's conservatism that drove him to participate in a splinter reform movement in the early 1870s, a movement aimed at ending corruption in public offices and reinvigorating the limited government ideals of an earlier age. By 1875 Ranney was back in the party's good graces, chairing the Democratic state convention, but he never again ran for elective office. Instead he concentrated on his law practice and the development of the legal profession, associating with legal and business elites, representing railroads and Standard Oil, and presiding over the state bar association. How the Radical Jacksonian Democrat came to be one of John D. Rockefeller's favorite attorneys, and what that turn of events meant for Democratic ideology, are intriguing questions. The answers must be speculative because Ranney stepped back from the limelight and left little record of his political or legal thought in the last fifteen years of his life. But the attitudes of Ranney and some other old Jacksonian jurists in the Gilded Age showed a remarkable continuity with the positions of their younger, radical selves in favor of limited government, laissez-faire economics, general incorporation laws, and, at least in Ranney's case, judicial review, legal science, and an educated bar.

This book, a study of Ranney's public life, is based on newspaper reports, the published proceedings of the Ohio constitutional convention, the reported opinions of the Ohio Supreme Court, and the records of the Ohio State Bar Association. Finding out about Ranney's personal life or his behind-the-scenes role in law or politics is impossible. No cache of Ranney correspondence appears to have survived. Ranney may not have been a prolific letter-writer, and he apparently did not keep letters he received. When an autograph collector asked him for a letter signed by Ranney's one-time law partner Benjamin F. Wade, Ranney replied that he had seen no reason to keep Wade's letters because they did not relate to business. "Besides," he continued, "I have several times destroyed piles of papers that were no longer of value to any one, to get handily at those which were."[25] Searches of the usual sources have turned up almost nothing. Newspapers from Portage, Ashtabula, and Trumbull Counties, where Ranney lived before 1850, have survived incomplete, and those were mostly Whig papers that gave little space to Democrats. Ranney apparently never set down his ideas on politics or law in systematic fashion. He wrote no books, and the indexes to nineteenth-century law journals contain no entries for him as an author, although he was for a few months a department editor of a short-lived legal periodical.[26] But even without documentation of Ranney's inner world, a study of Ranney's long and noteworthy public life reveals the durability of the relationship between Jacksonian political and legal thought and the Jacksonian contribution to American conservatism in the second half of the nineteenth century.

ONE

Western Reserve Democrat

AT TWO O'CLOCK in the morning on February 22, 1839, Benjamin F. Wade delivered a scathing attack on the Ohio Fugitive Slave Bill to a half-empty state senate chamber. Introduced at the behest of Kentucky slaveholders, the bill would make it easier for masters to recover runaways who sought freedom in Ohio. "[U]ntil the laws of nature and of nature's God are changed," Wade vowed, "I will never recognize the right of one man to hold his fellow man a slave." Let the slaveholders, with their doctrine of states' rights, "shrink back beyond their own dark borders, and there remain, a plague spot on the body politic," roared the future Radical Republican; let them not look to Ohio for aid and sympathy. As a member of the Whig minority, Wade could not defeat the Fugitive Slave Bill. If he hoped at least to influence his young law partner with his speech, he was disappointed there too. Rufus P. Ranney was and always would be a Democrat, an advocate of states' rights, and unsympathetic toward abolitionism. When Ranney ran for governor in 1859, Wade campaigned against him.[1]

Ranney rose to local prominence in the 1840s as a Democratic politician and lawyer, but his early life is mostly a mystery. He was born to an undistinguished descendant of Thomas Ranny, who immigrated from Scotland in the seventeenth century and settled in Middletown, Connecticut. Ranney's grandfather Elijah moved to Blandford in western Massachusetts in 1773, where his wife Mary gave birth to their son Rufus in 1779 or 1780. Rufus married a local girl, Dolly D. Blair, with whom he had eight children. The Ranneys were farmers in an area not noted for rural prosperity. Hampden County was a region of hardscrabble farms around the time Elijah Ranney settled there and no better off in the early nineteenth century.[2]

Rufus and Dolly's third child, Rufus Percival Ranney, was born October 30, 1813. Nothing is known of his life in Blandford: his health, education, religious training, or anything else. In 1824 the Ranneys moved to Freedom Township in Portage County, Ohio. Portage County was part of the Western Reserve, a large swath of northeastern Ohio once claimed by Connecticut and settled largely by New Englanders. Freedom Township was still a wilderness, lacking roads, schools, and churches. When the Ranneys came, Rufus senior "cleared four acres, built a cabin, and for a year they lived on the game killed." The elder Rufus, "an honest, industrious farmer . . . in humble circumstances," could not spare young Rufus's labor or afford to send him away to school. The boy received only one winter of formal education in Ohio. He may have acquired some learning from his mother, who, according to one source, "had received a good education" and "was very attentive to her children."[3]

Notwithstanding the paucity of information about Rufus P. Ranney's youth, one thing is clear: he hungered for knowledge. A Lincolnesque story has it that Ranney, unable to go to school, chopped wood for a local merchant to earn money for a volume of Virgil.[4] In 1833 he headed off to Western Reserve College in Hudson, a small Presbyterian school founded just seven years earlier. Ranney showed up "in a suit of homespun butternut." The college supposedly had the same admission requirements as Yale, including knowledge of Greek and Latin, but it is doubtful that the college adhered to those standards; Ranney learned to read French on his own, but no one ever claimed that he knew the classical languages. Ranney taught and performed manual labor, as all students were expected to do, but gave up in the spring of 1834. He may have been disappointed with the college, although his attachment to the school in later years suggests a lifelong fondness for the institution. Perhaps financial hardship impelled him to turn to more practical pursuits. There is no way to tell if the college left any significant impression on Ranney, but possibly it helped shape his views on one issue that would become crucial for his political career. Shortly before

Ranney's arrival, the college became a center of antislavery agitation. Abolitionist proposals set off heated debates, but the idea of colonizing American blacks in Africa enjoyed nearly universal support. Ranney's experience at the college during the formative days of the organized antislavery movement possibly implanted antislavery ideas in his mind, but the political record of his postcollegiate career reveals no sympathy with abolitionism.[5]

Perhaps it was through political activities on campus or in the village that Ranney met lawyers and future abolitionist stalwarts Joshua R. Giddings and Benjamin F. Wade. Giddings and Wade, like Ranney, were the sons of farmers who had moved to the Western Reserve. Also like Ranney, they had had little formal education when they took up the study of law. In 1831 Giddings and Wade formed a law partnership in Jefferson, in Ashtabula County. In 1834 or 1835 the flourishing firm took Ranney on as a law student. He walked from his home to Jefferson, arriving with just the clothes he was wearing and an extra shirt tucked into his hat. In those days lawyers typically received their training as apprentices in the offices of established attorneys. They read whatever law books their mentors might possess, copied documents, ran errands, and generally observed the business of the office. After a time they presented themselves to an examining committee for admission to the bar. In Ohio the aspiring lawyer had to obtain a certificate from an attorney stating that the applicant had "regularly and attentively" studied law for two years, was of good moral character, and had the knowledge and ability to perform his professional duties. Two justices of the supreme court, or attorneys designated by them, then conducted an examination. According to Albert G. Riddle, another Western Reserve lawyer and politician, these requirements were not mere formalities. "The examinations were thorough and searching," Riddle remembered, "often conducted by the judges themselves." On the other hand, in 1845 future Ohio governor John Brough reportedly gained admission to the bar by treating the examining committee to the best bourbon in town. The nature of Ranney's exam is unknown, but he passed, was admitted in Trumbull County in 1836, and set up practice in Warren.[6]

There are no contemporary portraits, in pictures or words, of Ranney as a boy or young man, but two men who knew him provided descriptions in later years. In remarks at a banquet of the Cleveland bar in 1881, Portage County probate judge Daniel R. Tilden, a native New Englander several years older than Ranney, recalled Ranney as solemn-looking and "a little unsociable," with "a sort of prescience . . . of the dignities and honors that awaited him in his profession." Riddle, who was born in Hampden

County, Massachusetts, less than three years after Ranney and was brought to Geauga County as an infant, made the real-life Ranney a character in a novel. *Bart Ridgeley: A Story of Northern Ohio,* published in 1873 but set in the 1830s, tells the story of a young law student who becomes Ranney's close friend. Riddle describes Ranney as "above the usual height, broad and heavy-shouldered, with a massive head and strong face, a high narrow forehead; rather shy in manner, and taciturn," yet able to indulge in a good laugh with friends. Ranney already had a reputation as "a man of strong, profound, ingenious mind, with much power of sarcasm," and seemed "destined to a distinguished career." Although Ranney went to church with Bart, he and Wade were suspected of having "no religion of any kind."[7]

Riddle attributes to the young Ranney a mature legal philosophy. When Bart asks whether "his lamp of genius" would aid a lawyer in his work, Ranney replies:

> It might, and he might be misled by its flare. He would do better to use the old lights of the law. Some are a little lurid, and some a little blue, but always the same in tempest or calm. The law, as you have doubtless discovered, is founded in a few principles of obvious right. Their application to cases is artificial. The law, for its own wise purposes, takes care of itself; of its own force, it embraces everything, investigates everything, construes itself, and enforces itself, as the sole power in the premises. Its rules in the text-books read plain enough, and are not difficult of apprehension. The uncertainty of the law arises in the doubt and uncertainty of the facts; and hence the doubt about which, of many rules, ought to govern. A man of genius, as you describe him, ought to become a good lawyer; he would excel in the investigation and presentation of facts; but none but a lawyer saturated with the spirit of the law until he comes to have a legal instinct, can with accuracy apply it.[8]

That Ranney had come to such conclusions at an early age is possible, but Riddle may have been projecting the thought of a mature and experienced lawyer and judge back in time onto a man in his twenties. The foundation of a few, unchanging principles, the importance of careful investigation and presentation of facts, and the recognition of the "spirit" of the law would all find a place in Ranney's jurisprudence.

Giddings and Wade had a falling out in 1836, and Ranney soon replaced Giddings as Wade's partner. The new firm remained intact for ten years despite Wade's election to the Ohio Senate as a Whig and Ranney's run for Congress as a Democrat. "The firm of Wade & Ranney had quite the lead in Ashtabula," recalled Riddle years later. "The rapid rise of Mr. Ranney at the bar and the constant calls to Trumbull, were such as to warrant, require, the opening of an office at its shiretown—Warren." Ranney moved back to Warren, "which soon brought the partners to the lead in that wealthy and important county also." The partnership finally dissolved with Wade's election to the court of common pleas in February 1847. Soon thereafter Ranney seems to have entered into a short-lived professional association with Ebenezer Spalding, a thirty-year-old graduate of Yale who had attended Harvard Law School for a time before moving to Ravenna, Ohio, in 1840. He then formed a more durable partnership with Charles S. Simonds and Darius Caldwell, both of whom had studied law in the office of Wade & Ranney.[9]

Ranney's legal practice probably involved a great deal of commercial and property law. The growing population of the Western Reserve and thriving trade of Lake Erie ports produced lots of litigation. "It was not until comparatively recently that the admiralty laws of congress were extended to the great lakes," wrote Riddle.

> Their want in the meantime was supplied by legislation of the state, which permitted suits for supplies, wages, claims for damages, for all causes of action against a craft by name, in any county along the lake coast, in whose water service of process could be made, no matter where or by whom owned. Geauga had a port, Ashtabula had two. There was power in the courts to change the venue of marine cases, as of others. Shipping increased. Lake Erie was stormy. There were many cases for collisions, especially between steamers and sailers, as between steam vessels or sailers. Many of these became famous cases. They paid well.[10]

Wade served for two years as prosecuting attorney of Ashtabula County, so perhaps he brought a criminal defense practice to the firm after his term ended. The Panic of 1837 generated legal business, including "[j]udgments innumerable, followed by creditors' bills, to uncover properties and reach equities." Much of this business, though, was unremunerative. The new firm of Wade & Ranney "had its full share of this unsatisfactory business, procured its full share of never to be satisfied judgments." The twenty reported cases between 1836 and 1851 in which Wade & Ranney or Ranney alone appeared as counsel before the Ohio Supreme Court involved a wide range of subjects.[11]

On May 1, 1839, Ranney felt secure enough to marry. His bride, Adeline Warner, was the daughter of a lawyer, local politician, and soon-to-be judge of the Ashtabula County Court of Common Pleas. Between 1840 and 1859 the couple had six children, but only three survived into adulthood and one of those died at the age of thirty. One of the two remaining children, John Rufus, would practice law with his father. The other, Charles Percival, became a successful Cleveland businessman. Rufus and Adeline also raised Henry Clay Ranney, whose father, Rufus's brother Elijah, died in 1836 when Henry was seven. H. C. Ranney achieved prominence as a lawyer and businessman.[12]

Ben Wade, Joshua Giddings, and their mentor, Elisha Whittlesey, were all Whigs, and from the name of Ranney's nephew it appears that the Ranney clan included enthusiastic supporters of the National Republican and later Whig hero Henry Clay. The Whigs did not share the Democrats' limited-government views. They believed that government had a positive role to play in the economic development of the nation and the moral improvement of individuals. Most Whigs had less sympathy for foreign immigrants, especially Catholics, than Democrats did, but they tended to be far less racist. By the 1830s the Western Reserve was well on its way to becoming a Whig stronghold and a hotbed of political abolitionism. But Rufus P. Ranney became a Democrat even before he could vote. Budding politicians typically began their public careers by engaging in civic activities. Ranney belonged to an independent militia company, helped found the Historical and Philosophical Society of Ashtabula County and the Jefferson Library Association, and was twice elected a trustee of the Village of Jefferson. In 1843, not yet thirty years old, he received the Democratic nomination for United States representative from Ohio's newly created twentieth congressional district.[13]

The odd-year congressional election resulted from a law that gave Ohio two additional representatives and required that all House districts throughout the country be single-member districts. Ranney ran against Giddings and Ben Wade's brother Edward, candidate of the antislavery Liberty Party, in Ohio's new twentieth district, comprising Ashtabula, Cuyahoga, Geauga, and Lake Counties. History books and surviving newspapers reveal little about the issues discussed in the race, but the party platform adopted a few months later in anticipation of the gubernatorial and presidential elections shows where the Democrats stood on national issues: against a national bank, paper currency, a protective tariff, distribution of the federal surplus revenue to the states, and the assumption of state debts by the federal government; in favor of "immediate possession" of all of the Oregon Territory, then being disputed with Great Britain.[14]

Notwithstanding the existence of a soft-money, pro-banking wing of the Democratic Party, these were all standard Democratic positions. There is no reason to think that Ranney disagreed with any of them. But 1843 was a Whig year, and Ranney was running against a firmly ensconced Whig in a resolutely Whiggish part of the state. Whigs carried the state elections, and although Democrats won a majority of the congressional races, helped no doubt by gerrymandered districts, Ranney lost to Giddings in a landslide. Ranney pulled in just 35.13 percent of the vote, but that was a higher percentage than all but one of Giddings's opponents polled in seven subsequent races, and that one received 35.17 percent.[15]

Ranney returned to Warren in Trumbull County in 1845. In September 1846 the Democratic convention for the nineteenth congressional district (Portage, Summit, and Trumbull Counties) unanimously nominated him for the U.S. House of Representatives. The convention adopted a platform containing the usual Democratic planks in favor of low tariffs and against special privileges for banks, but it also recognized two new realities: the Mexican War and the rise of political abolitionism. The convention approved a "vigorous prosecution" of the war and condemned "the course and conduct" of Giddings and Daniel R. Tilden, the nineteenth district's Whig incumbent, "to embitter the North towards the South." The sectional conflict, the convention declared, required "concession and compromise." Ranney's acceptance speech, reported the *Portage Sentinel*, reinforced "the abiding confidence reposed in him by the democracy of the district, and to his well established reputation as a man of the highest order of talent."[16]

Ranney's opponents were Whig John Crowell, another antislavery lawyer of New England provenance, and Liberty Party candidate John Hutchins. Ranney ran slightly ahead of his party in all three of the district's counties, carrying Portage and Trumbull by small margins but losing overwhelmingly in Summit. In the district as a whole he lost to Crowell by fewer than four percentage points. It was the closest he would come to winning legislative office. The narrowness of the loss is misleading, however. Hutchins received more than 7 percent of the votes. Had he not been in the race, almost all of his support surely would have gone to Crowell.[17]

Ranney got one more shot at Congress in 1848, when, the *Western Reserve Chronicle* tartly remarked, the Democrats were "again deceived into the fallacious hope of his success at the ballot box." As election day neared, the Democratic *Portage Sentinel* trumpeted the Democratic Party's national principles, including the traditional opposition to a national bank, a protective tariff, and special legislation that bestowed "exclusive charters and privileges" on banks. But slavery trumped all the old issues, especially in the Western Reserve. The *Sentinel* listed popular sovereignty—"the rights of the people of States and Territories of framing their own institutions"—as a national Democratic principle, along with "[o]pposition to all principles of a sectional character" and "to all fanatics who seek the dissolution of the American Union." (Fanatics, in the parlance of the time, meant abolitionists.) However, no one who advocated such positions stood any chance of election in the Reserve. Giddings had gone over to the new Free Soil Party. Crowell, running as a Whig, openly avowed his support for the free-soil movement.[18]

The Free Soil Party grew out of a huge antislavery convention held in Buffalo, New York, in August 1848. Disaffected Whigs and Democrats with divergent views on various issues, along with Liberty men looking for a more effective antislavery vehicle than their existing party, adopted a "national platform of freedom." The platform declared that slavery's existence depended solely on state law, which the federal government lacked the power to annul. The Free Soilers asserted, however, that the federal government had no authority to establish slavery, and that it had a duty "to relieve itself from all responsibility for the existence or continuance of slavery wherever that government possesses constitutional authority to legislate on that subject." The platform had little to say about the plight of slaves in the South, but it evinced deep concern for the condition of white settlers in the western territories, including the lands acquired in the Mexican War. "Let the soil of our extensive domains be ever kept free, for the hardy pioneers of our own land, and the oppressed and banished of other lands, seeking homes of comfort and fields of enterprise in the new world," the convention resolved. "[W]e demand freedom and established institutions for our brethren in Oregon, now exposed to hardships, peril and massacre, by the reckless hostility of the slave power to the establishment of free government for free territories, and not only for them, but for our new brethren in California and New Mexico."[19]

On September 30 antislavery activist Benjamin F. Hoffman challenged Ranney to state publicly his responses to a series of questions: on the power of Congress over slavery in the territories and the District of Columbia; on his attitude toward the use of such power and toward the Free Soil platform; and on his preference in the approaching presidential election. Although Ranney did not directly answer Hoffman's query about the Buffalo platform, most of his replies should have warmed the hearts of Free Soilers. "[O]ur flag should never float over another foot of slave territory," Ranney declared. It was well-settled that slavery existed in a state by virtue of local law; neither Congress nor a territorial legislature had the power to establish it. More than a decade ago he had publicly called upon Congress to abolish slavery in the nation's capital, and time had only strengthened his opinion. As for the newly acquired territories, Ranney had no doubt of the power of Congress to prohibit slavery there, and he was "in favor of and would support such prohibition." Keeping New Mexico and California free was "due to humanity, to republican principles, to our character and interests as a people, to Mexico, and above all to the poor of our own and other lands, who shall go there to find homes for themselves and their families, and who would be beggared and disgraced by the contact of slave labor." Furthermore, Ranney recommended that public lands in the West "be *freely* granted, in limited quantities, to actual settlers *only*. This . . . would secure them against monopolists and speculators of all kinds; and would settle them with a hardy and industrious population of *freemen*." If elected, Ranney promised, he would "support all such measures as were calculated to maintain" his antislavery views, "taking care at all times not to overstep the limits of the National compact, or to encroach upon the reserved rights of the States."[20]

The one reply of Ranney's that must have stuck in the craw of Free Soil men was his support of Democrat Lewis Cass for president. Cass, a former governor of the Michigan Territory, secretary of war, and minister to France, advocated popular sovereignty in the territories, which allowed for the possibility that some or all of the territories would embrace slavery. The Whigs had nominated Louisiana slaveholder and Mexican War hero Zachary Taylor, a man with no political experience or principles until he discovered in 1848 that he was "a Whig but not an ultra Whig." The Free Soilers in Buffalo, abhorring both candidates, nominated former president Martin Van Buren. Crowell, a four-square supporter of the Buffalo platform, announced that he would not vote for either Cass or Taylor. Ranney knew that Van Buren could not win. Of the two major-party candidates he preferred Cass, a "tried Statesman" whose views were known and whose "education, habits, location, and associations must all incline him to detest

Slavery." A Democratic vote for Van Buren, Ranney declared, would simply help elect the political cipher and southern slaveholder Taylor. Of course, Whigs made the same argument in reverse. Addressing the Whigs of the Western Reserve, former New York governor and soon-to-be U.S. senator William H. Seward declared that "seceding Whigs can only give success to the party of Lewis Cass."[21]

Democratic papers professed confidence in Ranney's candidacy. One pointed out that Ranney was "the uncompromising opponent of every species of slavery." But the Whig *Western Reserve Chronicle* mocked the Democrats' persistence in nominating Ranney for Congress and, on the very day on which the paper published Ranney's reply to Hoffman, it also printed the claim of Whig Party committeemen that Ranney denied the power of Congress to prohibit slavery in the territories and the District of Columbia. The *Chronicle* believed that the claim was unfounded, but it questioned the honesty of someone who professed to oppose the extension of slavery and yet supported Cass for president.[22]

Ranney stood no chance of election. He lost all three counties, receiving 44 percent of the vote in the district as a whole, the same as the Democratic candidate for governor and a few points higher than Cass's plurality in the three-way presidential race.[23] After three straight defeats, Ranney gave up the hopeless cause. The nineteenth district would not elect another Democratic congressman until the twentieth century. But Ranney's defeat meant that he was available for election as a delegate to the state constitutional convention in 1849. His espousal there of Radical Democratic principles would bring him statewide prominence and a seat on the Ohio Supreme Court.

TWO

The Constitutional Convention

Corporations and Citizens

IN 1864 the Union Pacific Railroad, chartered by Congress to build a railroad from Missouri to the Pacific, created the secretly affiliated Crédit Mobilier of America to serve as its construction contractor. Through bribes of cash and stock, Crédit Mobilier ensured that Congress appropriated money to pay inflated invoices, to the immense profit of Union Pacific's shareholders. The scandal came to light during the 1872 presidential campaign, by which time Rufus P. Ranney had been decrying the chumminess between corporations and Congress for years. In a widely noted speech in 1867, Ranney lambasted the corruption of the Republican administration, claiming that "vast manufacturing interests," their agents loaded with money with which to promote their clients' interests, "clustered around the Government" demanding legislation for the benefit of the industrialists. The problem was hardly confined to the federal government. As Luke P. Poland, the antislavery Democrat-turned-Republican who chaired the House committee investigating the Crédit Mobilier affair, lamented, "gigantic corporations" had gained such control over state legislatures that in some states they had become "the ruling power." Ranney's concern about the baleful influence of corporations on both the political process and the economic well-being of individual citizens long predated the postbellum rise of huge industrial and railroad enterprises. It impelled some of his most dogged argumentation at Ohio's constitutional convention in 1850–51, argumentation that cemented his reputation as a Radical Democrat.[1]

After suffering his third straight defeat in pursuit of a seat in Congress, Ranney won a place in the forthcoming convention in a popular election of delegates. Ohio's first constitution could be amended only by a convention, for which proponents of judicial reform and biennial legislative sessions had called in vain before 1846. In the late 1840s an accumulation of judicial backlogs, financial crises, partisan conflicts, and bribery and election scandals raised the pressure for a convention to an irresistible level.[2]

Whigs viewed the prospect of a convention with foreboding. Whig state representative Miller Pennington warned against "rush[ing] headlong upon the wild sea of experiment." But Democrats denounced apprehensions about the "ghosts of anarchy and confusion and agrarianism and disorganization and civil strife." If the people could not be trusted to address acknowledged defects in the constitution, then the American adventure in popular government must be deemed a failure. The Democratic *Portage Sentinel* listed the constitutional reforms demanded by Democrats: a state legislature that would meet only once every two years; popular election of judges and other state and county officers; a prohibition on the incurrence of state debt and the creation of banking corporations without popular approval; "equal distribution" of the "burdens of taxation," with no special favors for stockholders of banks or other business corporations; judicial reform to make the operations of the legal system simpler and more expeditious; referral of all proposed legislation of a local or private character to a special county tribunal; and a general school law to ensure a good education for poor children, funded by "an equal tax upon all the property within the State."[3]

Advocates of a convention finally succeeded in 1849, when partisan passions had reached a fever pitch and popular disenchantment with government seemed deeper than ever. The General Assembly set April 1, 1850, as the date for the election of convention delegates and created special election districts, with each district choosing a number of delegates equal to the number of its state representatives and senators. Trumbull and Geauga counties formed one district, with three delegates to be elected in common. The Whigs and Democrats of Trumbull County called for interparty cooperation to choose delegates on a nonpartisan basis. According to the free-soil *Western Reserve Chronicle*, the central committee of the Free Democrats, as Ohio's Free Soilers called themselves, responded by sending a questionnaire on the issues to likely nominees, to which all but Ranney responded. The paper accused Ranney and other major-party politicians of striking a bargain by which Whigs Peter Hitchcock of Geauga and Jacob Perkins of Trumbull would be nominated along with Ranney and then of managing poorly attended county conventions to consummate the deal. In their lust for office, charged the *Chronicle,* the Whig and Democratic Party leaders had forfeited all principle. "Can the whigs support [Ranney's] radical notions, which they believe he entertains? . . . Are the whigs really in love with Ranney, and the democrats in love with Hitchcock? If there are two politicians in the district who stand farther apart than Hitchcock and Ranney, we are unacquainted with them." The Free Democrats, unwilling to participate in an "unholy alliance," nominated three candidates of their own.[4]

In the election Ranney, then living in Trumbull, led all candidates by a wide margin in both counties. Two of the Free Democrats ran neck-and-neck with Hitchcock and Perkins in Geauga, but the combined Whig-Democratic slate comfortably outpolled the Free Democrats in Trumbull and secured all the district's seats at the convention. In the state as a whole Democrats won a majority of the seats. A minority of Conservative Democrats occasionally combined with Whigs to stymie some of the more Radical proposals, but the document that emerged from the convention represented a victory for the mainstream of the Democratic Party.[5]

At thirty-six years of age Ranney was one of the younger convention delegates. Familiar to voters in his congressional district and to lawyers in the Western Reserve, he was probably little known in the rest of the state. His prominent role at the convention would give him a statewide reputation as a staunch Jacksonian Democrat. At the convention Ranney praised Andrew Jackson as "the greatest man of this age," whose "great and glorious deeds" entitled him "to the highest niche in the temple of fame!" A disgusted adversary labeled Ranney "a good representative of the Locofoco, destructive agrarian party of this country." The harshness of this characterization no doubt stemmed in part from Ranney's tendency to antagonize men with whom he disagreed, including some fellow Democrats. Taking criticisms of his political positions as personal affronts, he sometimes responded with uncivil barbs. From the Whig point of view, the characterization had a firm basis in political principle. Ranney went into the convention as a known Radical.[6]

In an age when "liberal" was rarely used in political discourse, American commentators usually divided the political world into two groups, conservatives and radicals. There were, said the Whig *American Review,* two parties, the cautious, conservative Whigs and the rash, radical Democrats.[7] There were genuine radicals in Jacksonian America: socialists and Transcendentalists who formed rural communes; workingmen who denounced private property and organized their own political parties; abolitionists who saw the Constitution as a pact with the devil and who would sooner sunder the Union than live within it with slavery. But the so-called Radicals of the Democratic Party were what would later be called classical liberals; they were, said the *Democratic Review,* simply more "ardent spirits" who sometimes "carr[ied] their ideas to the verge of extravagance"—a necessary "counterbalance [to] the opposite tendency to anti-liberal opinions." They were followers of Jefferson, Madison, and "accredited writers upon political economy"; nothing they proposed, "when fairly understood, with proper allowances, should excite the apprehensions of the most sober-minded republican." The Radicals' creed, shared with all Democrats, was individual liberty, respect for the rights and property of all, and no "exclusive privileges" or "selfish monopolies." Their notion of government was "[a]s little government as possible; that little emanating from, and controlled by, the people; and uniform in its application to all." Even the Whig *American Review* called Radicals rather innocuously "the party of change and reform" and "a spur to the progress of the State and of society."[8]

Whigs often used the term "radical" disparagingly. Just as Democrats routinely referred to Whigs as Federalists in order to tar them with what they saw as a discredited, antidemocratic political creed, Whigs frequently called the Democrats radicals as a way of deprecating their gravitas. But the Whigs also had a more pejorative term at their disposal: loco-foco. "Loco-foco" was the name of a match used by real New York City Radicals in 1834 to provide illumination at a Democratic meeting after party regulars turned off the gas lights. From then on stridently egalitarian, antibank Democrats were called loco-focos by their political adversaries. Whig editors lumped the loco-focos together with a variety of perceived social disorganizers: the radical equalizers and land redistributionists known as agrarians; the feminist and abolitionist social reformer Fanny Wright; and others whom they plainly regarded as dangerous and possibly crazy. In 1836, when Andrew Jackson's chosen successor, Martin Van Buren, was running for president, a Whig newspaper in Maine expressed relief that Van Buren would "oppose the measures of the loco-focos, agrarians, and Fanny-Wright-men of our country." As bad as Jacksonism was, declared the paper, it was "infinitely preferable to the disorganizing doctrines and dogmas of the infidels and anarchists who compose this lowest of all political parties."[9] What the paper could not foresee was that the Democratic Party would soon move in a Radical direction.

The Democrats, like the Whigs, consisted of a mélange of interests. Jackson's war on the Second Bank of the United States and Van Buren's subsequent adoption of laissez-faire economics and the independent treasury, which removed federal funds from private banks, pushed a significant minority of influential Democrats into electoral alliances with the Whigs. The Democratic Party split into Conservative and Radical camps. Radical hard-money, anticorporate, laissez-faire thought came to characterize the mainstream of the Democratic Party. Conservatives—the designation applied by themselves and their antagonists—made up the minority within the party.

Nevertheless, some historians have detected in Jacksonian Democracy a conservative, backward-looking disposition. The market-oriented and commercially minded Whigs, with their economic program of banks, tariffs, and publicly sponsored internal improvements, wrote Marvin Meyers, "spoke to the explicit hopes of Americans"; the Democrats, yearning for a restoration of the republican virtues of Jefferson's time and a simple society that rested on the sturdy shoulders of the independent farmer, "addressed their diffuse fears and resentments." According to Meyers, even the radical libertarian William Leggett shared this essentially conservative Democratic theme of restoration, an appeal to undo "the errors of the past generation" and recover "free trade and equal rights." Similarly, Harry L. Watson writes that "Whigs advocated the rapid transformation of America's economy and Democrats tended to resist it." Jacksonian Democrats "embraced what they thought to be the cause of the many against the few, and battled for the restoration of better days."[10]

But Ranney did not seem conservative to his fellow convention delegates. He made clear his Radical Democratic proclivities from the start. The statute that provided for the holding of the convention directed the delegates to secure for the state the copyright of the report of the debates and proceedings. Whig Henry Stanbery offered a resolution declaring it "inexpedient" for the convention to comply with the statute. Pursuant to the statute the convention had already provided for the daily publication of the debates in the *Ohio State Journal* and the *Ohio Statesman.* Once the debates were published in the papers, said Stanbery, it was too late to secure the copyright. Furthermore, there was "a higher object than profit" in the publication of the debates: to inform the people as fully as possible of proposed changes to the constitution. Ranney agreed with both points, but in the creedal antimonopoly and laissez-faire language of Radical Democrats. He questioned whether the debates of public bodies could be "put under the screw of monopoly" and doubted that the state would profit from sales of the books. "We have already tried our hands in several schemes for making money, in constructing roads and canals, besides a variety of other things, in all of which the State has failed to prosper" (1:18, 60–61, 83–84).[11]

About a month into the convention, Ranney set forth his political principles in arguments over the report of the committee on nonbanking corporations. Many Democratic delegates displayed deep hostility toward business corporations. Animosity toward banks had been a staple of mainstream Democratic rhetoric since the 1830s. Other corporations, especially those created for the purpose of constructing roads, bridges, or canals, tended to be seen as quasi-governmental in nature and thus attracted less criticism, at least before the Panic of 1837. The General Assembly spent much of its time before 1850 enacting or amending special laws that granted corporate charters. The charters of business corporations often included "special privileges," such as the power to take property through eminent domain, the limitation of shareholder liability for corporate debts, or freedom from competition. After the Panic of 1837 and the heavy losses sustained by the state and by local governments that had invested in corporate enterprises, many Democrats developed a burning antipathy toward corporations. At the constitutional convention, they strove to put limits on corporate power into Ohio's fundamental law.[12]

The debates over business corporations occupied much of the convention's time. Ranney spoke out forcefully and with his wonted acerbity on two significant issues, the liability of shareholders for corporate debts and the power of the legislature to repeal corporate charters. Jacksonian Democrats had long appealed for support to independent artisans and shopkeepers whom corporate enterprise threatened to destroy. In 1835 Connecticut Democrat Gideon Welles warned that "[t]he unobtrusive work-shop of the Mechanic, the residence of freedom, is beginning to be abandoned, because he cannot compete with incorporated wealth." Corporations, Welles continued, were "destroying that equality of condition, which is the parent of independence." Individuals could not hope to compete with capital "entering the field, under privileged laws." Less than two years after the Ohio constitutional convention adjourned, the Democratic *United States*

Review complained that the incorporation of manufacturing companies had concentrated capital and labor in a few hands, whereas previously these resources had been "diffused among all classes, and contributed equally to the prosperity of millions of industrious people," who were "always improving their condition." Corporations had "banished the loom and the spindle from the fireside," driven housewives and mothers out of their homes and into factories, and turned independent mechanics, previously the "sole masters of their time and of themselves, into slaves of the steam-engine and spinning-jenny."[13]

Ranney declared that he had no objections to corporations created for "proper purposes," by which he seems to have meant the construction of "public improvements"—he himself had recently been among the incorporators of two plank road companies—but he feared that "their introduction into all the departments of ordinary business" would "depress private enterprise, and break down men of small capital." Without protection from the aggrandizement of corporations, said Ranney, mechanics (artisans) and small businessmen would soon be compelled "to find employment under the overshadowing power and influence of associated wealth." The growing tendency "to engulph every branch of business in the vortex of corporations" had to be resisted with "guaranties against their frauds." Two of the most important of these guarantees, he insisted, were shareholder liability and the right of repeal. Writing these two protections into the constitution would go a long way toward making "[e]qual rights to all, exclusive privileges to none . . . an operative, living principle" (1:370).[14]

The first report of the committee on corporations other than banks proposed changing the method of creating corporations. The General Assembly would no longer be able to grant corporate charters by special acts of incorporation. Instead, it would have the authority to pass general laws under which any group of individuals could set up a corporation. However, all such general laws might "be altered from time to time, or repealed." Upon repeal, "the property or credits legally acquired" by the corporation would "rest in the individual corporators, subject to the liability of the corporation." The liability of each incorporator or shareholder would never be less than the amount of stock subscribed by that individual. Despite his concern that general incorporation laws would encourage the proliferation of corporations, Ranney reluctantly assented to the idea because they would eliminate legislatively granted monopolies and allow anyone who wanted to form a corporation to compete on an equal basis

(1:260, 369–70). But he believed these provisions to be inadequate protections against corporate rapacity.

On its face the clause establishing minimum shareholder liability allowed the legislature to saddle shareholders with full liability for corporate obligations. Critics of the clause, though, took it for granted that the minimum would prove to be a maximum.[15] And if a shareholder's maximum liability were the amount of his investment, a corporation could run up enormous debts, beyond the value of its outstanding shares, while those individuals who owned the corporation would escape responsibility to the creditors. (The owners were not the thousands or millions of anonymous shareholders who invest in giant corporations today; they were usually a relative handful of men personally involved in the operations or general oversight of the business.[16]) Ranney moved to amend the report to make each shareholder liable for double the amount of his or her shares, and, in the case of a business corporation that was not created "to construct public improvements," the stockholders would be "individually liable for all the debts and liabilities" of the corporation (1:369).[17]

Ranney thought it outrageous that every individual or group of individuals associated for business purposes except those with a charter was fully liable for debts incurred. A merchant who lost a ship or a farmer whose crops were ruined by drought had no exemption from liability, he observed, but a shareholder had the shield of corporate privilege. The shareholders might have taken five times the amount of their stock subscriptions in dividends or profits, but once their stock was gone, their liability was gone. They could "revel in wealth and luxury, while hunger and destitution were grinding in the dust those who had labored for the corporation." Ranney believed it useless to leave to the General Assembly the matter of liability beyond the amount of the stock subscribed. The shareholders of the numerous corporations formed under general corporation laws would all seek to avoid liability. "They will be in the ear of every member before he comes here, and in his bed after he comes here, if necessary to effect their ends. They will be able to form the most powerful combinations, and raise any amount of money required for corruption purposes." There would be no hope for "legislative purity" or "honest principle" (1:371).

Members of both parties questioned whether any capitalist would invest in a corporation without knowing the limits of his liability. Democrat Edward Archbold even denied that individual liability, as proposed by Ranney, was sound Democratic doctrine. "The principle, that a man worth

$2000, with a family of 7 or 8 children, who wishes to contribute 50 or 100 dollars, towards the construction of a turnpike, or a plank road, shall thereby put to hazard his whole property, is not Democratic nor is the principle that he shall know the amount of his own engagements, and be liable to that extent only, Aristocratic," Archbold maintained. The question really boiled down to one of expediency. Archbold recommended that the extent of shareholder liability for corporate debts be left to the people's representatives to determine in the light of changing circumstances and experience (1:373, 387).

Ranney emphatically rejected these contentions. The principle of equal rights, he declared, "lies at the foundation of our institutions," and he would not sacrifice principle to expediency. (Ranney conceded, though, that in his amendment he had limited liability in cases of public improvements to double the shareholders' stake "more from the suggestions of others, than the dictates of my own understanding.") Moreover, no such sacrifice was necessary. Fear of unlimited liability had never prevented men from engaging in enterprises they thought would produce a profit; if a road was worth building, it would be built and pay for itself (1:405).

When Ranney's amendment finally came to a vote, the committee of the whole accepted the first part, which established minimum shareholder liability at twice the amount of stock subscribed, by a vote of 43 to 33. However, the delegates overwhelmingly rejected the portion that subjected to unlimited liability the shareholders of corporations other than those created to construct public improvements. Just before the vote was taken, Whig Benjamin Stanton noted that the standing committee had considered the matter and had been unable clearly to establish a principle by which to distinguish the different types of corporations. The amendment as adopted by the committee of the whole remained in the constitution (1:429).[18]

Besides trying to increase shareholder liability, Ranney sought to limit corporate privilege by enabling the General Assembly not just to repeal general incorporation laws but to revoke any corporate charter obtained under such laws. The committee of the whole agreed to the principle. Section 35 of the proposed legislative article prohibited the General Assembly from passing retroactive laws. The committee of the whole, with Ranney's support, amended the section to allow the lawmakers to amend or repeal any corporate charter granted by any previous General Assembly (1:363, 282; 2:165).

Stanton found it incongruous that a provision forbidding the enactment of retroactive laws allowed the legislature to amend or repeal legally obtained corporate charters. Moreover, he believed that a charter constituted a contract between the incorporators and the state and that a repeal would violate the constitutional prohibition against impairing the obligations of contract. To protect rights that had vested under law before the passage of a repealing act, the convention, on Stanton's motion, amended Section 35 to say that upon repeal, "the title to property and credits legally acquired under any former law, shall not be affected by such repeal" (2:165–66).

The question now before the delegates was whether to adopt the latest version of Section 35 as part of the report of the committee on the legislature. A motion to reconsider the vote on Stanton's amendment passed, whereupon Elijah Vance moved to amend Stanton's amendment to read that on repeal of a corporate charter, "the property or credits legally acquired by any corporation, or holder of a franchise, shall rest in the individual [corporators], subject to the liability of the corporation." In the ensuing debate delegates argued over whether a corporate franchise was property, a contract, both, or neither. Ranney characterized charters as property—and property, he noted, could be seized by the state in case of public necessity, provided the state compensated the owner. Adverting to the U.S. Supreme Court's decision in the *Charles River Bridge* case, Ranney declared that the right of the state was "paramount to every private right." He voted against Vance's amendment to Stanton's amendment, then against Stanton's amendment, and then, finally, in favor of the amendment (as amended by Vance and Stanton) made by the committee of the whole. He came out on the short end of three close votes. In other words, the attempt to give the General Assembly the explicit power to repeal corporate charters had failed (2:167, 169, 173–75).

But the fight was not yet over. Three days later Samuel Humphreville returned to Section 35, moving that it be amended to give the General Assembly the authority to repeal any corporate charter upon "just and equitable terms," as determined by the lawmakers. Ranney moved to add language to specify that the right of repeal applied to existing as well as future charters. His purpose, he said, was to guard against court decisions, "founded in error," holding corporate charters to be contracts that enjoyed constitutional protection from impairment by the legislature. The chief such erroneous decision was *Dartmouth College v. Woodward*, rendered by the United States Supreme Court in 1819. In the face of arguments that the Supreme Court had already decided the issue, Ranney's amendment to Humphreville's amendment passed. But the convention then rejected Humphreville's amendment by a two-vote margin (2:185, 188–89, 191, 210).

Proponents of the right of repeal kept trying. Vance sought to amend Section 35 to provide that all acts granting corporate franchises could be amended or repealed "upon such terms and conditions pertaining to the inviolability of private property, as is provided in other cases in this Constitution"—in other words, upon payment of compensation as in cases of eminent domain. Ranney favored a declaration of the General Assembly's power to repeal corporate charters, a power he believed the legislature possessed even without such a declaration, but he objected to the compensation requirement. Vance's amendment, said Ranney, would require the state to pay a corporation for its franchise regardless of how much harm the corporation had caused to the community. (There followed a testy exchange between Ranney on one side and Archbold and Lucius Case on the other as to whether Ranney's position was that of "the highwayman.") Ranney then discoursed on the distinction between corporate franchises and property, throwing in along the way further remarks on the dangers of corporations and the injustice of "exclusive privileges." The state, he said, was bound to protect the natural right to acquire and enjoy property, but it could not create property. A corporate franchise was nothing more than a privilege granted by the legislature to operate in association as an artificial person. The legislature could give it or take it away as the public good required (2:242, 249, 250–51).

After protracted arguments on the legal nature of corporate franchises, on the debaters' political partisanship and fidelity to party principle, and on the allegedly biased newspaper reports of the proceedings, the convention decided to recommit the report on the legislative department, along with pending amendments, to the standing committee (2:286–87).

Ranney's latest arguments over the right of repeal involved him in a paradox and a contradiction. In debates on other issues he had expressed deep distrust of the legislature. Now he insisted that the General Assembly, the "people's representatives," could be trusted to do right in determining whether the public good required the repeal of a corporate charter. Stanbery made a point of the apparent conflict (2:251, 264). But Ranney was not inconsistent in this instance. He sincerely opposed the concentration of power in the General Assembly, but he opposed concentrated power in private hands as well. For all its shortcomings, the legislature could still serve as a counterweight to associated wealth.

Ranney's insistence that a corporate franchise was not property, however, flatly contradicted his prior statements. The subject came up again during debate over the second report of the committee on the legislative department. In that report the controversial section on corporate franchises, Section 33, read: "The General Assembly shall have no power to pass retroactive laws, or laws impairing the obligation of contracts, provided, however that acts of incorporation, or corporate franchises, privileges or immunities, whether granted by a general or special law, shall never be deemed contracts or irrepealable" (2:319).

The debate resumed with all its former fury. Tempers flared. On February 5 Case declared that any lawyer who, after reading Blackstone, could assert that a franchise was not property was "unfit to belong to the profession." Case quoted "a very eminent lawyer" to the effect that any attorney who made such an argument "must be either a fool or a knave." Although Case claimed not to endorse such language, and went on to quote Ranney and other Democrats who had stated during the debates that franchises were indeed property, his meaning could not be missed (2:487–88).

Ranney reacted in characteristic fashion. He denied ever asserting that a franchise was property (although he later conceded that his remarks had been reported correctly) and insisted that if he had uttered such words Case was now taking them out of context. Indeed, Ranney quoted numerous instances in which he had made clear his position that corporate franchises were not property and insisted that no one at the convention could possibly have misunderstood his position. He castigated Case for referring to him, however obliquely, as "a knave or a fool" and retorted that "[i]f a man will make a blackguard of himself, he must not complain if he is treated as such." Along the way he picked a fight with fellow Democrat William Hawkins over an innocuous remark Hawkins had made in an attempt to excuse Ranney's apparent inconsistency (2:488, 492–93, 596).

On February 11 the committee of the whole punted, informally passing Section 33 with the understanding that the fight would continue in convention. Two days later Case reignited the personal feud. Having missed Ranney's "blackguard" comment in the heat of the debate on February 5, he now challenged Ranney to declare whether or not it was meant to apply to him. His honor affronted, Case would not accede to the requests of other delegates to let the matter go. Ranney refused to be drawn again into "this small potatoe business," but Case announced that if Ranney "intended to apply to me that dirty word 'blackguard,' I hurl it back into his teeth—yes, I cram that filthy word down his very throat, to the place from whence it came—filth to filth." Case sat down to cries of "order, order," and the convention at last proceeded with its business (2:569, 595–96).

For the rest of the convention Ranney strove valiantly but futilely to get an explicit, unrestricted right of repeal into the constitution. He lost the key battle when the delegates voted to strike the proviso from Section 33 and rejected attempts to replace it with language that Ranney and his friends considered more suitable. After Section 33 was ordered engrossed, the struggle for repeal shifted to the debate on the report of the committee on nonbanking corporations. Ranney let others carry the water in that phase of the fight, but he tried again in a debate on the bill of rights, proposing to include an express right of the General Assembly "to alter, repeal or abolish any law hereafter created by it" (2:605–33, 619, 621–22, 644–50, 659–62, 690–92). Ranney lost this round, too. He would have to be satisfied with a guarantee that "no special privileges or immunities shall ever be granted, that may not be altered, revoked, or repealed by the General Assembly," along with the suggestion by Justice Story in the *Dartmouth College* case that any corporate charter could be made repealable by the reservation of the right of repeal in the charter itself.[19]

Ranney's anticorporation animus showed up in the debates on other issues. He won a victory against tax exemptions for corporations. The report of the committee on corporations provided that the property of corporations would "forever be subject to taxation, the same as the property of individuals." Ranney moved that the section be amended to apply to corporations already in existence as well as those formed in the future. Notwithstanding the fact that the amendment might effectually modify the charters of corporations already in existence, a majority of the delegates agreed that the state could not barter away any aspect of its sovereignty, including the power of taxation. The amendment passed by a comfortable margin and became part of the constitution. But Ranney's attempt to limit the legislature's power to grant rights of way to corporations to cases "where the public good imperatively demands it" failed. Charles Reemelin complained that Ranney's proposal would reintroduce special legislation, allowing the General Assembly to decide on a case-by-case basis whether to grant a valuable right. In classic Jacksonian language, Reemelin insisted that legislative acts "should be like the dews of heaven, capable of being enjoyed by all." The General Assembly, he maintained, should no longer be "a dispenser of unequal laws, of special privileges and immunities." Ranney did not press the point (1:260; 2:665–66, 674–75).[20]

In his arguments against corporate privilege Ranney stood up for the ordinary citizen. Concern for the poor animated his remarks on other aspects of the convention's work. He supported a motion to specify in the constitution an amount of money that the General Assembly must raise for the support of the common school fund. Other delegates who agreed that the General Assembly should be required to provide funding for the support of a "thorough and efficient system of common schools" objected to enshrining the extent of that support, which Simeon Nash labeled a "mere [question] of policy," in the constitution. But Ranney, who had struggled to acquire an education, wanted to ensure that the legislature would "establish a system of education that shall reach every poor, every ragged, every destitute child in the State." When the committee on finance and taxation proposed that the legislature be prohibited from levying poll taxes for county or state purposes, as under the original constitution, Ranney urged a blanket prohibition. Under the existing law every citizen had to pay an annual tax of two dollars for highway maintenance or perform a certain amount of labor on the roads. The committee argued that the existing constitutional provision had worked well and generated no complaints, but Ranney demanded consistency of principle. If poll taxes were "grievous and oppressive," as the constitution declared, they ought to be outlawed for all purposes. To require a young man, living away from home, working by the month, with no spare time, to be under the same obligation as a rich person, was simply unjust. In both cases, the schools and the poll tax, Ranney failed to sway the majority of delegates (2:13, 16, 34–35).

Ranney's sympathy for the poor affected his attitude toward the criminal justice system, too. It was the one issue that elicited religious sentiment from him. He supported Reemelin's proposal that inmates of the state penitentiary be paid for their labor while confined. Ranney believed that reformation of the criminal was one of the chief objectives of punishment. To deny the offender his wages deprived him of "all hope of reformation" and "consigned him to irretrievable ignominy." If the prisoner had a family, "his wife and children are beggared, and pining and starving from want." Ranney did not fear being labeled a friend of rascals, for "the greatest of all philanthropists" had been reproached as "a friend of publicans and sinners." "[H]owever poor, degraded, and down-trodden the citizen may be," declared Ranney, there remained the "great rule of justice, that, to the laborer belongs the proceeds of his labor." The convention rejected Reemelin's amendment, as Ranney knew it would (1:542, 545–46, 549).

Ranney argued with equal earnestness, and equal futility, for a constitutional prohibition of capital punishment. He again insisted that one of the objects of punishment was reformation of the criminal; the death penalty left nothing to reform. Those who would maintain that murderers were beyond reformation, he said, would "deny the power of the divine arrangement to reform the heart of man." Nor was vengeance a legitimate purpose of punishment, because vengeance belonged to God. He conceded that capital punishment might deter would-be offenders, but he "held human life more sacred." Ranney saw no need for the state to follow a murderer's bad example. He had witnessed one hanging, and that had been enough—the worst possible spectacle from which to learn a moral lesson (2:23).

As the official record of the convention's proceedings reveals, Ranney was one of the most active and vocal members of the convention. Given the scope of delegates' duties and the division of labor among numerous committees, neither Ranney nor anyone else could have played a leading role in every area. In light of the havoc that temperance and slavery were already wreaking on the existing party system of Whigs and Democrats, Ranney's active involvement with those issues would have been enlightening. However, he had little to say about them. He proclaimed himself a supporter of temperance but questioned the wisdom of prohibiting the sale of liquor in the constitution. The success of the temperance movement, said Ranney, depended upon moral suasion, not legal force (2:875–76). Ranney may have taken this position in all sincerity—it did, after all, accord with the general Democratic view that "there are *some* subjects unfit for legislation, and among them is 'what we shall eat and what we shall drink and wherewithal we shall be clothed'"—but it also conveniently allowed him to sympathize with a popular movement without alienating important political constituencies.[21]

Slavery was not an issue at the convention; it had always been outlawed in Ohio. But the convention did confront ancillary matters of political and legal rights for blacks. The General Assembly had repealed most of the notorious "blacks laws" in 1849 as part of a political deal between Free Soil and Democratic legislators, but Ohio's blacks still did not have the right to vote. At the convention the committee on the elective franchise, following the precedent of the 1802 constitution, recommended that suffrage be limited to whites. On Saturday, February 8, 1851, the delegates took up Humphreville's motion to eliminate the racial restriction. When they reconvened at 3:00 p.m. following a recess, Ranney joined in defeating a motion to adjourn. But when the convention turned to Humphreville's motion, Ranney took no part in the debate and did not vote. Nor did he ask on Monday, as did several other delegates who missed the vote, to have his vote recorded (2:352, 550, 554–56).[22]

There is no way of knowing whether Ranney deliberately avoided putting himself on record or missed the vote for some other reason, but he seems to have stayed away from racial issues. When the question of desegregating the public schools arose, he took little or no part in the debates,[23] but his votes on motions put him in a minority of antisegregation delegates. The report of the standing committee on education required the legislature to provide for a system of free common schools for all children in Ohio. Committee member Otway Curry drew up a minority report, Section 4 of which would have prevented blacks and mulattoes from attending white schools "unless by common consent." The committee of the whole decided to recommit the majority report to the education committee. Some members wanted to instruct the education committee to incorporate Curry's Section 4. Ranney voted against striking the phrase "unless by common consent" from the section, which would have left a blanket prohibition of racial mixing, and for a motion to delete the whole proviso dealing with black and mulatto children. In both cases he was on the short end of a lopsided vote. However, the committee of the whole decided to recommit the report without instructions, and the standing committee's second report omitted all mention of race (1:693–94, 2:18–19, 663).[24]

On September 18, 1850, during the five-month break between the first and second sessions of the convention, Congress passed the Fugitive Slave Act as part of the Compromise of 1850. The party leaders who shepherded the compromise through Congress hoped that the measures would end the agitation over slavery and with it the threat of disunion. The act required all citizens to cooperate in its enforcement. It authorized the appointment of federal commissioners to hear claims to the ownership of alleged runaways. Blacks who were seized and hauled before a commissioner had no right of habeas corpus, no right to testify, and no right to trial by jury. The commissioner could order the rendition of the captive upon nothing more than an affidavit sworn to before an officer of a southern court attesting to the claimant's ownership of the alleged fugitive.[25]

At public rallies abolitionists and other opponents of slavery attacked the Fugitive Slave Act for depriving seized blacks of their constitutional rights and encroaching upon the rights of the states. The *Mahoning Index* reported that, at an "indignation meeting" in Canfield, Ranney joined his old law partner Wade and other prominent Whigs, Democrats, and Free Soilers in denouncing the law. Ranney, said the paper, "exposed not only the INFAMOUS MANNER in which the bill was rushed through the House under the gag rule of the southern and infamous oppression but in SCATHING AND BLISTERING CURSES denounced the whole bill as UNCONSTITUTIONAL (!) and the MISCREANTS who assisted in its inception and passage by their votes, or fleeing when God and their duty required their aid in behalf of liberty and the rights of blood and life, as unworthy of our regard—as UNWORTHY OF OUR SUFFRAGE—now or hereafter!"[26]

During Ranney's gubernatorial campaign of 1859, Ranney would deny the *Index*'s version of events, and the *Ohio Statesman* would condemn it as a pack of lies.[27] But that was in the future, when Ranney was the conservative candidate for governor. At the convention, he burnished his Radical image not only with attacks on corporate privilege and advocacy for society's underdogs but also, as we will see in the next chapter, with populist notions regarding the judicial system and future amendment of the constitution.

THREE

The Constitutional Convention

Government

THE FIGHT at the constitutional convention by Democrats such as Ranney and Reemelin to end legislative grants of "special and exclusive privileges" revealed the Radicals' fundamental distrust of government. Anxious to secure equal rights and equal liberty for all—or at least all white males—they loathed to give to a legislature that was susceptible to corruption by the rich and powerful the authority to do much of anything. Early in the convention proceedings Reemelin predicted that the convention would produce "a General Assembly reduced materially in power and the scope of duties, in all its arrangements; and we shall thus take away from them as much as possible all temptation to the abuse of their powers" (1:174).

Ranney insisted on severe limits to legislative discretion. "I am practically in favor of the doctrine of democracy—using the word in no party sense," he declared. While the people had to delegate some power, political wisdom dictated that they delegate as little power as possible, because all delegated power was liable to abuse. The adoption of a constitution was "the act of the great democracy—the people themselves prescribing their own rule of civil action." But leaving fundamental laws to the legislature meant "placing the exercise of power one step further from the source; and the people possess no direct power to correct the decision" (2:49).

For all his reliance on the "people," though, Ranney was no more willing to trust them with power than he was to trust the legislators. Editor John O'Sullivan raised this basic question of Jacksonian majoritarianism in the first issue of the *Democratic Review* in 1837. O'Sullivan conceded the plausibility of the antidemocratic argument that "[m]ajorities are often as liable to error of opinion, and not always free from a similar proneness to selfish abuse of power, as minorities." "A strong and active democratic *government*," he averred, "is an evil, differing only in degree and mode of operation, and not in nature, from a strong despotism." Because majorities could no more be trusted with power than minorities, the "best government is that which governs least."[1]

At the Ohio constitutional convention the committee on public debt and public works incorporated this principle into its report by prohibiting the General Assembly from authorizing the state or any local government, "by vote of its citizens of otherwise," to be a stockholder in a private corporation or to aid private enterprise in other ways. Some Democrats objected to the ban as undemocratic. One, proclaiming "*vox populi, vox Dei*," demanded that the voters be allowed to decide whether the state should incur debt to finance internal improvements. Another contended that the prosperous portion of the state, having "waxed fat at the public crib," had no right to deny "their poorer, because less favored, fellow citizens, the humble privilege of helping themselves with their own money." But Ranney regarded the government's power of taxation as a "dangerous power" by which the "proceeds of the industry of the citizens" are put "at the mercy of the State." He denied the right of the majority to tax the minority for any purpose "beyond the support of government" and the execution of the laws. When a delegate moved to amend the committee's report to allow local governments to vote funds for the completion of works already begun, Ranney claimed that the amendment "amounted to about this: that where the minority has been robbed once, it shall be proper to do it again" (1:292, 2:123, 2:308, 1:530, 2:215–16, 2:310–11).

From the widespread distrust of the General Assembly arose many issues related to the legislature: annual versus biennial sessions, the manner of apportionment, the executive veto, legislative power over corporate charters, and so on. Ranney's positions marked him as a consistent and outspoken Radical Democrat, wary of government and very aware that the people were the fount of political authority. As one of his adversaries observed, "it is pretty difficult to get ahead of him in democracy" (2:430).

Ranney opposed annual legislative sessions because the greatest legislative evil was "too much legislation and the instability of the law"; or, as Ranney also said, echoing a popular phrase of the day, "the world was governed too much" (1:174–79; 2:145). He resisted proposals to extend state senate terms from two to four years because over such a long period of time, especially in a rapidly growing and changing state, the views of the people and their delegates might diverge (1:175, 179; 2:145). He wanted to fix the method of legislative apportionment in the constitution, leaving no discretion to flawed legislators who, as experience had shown, were too much tempted to gerrymander (1:144–45, 460; 2:708).

The widely held opinion at the convention that the General Assembly's authority needed to be curtailed did not lead to a significant transfer of power to the executive branch of government. Most notably, the delegates refused to confer the veto power upon the governor. Ranney could not deny that the General Assembly passed too many laws and often acted with undue haste. But the remedy, he thought, lay in reducing the legislature's power, not in giving more power to the governor (1:112).

Ranney also opposed what he considered an undue expansion of the governor's patronage power. The selection of public officers by the General Assembly had been fraught with unpalatable wheeling and dealing. Ranney believed that the legislature's "power to confer office" had done much "to discredit legislative bodies" and was a major source of "hasty and inconsiderate legislation" (1:112). Many delegates shared Ranney's view. As a result the convention took from the General Assembly and gave to the electorate the power to elect judges, the secretary of state, and the state auditor and treasurer. Ranney successfully fought an attempt to increase the terms of state executive officers, other than the auditor, beyond two years (1:325, 330–31; 2:290).

Notwithstanding the trend toward popular election of public officials, the delegates disagreed over the method of selecting lesser officials, such as the directors of the state penitentiary and trustees of the deaf and dumb asylum and other state benevolent institutions. Some thought that the election of lower-level administrative officers was too burdensome a responsibility for the voters (1:365, 540). Ranney believed otherwise, at least regarding the penitentiary. The management of the state prison, he asserted, was no mere ministerial function but one of the most important jobs in the state. The directors had in their hands the lives of hundreds of individuals, the safety of the public, and great patronage and pecuniary interests (by which Ranney probably meant the hiring of employees and awarding of contracts). Rather than subject such vital offices to party influences, Ranney wanted to have the directors of the penitentiary, and of any future state prisons, elected directly by the people (2:342, 1:541). The convention yielded to the extent of giving the legislature the authority to determine the method of selecting the directors of the penitentiary; the trustees of all other state institutions would be appointed by the governor, with the advice and consent of the Senate (2:340–43).[2]

Ranney's most notable, although largely unsuccessful, work at the convention involved the reformation of Ohio's third branch of government, the judiciary. A bipartisan consensus on the need to revise the constitutional article on the judiciary overshadowed all other reasons for holding a convention. The constitution of 1802 provided for a supreme court, courts of common pleas, and justices of the peace, but for the most part it left the jurisdiction of the courts, judicial salaries, the establishment of common pleas circuits, and other court-related matters to the General Assembly. At its first session in 1803 the General Assembly gave the supreme court exclusive jurisdiction over cases involving divorce, alimony, and capital offenses, concurrent jurisdiction with the courts of common pleas over other major offenses, original jurisdiction in important civil cases, and the power to hear appeals from the courts of common pleas where the title to land was in question or where the amount in controversy exceeded one hundred dollars. The legislature soon expanded the supreme court's appellate jurisdiction to cover all cases that originated in the courts of common pleas, possibly because the panel of common pleas judges that heard a case did not necessarily include a lawyer. This expansion of appellate jurisdiction imposed a heavy burden because in those days an appeal often meant a new jury trial in the supreme court. The common pleas courts had jurisdiction over all civil and noncapital criminal cases that were not relegated to justices of the peace, including probate and guardianship matters. Justices of the peace heard small civil and criminal cases.[3]

Constitutional limitations on the legislature's power to regulate the structure of the court system posed serious problems for the lawmakers. The constitution specified an initial supreme court of three judges—a fourth could be added after five years—and required it to hold a session in every county every year. The court simply could not keep up with the demands of a rapidly growing state and a legislative propensity to create counties willy-nilly.

In 1808 the General Assembly added a fourth judge and, as permitted by the constitution, divided the state into two districts. In each district two judges would hold sessions at the county seats. If the judges in a district disagreed on a question of law, or if they wanted the full court to consider a novel or particularly difficult legal issue, they could postpone the case. To hear postponed cases, at least three judges had to hold an extraordinary session in each district annually.[4]

The innovations did not relieve the weary judges. Moreover, the split court presented other problems. A disagreement between the two judges in a district led to a postponement and a new hearing at which one or both of the same judges would sit. Furthermore, there were in effect two supreme courts which could produce different bodies of law for the two districts. In 1810 the General Assembly restored the supreme court to its original form. In the ensuing years the lawmakers again added a fourth judge, allowing the judges effectively to reinstate the two-district solution (because two judges made up a constitutional quorum), and required annual sessions of the court in bank (as a whole) to resolve conflicts and difficult questions of law. Nothing seemed to help. According to Judge John C. Wright, in 1834 the supreme court had 1,459 cases on its trial docket. To hear these cases the judges had to travel 2,250 miles through seventy-two counties. After deducting travel time, Sundays, and the month required for the court's meeting in bank, Wright calculated that the judges had to decide seven cases per day, every day, for the rest of the year to keep up with the caseload.[5]

The common pleas courts also came in for criticism. As required by the constitution, the General Assembly initially divided the state into three common pleas circuits, each headed by a president judge. A court of common pleas, with two or three associate judges, sat in every county. The lawmakers added common pleas circuits until by 1851 there were twenty, but the courts still wallowed in a mass of business. The associate judges, often laymen with little legal experience, did not much ease the burden of the president, even though they could form a quorum without him. The presence of lay judges poorly versed in the law brought numerous complaints.[6]

Legislative "fixes"—the creation of several trial courts known as superior courts, abolition of the supreme court's original jurisdiction in civil actions at law and in the trial of capital crimes, and elimination of the right of appeal to the supreme court—failed to satisfy anyone.[7] When the constitutional convention opened, the courts remained mired in a bottomless bog of cases.

The president of the convention appointed Ranney to the committee on the judicial department, a thirteen-member body that included some of Ohio's most prominent lawyers and politicians (1:64). Records of the work of the convention's committees have not been preserved, but the published report of the convention debates suggest that the work of the judiciary committee did not always proceed harmoniously. On the question of whether district courts should meet in every county or only at two or three locations within a district, for example, the committee split 7–6, so that members had to "yield their own extreme views" to reach a compromise. However, Ranney never gave in on this point. Indeed, he refused to go along with the majority report as a whole. Henry Stanbery defended the majority report as "the result of long and arduous labor—of much discussion—of examination and comparison of a multitude of plans" that had "united the opinions of more than three-fourths of all the members of the committee, composed of gentlemen who have been for a long time in the practice of the law." But Ranney submitted a minority report on behalf of himself and perhaps Samuel J. Kirkwood and Samuel Humphreville, two other Democrats who refused to sign the majority report (1:430–31, 592–93, 551).

Ranney ruffled his fellows' feathers when he moved to amend the majority report to require each district court to meet in every county in the district. Joseph Swan argued that the majority plan would produce a more respectable bar. "[I]nstead of being insulated, as now, to each county," he maintained, lawyers would get together in large numbers at the sessions of the district court. The bumpkins would be exposed to more learned and intelligent lawyers, and the court, which "seldom rises above the bar in learning and legal attainment," would benefit in turn (1:591). Ranney took personal offense at Swan's remarks. Swan, he said, expected "extreme temerity" from those with positions contrary to his own and described the men who practiced in the county courts "in no very flattering terms." When Swan denied that he had directed his remarks at Ranney or any other member of the convention, Ranney retorted, "what difference does it make, when their marks will apply to any one who insists upon the establishment, of such a county court." The tenor of the debate suggests that personal friction between Ranney on the one side and Swan and Stanbery on the other characterized discussions in committee as well (1:605).

Politics also intruded into the committee's deliberations. Chairman William Kennon, a Democrat, complained that "it seems from the statement of the gentleman from Trumbull, [Mr. Ranney] the whigs have over-reached us—the democrats of the committee have been over-reached by their whig associates. We—that is—a part of us have had our sagacity discredited." While Ranney argued for his minority report in Jacksonian terms, he did not, at least in the reported debates, accuse the committee's Democrats of knuckling under to the Whigs. Perhaps he leveled such charges during committee meetings or out of session; he insinuated as much in the convention's second session. Or Kennon may have attributed to Ranney the comments of Democrat Daniel A. Robertson, a vociferous opponent of the majority plan. Robertson in essence accused the committee majority of gerrymandering in its proposal for judicial districts. "The gentlemen of the whig party in the Convention," avowed Robertson, "could not have devised a better plan than this, to control the judicial system of Ohio" (1:631, 627).

The majority report proposed a judicial system that Ranney portrayed as too complex, too expensive, and too distant from the people. On one key point, though, everyone agreed: the judges would all be chosen by popular vote instead of by the legislature. The committee took this for granted from the start.[8] On the lowest rung of the judicial ladder, as recommended in the majority report, stood the township justices of the peace, whose powers and duties would be established by the General Assembly. Then came a county court in each county, with jurisdiction over probate matters and with jurisdiction over such civil appeals and such original and appellate criminal matters as the legislature might provide. Above the county courts were the courts of common pleas. The committee left their jurisdiction entirely up to the legislature, although it apparently contemplated that these would continue to be the trial courts of general jurisdiction. The report called for the state to be divided into nine common pleas districts, in each of which the voters would elect three judges, one or more of whom would hold court in every county in the district as often as the legislature might require (1:586, 51, 431).

The majority report created a new intermediate appellate court called the district court. Each of the nine common pleas districts would have a district court consisting of the three common pleas judges and one justice of the supreme court, with any three of the judges making up a quorum. The district courts would have the same limited original jurisdiction as the supreme court, but their chief purpose would be to hear appeals. In a sentence that would provoke Ranney's criticism and intense debate in the committee of the whole, the report required that district courts "shall be held in and for each district . . . as often in each year, and at such places in said district as may be prescribed by law" (1:431).

At the apex of the judicial hierarchy envisioned by the majority report stood the supreme court, with a chief justice and three associates. Any three of the justices would constitute a quorum. The report limited the court's original jurisdiction to special writs and left its appellate jurisdiction up to the General Assembly. The court would hold at least one term annually in the capital and other terms whenever and wherever the legislature might require by law. The electors of the whole state would choose the chief justice. For the election of the associates the nine common pleas districts would be combined into three districts "of compact territory," each of which would elect one justice. Every additional justice that the legislature might create in the future would be elected by the voters of the entire state (1:430–31).

Ranney's plan differed radically from the majority proposal. His judicial system consisted of township justices of the peace; a county court in each county having jurisdiction over probate matters and both original and appellate jurisdiction over civil and criminal cases in which the amount in controversy did not exceed three hundred dollars; and a twenty-member supreme court whose original and appellate jurisdiction would be established by law. The General Assembly would be able to create a separate probate judgeship in any county having forty thousand or more people as well as other courts inferior to the supreme court (1:551).

Ranney recommended that the state be divided into ten judicial districts bounded by county lines. Each district would elect two supreme court judges, at least one of whom would hold court in each county in the district two or more times each year. The state would also be divided into a minimum of three "convenient districts" in each of which the supreme court in bank would hold session at least once annually for the sole purpose of hearing appeals. Under Ranney's scheme, five judges would make up the court in bank. The judge in each of five alternating judicial districts with the shortest time to serve would sit in bank one year, and a judge from each of the other districts would serve the next. The chief judge would be chosen from among the members serving as provided by law (1:551).

On June 26, 1850, the committee of the whole took up the majority report. After the committee agreed to have all supreme court judges elected on a statewide basis, Ranney moved to require every district court to meet annually in each county in the district. The motion touched off a strenuous, ill-tempered debate. In an extended defense of the majority's position, which did not have the district court meeting in each county, Swan observed that the district court, as an appellate body, would be a "mere paper court," a "lawyer's court," at which there would be no need for parties, witnesses, or jurors. It would be a waste of time and money to have this court traipse around from county to county. Swan then made it clear that the biggest problem with the existing judicial system was the workload of the supreme court. That tribunal, he said, was "emphatically a stirrup court, chasing from county to county," and forced "to decide promptly and without careful deliberation" in order to avoid "deny[ing] justice by delay." Under the majority proposal, the district courts would be a "breakwater to prevent the flow of business into the supreme court." Indeed, the only reason for the supreme court to meet in bank would be to settle differences among the circuits (1:586, 590–92).

Stanbery and fellow Whig Simeon Nash also assailed Ranney's proposed amendment. It would, they said, leave no discretion to the legislature to make adjustments to suit the needs of different districts. It would encumber the supreme and common pleas judges who made up the district court with impossible schedules. The amendment would in effect restore the old system that had caused all the problems in the first place and led to the calling of the constitutional convention. Even Peter Hitchcock, who sympathized with Ranney's insistence that the court remain close to the people, opposed the amendment. Noting that the district and supreme courts were chiefly courts of appeal, Hitchcock denied that the judges would be too pressed for time to travel to every county in the district. However, he objected to fixing the meeting times and places in the constitution. He preferred to leave those matters to legislative discretion (1:595–97).

The debate ranged well beyond Ranney's proposed amendment to embrace the cost of the majority plan, the need to attract competent lawyers to the bench, and other issues. With the discussion covering so much ground, Ranney reentered the fray, insisting that his constituents had sent him to the convention to represent their opinions and that he would do so "without fear, favor or affection," notwithstanding the eminence of his opponents on the judiciary committee. The people demanded reform of the judiciary. Before defending the specific proposals of his report, Ranney laid out its animating principles. "[T]he practical operation of the law through the Judiciary," he declaimed, "is the most important of all the operations of our government." Without it, the other branches of government "can do nothing towards carrying justice home to the people." Justice delayed was justice denied and fostered disrespect for the law. "Delay in the administration of justice to those who are seeking to recover their rights," he said, "is calculated to destroy their peace of mind, diminish their regard for, and confidence in, the judicial tribunals, and to keep convulsed whole neighborhoods, embittering the fountains of social life" (1:604–5).

Ranney saw the majority report's appellate process as a big obstacle to speedy justice. There ought to be as few appeals as possible. Yet the majority report proposed that an unnecessary supreme court sit atop the judicial hierarchy. The court would have little to do and would have no jurisdiction that could not be better exercised at the district level. It would have a chief justice elected by the voters of the whole state and associates conscious of having "com[e] up from the districts"—a sort of grand pooh-bah presiding over a bunch of provincials. It would have an even number of justices who, if evenly divided, would in essence be confessing to the parties "that the court is powerless to decide between them—that the law is struck with a paralysis." It would be a purely "paper court," excluded from "participation in the every day business of judicial duty" and separated from daily familiarity and practical application of legal rules. The majority report, Ranney declared, envisioned an "august" court surrounded by a "luminous" bar sitting in the capital, "[i]ts dazzling appearance . . . such, that no county court lawyer could ever look upon it and live." But the greatest judges, from Lord Mansfield to Chief Justice Taney, had been "stirrup judges," riding the circuit and catching the spirit as well as the letter of the law (1:605–7).

Ranney had little use for the district appellate courts proposed by the majority. Outside of Hamilton County they would sit in only two places in each of eight large, multicounty districts, forcing attorneys and parties to travel great distances and making even the filing and copying of papers a burden. Moreover, appeals would be "as liberal as before," and every equity case would be the subject of an appeal, which Ranney regarded as a major flaw in the majority's system. "Who does not see," asked Ranney, "that in all this you will experience great delay, to say nothing of the increased expense in bringing the cause to hearing." Under the proposed system the appellate court would meet twice a year, "but to get the benefits of it without waiting a whole year, you may have to go to a remote part of the district, and you will of course have a greater delay, than if the cause was settled in the county in which it originated." Under his own scheme, Ranney continued, appeals would be decided "on the spot, in the same county where the suit first commenced, by the two judges of the supreme court—the same number that now decide finally; all the difference is, they now decide on appeal, they will then decide in the first instance" (1:608–9).

Ranney also attacked the county courts proposed by the majority. They had insufficient jurisdiction to gain the respect of the community. Their judges' compensation was fee-based, which could only induce them to corruption and an encouragement of litigation (1:609–10).

In defense of his proposed substitute plan Ranney declared it to be "simple and plain, and easily understood." It provided for good courts in the first instance, rather than relying on good appellate courts to correct errors. It provided for no "unnecessary judges" and brought the courts to the bar, the parties, and the people. And, he contended, it was cheaper than the majority's system, an assertion that Kennon rejected (1:610–11).

In response to Ranney's attack members of the judiciary committee noted that nothing in the majority report prevented the legislature from requiring the district courts to meet in every county. They pointed out that the matter of whether a district court should be required to meet in every county in the district had been the most contentious issue in committee and claimed that Ranney was the only member who had refused to go along with the compromise embodied in the majority report (1:612–14, 617).

After further sharp debate the committee of the whole rejected Ranney's amendment by a vote of 42–35 (1:621–22, 626). That was on June 28, 1850. On July 9 the convention, fearful of the cholera epidemic then sweeping the state, adjourned until December, when it reconvened in Cincinnati. Not until January 21, 1851, did the convention again take up in earnest the judiciary committee's report.

Once again Ranney offered an amendment that provoked heated argument. This time Ranney sought to compel the supreme court to meet at least once annually in each of nine districts. His aims, as before, were to expedite justice, reduce costs, and bring the courts closer to the people. No one else from the judiciary committee spoke in favor of the amendment, and only Humphreville voted for it. The amendment went down to defeat 50–45. But Ranney vowed to keep offering amendments to have the supreme court sit in different places throughout the state—five, and if that failed, four, and if that failed, three. And he promised to demand the yeas and nays each time so that the voters could see who supported "centralization" and who favored "the equalization of the benefits of the judicial system." Ranney kept his promise, at least to the extent of demanding that the supreme court sit in four different places, but the convention soundly defeated his proposal (2:368, 365, 376, 685–86).[9]

After Ranney lost his first bid to create a traveling supreme court, another delegate offered an amendment to require the district courts to meet every year in every county. In the course of another bitter debate, Ranney accused the Whigs of concocting a judicial system so objectionable that even the Whig papers opposed it. The Whigs knew that the constitution produced by the convention would be "likely to cut up monopoly and exclusive privilege." If they could get the Whig papers to stir up popular animosity toward the proposed judicial system, they could send the whole constitution down to defeat. When the time came to vote, Ranney finally triumphed (2:368, 376, 383–86). The victory, however, was short-lived; the convention adopted a Whig modification allowing the General Assembly to authorize at least three annual sessions in at least three places in any district where annual sessions in each county would be "inexpedient." Ranney of course voted against the amendment, but it passed by two votes and ultimately found its way into the constitution (2:388).

Despite his objections to the judicial article of the new constitution, Ranney announced during the convention's second session that he would vote for the constitution because he expected it would allow for easy amendment. Ranney chaired the committee on future amendments, was "the father of the [committee's] report," and was the only member of the committee to take part in the debate over the amending process (2:432, 427–36, 446).

The committee report retained, with slight modification, the provision of the 1802 constitution that authorized the electors to call a constitutional convention upon the recommendation of two-thirds of the members of each legislative chamber. Moreover, it required that the question of calling a convention be placed on the ballot every twenty years. The report's great innovation, though, was to allow either house of the General Assembly to initiate constitutional amendments. Under Section 1 of the report a proposed amendment would have to receive a three-fifths majority in each house and be published in a newspaper of every county having a paper once a week for six months before the next general election. The amendment would then appear on the ballot and become law if a majority of electors voting at the election approved it (2:339).

The report proved contentious. One delegate thought that Section 1 would turn the General Assembly into a "perpetual constitutional convention." The possibility of a convention being called every twenty years agitated conservatives even more than the prospect of legislative meddling with the constitution. Ranney, however, pointed out that the provision had "its origin in the theory that there should be some power in the people themselves, to originate amendments to the Constitution." Future generations would inherit the constitution then being drawn up. "Is it not justice then to declare that when we deliver it into their hands, they shall have the privilege to say, whether or not, they will be bound by it?" (2:428–30).

As usual when Ranney took part in debate, the discussion turned sharp and personal. Ranney accused Simeon Nash of being congenitally opposed to every form of progress. Nash, he declared, "would have made a first rate member of Parliament for the times of James the First. For, being admonished that he should not meddle with matters of State, he would be a very obedient man." As it happened Ranney could have curbed his acerbic inclinations without harm to his cause; the committee of the whole made only one small change to Ranney's report, and the convention adopted all three sections with little opposition (2:430–31, 446).

After approving the report the convention referred it to the committee on revision, enrollment, and arrangement. That committee, also chaired by Ranney, was responsible for cleaning up the language of the reports of standing committees as adopted by the convention and locating the provisions logically within the final document. Although the committee's work was largely housekeeping in nature, its proposals could have serious consequences, and disputes over its reports occasionally broke out. A short but acrimonious argument erupted on the convention's last day when committee member Samson Mason moved to strike a section from the report on nonbanking corporations. For once, the bitterest exchange involved other delegates, but Ranney managed to irritate Henry Stanbery, a distinguished Whig attorney, by characterizing Stanbery's contentions as "all a fudge" (2:435, 314, 748, 849).

The convention concluded its business on March 10, 1851, with a resolution adopting the proposed constitution by a vote of 79–14. A fellow Radical delegate later recalled that Ranney, more than anyone else, had "distinguished himself in debate" and brought "the majority of the convention to form the present admirable constitution of Ohio."[10] Ranney had the last word in the last argument, precipitated by the gloating tone of his response to Whig delegate John L. Green's concern that the constitution might be defeated at the polls. Noting that Ranney had spoken "with an air of triumph that must have excited the attention of all," Green explained that his main reason for opposing the constitution was the section prohibiting counties from lending their credit to private enterprise for the construction of internal improvements. Characteristically, Ranney took Green's explanation as an "attack" and insisted on responding. But he assumed a conciliatory tone toward Green and concluded with praise for the convention's handiwork. He regretted some omissions and would have modified some provisions, but on the whole he believed "before God and man that it is one of the best, if not the best of the Constitutions of American States," and he vowed to work earnestly for its ratification by the voters (2:870, 815, 869).

Ranney's biggest disappointment with the constitution was the article on the judiciary (2:815). He had labored long and hard to keep the courts close to the people, but lawyer-delegates of both parties successfully resisted his plan. Ranney also failed on other fronts. For example, he could not persuade the convention that the people ought to have a direct say—that is, the right of referendum—on all legislation (2:215–16, 227–28). But he had his successes, too. It was on Ranney's motion that the convention added to the eminent domain clause the requirement that compensation for private property taken by the government be assessed by a jury and that it not be reduced by the value of any benefits of the taking to the owner (1:290), and Ranney succeeded in eliminating restrictive qualifications for the office of governor (1:299, 302, 306; 2:290–91). More generally, the popular election of judges and the major executive branch officials, restrictions on public debt and governmental assistance to private enterprise, and prohibition of special acts of incorporation satisfied Ranney's Radical Democratic principles. The constitution represented a triumph of mid-nineteenth-century popular, small-government, laissez-faire constitutionalism.

FOUR

Supreme Court Judge

ON MARCH 11, 1851, one day after the constitutional convention closed, the Ohio Senate and House of Representatives received notice from Governor Reuben Wood that Edward Avery had resigned his seat on the state supreme court.[1] The constitution just adopted by the convention, with its provisions for the popular election of judges, would not take effect unless and until it received approval from the electorate. Therefore, the task of choosing Avery's successor fell to the General Assembly.

The lawmakers had many posts to fill besides the seat on the supreme court: lower court judgeships, generals of militia, state auditor, acting commissioner of the canal fund, state librarian, register and receiver of the state land office, and, most significantly, United States senator.[2] On March 13 the senators trooped down to the representatives' hall in the old statehouse and a joint meeting of the members set to work. It was difficult business. The legislature was evenly divided between Whigs and Democrats, with Free Soilers holding the balance of power. The previous session of the General Assembly had been paralyzed by the failure of the two major parties to agree on the seating of members from Hamilton County and by bargaining for the support of the Free Soil contingent. The acrimony carried over to the

1850–51 session. The legislators took ten ballots to elect the state auditor and twenty-seven to elect a U.S. senator.[3]

On March 17 the lawmakers finally got around to the supreme court seat. The Whigs nominated Charles C. Convers, Speaker of the Senate, while the Democrats put forward Urbana lawyer John A. Corwin, "a very eccentric man, and not possessed of good habits."[4] Convers received thirty-eight votes from the seventy-eight legislators present, two shy of the required majority, to just twenty for Corwin. Eight members voted for Ranney, five for Toledo lawyer John Fitch, and seven cast blank ballots or voted for other men. Ranney's limited support might have been due to the fact that he was unaware of Avery's recent resignation and therefore expressed no interest in the position.[5]

The Democrats needed someone other than Corwin. Ranney had been a Democratic stalwart for years, had been prominent at the constitutional convention, and could attract Free Soil support. The Democratic tide shifted from Corwin to Ranney. According to the House and Senate journals, Ranney won on the second ballot. However, the *Ohio State Journal,* the state's leading Whig paper, presented a different picture. In the newspaper's account Convers and Corwin remained the party nominees. Convers led the second round of balloting with thirty-seven out of seventy-nine votes, but Corwin's figure dropped to ten while Ranney's rose to nineteen. At this point the Democrats withdrew Corwin's name and officially nominated Ranney. Two members left the hall before the third vote was taken, leaving no more than seventy-seven members present. Round three, at first count, produced a 37–37 tie, with five blanks. Obviously, too many votes, including abstentions, had been cast. A revote resulted in thirty-eight votes for Ranney, thirty-seven for Convers, and five blanks. Again there were too many votes. The third ballot had to be taken a third time. Now Ranney appeared to win with thirty-nine votes to thirty-six for Convers and two blanks. According to the *Journal* Ranney had triumphed with Free Soil assistance because he had pledged to support their position on the constitutionality of the federal Fugitive Slave Law, whereas Convers had refused to make any pledges "on the eve of an election."[6]

The Whigs would not yet concede. Representative Ephraim R. Eckley claimed there had been a mistake in the last vote and demanded another do-over. "Great commotion" followed Eckley's demand. The *Journal* did not report the basis for Eckley's claim, but it may have been that the total number of ballots cast was seventy-seven, leaving one ballot unaccounted for. If there were in fact seventy-eight members present, Ranney's total was one short of a majority. Democrats called out for Whig senator Harvey Vinal, occupying the Speaker's chair, to "announce the result . . . or leave the chair" and threatened a walkout if the vote were retaken. Vinal was at a loss; he knew the rules in the Senate, but not in a joint session of the legislature. Convers finally ended the confusion by graciously requesting that Vinal announce the result "as it now stands." Vinal declared Ranney the winner.[7]

Ironically, Ranney, who had so strenuously demanded the popular election of judges at the constitutional convention, thus became the last supreme court judge to be chosen by the General Assembly. The lawmakers elected Ranney to a seven-year term, but when the voters approved the new constitution in a special election in June, they subjected all judges to popular election that fall and terminated existing terms of office as of the second Monday in February of 1852. In August the Democratic state convention nominated candidates for the five supreme court judgeships created by the constitution. Ranney led the vote-getters, followed closely by William B. Caldwell. Corwin, Thomas W. Bartley, and Allen G. Thurman rounded out the slate.[8]

Ranney and Caldwell were also nominated by the Free Democrats, the name taken by the former Free Soilers whom Salmon P. Chase had been trying unsuccessfully to unite with the Democratic Party. Ranney's nomination provoked a "spirited discussion" at the Free Democratic state convention. One member thought Ranney was "too ultra—too much of a party man"; that is, more committed to the Democratic Party than to the antislavery cause. However, B. F. Hoffman urged the convention to endorse the best judicial candidates put forward by the Democrats and Whigs, "independent of party considerations." Ranney received his nomination by a "fair majority."[9]

Caldwell, like Ranney, was essentially running for reelection. He had been placed on the court in 1849 after serving as prosecuting attorney and common pleas judge for Hamilton County. At forty-three years of age, he was by nearly five years the oldest of the Democratic candidates. Bartley, of Mansfield, was one of Ohio's most prominent antibank Democrats, a former prosecutor, state representative, state senator, governor, and United States attorney. Thurman, too, was an influential Democrat, but his public career, which would culminate in the Democratic nomination for vice president, did not begin in earnest until his election to the supreme court.[10]

The Democrats swept to a crushing victory in 1851, capturing the governor's chair, both houses of the legislature, and all five seats on the supreme court. The Whigs never recovered and soon disappeared as a party. Historians disagree over the cause of the Whigs' demise, with some blaming primarily the sectional crisis and the defection of antislavery Whigs and others stressing the rise of prohibition and nativism, which sympathetic Whigs embraced at the peril of losing their German constituents. Whatever the reasons, there was "no denying the fact," as a Whig newspaper moaned, that the Whigs were "used up."[11]

The constitution provided for five-year terms of office for supreme court judges. However, it required that the initial terms of the five judges be of one, two, three, four, and five years, with the judges deciding by lot who got which term. The General Assembly then created a rotating chief judgeship by mandating that the judge with the shortest time to serve would be chief. Ranney drew the five-year term, which meant that he would not have to run for reelection for five years but would have to wait four years to head the court.[12]

Under the new constitution the supreme court was primarily an appellate court. It had to hold at least one term annually in Columbus and such other terms as the General Assembly might require. The supreme court judges also served on district courts, each of which consisted of one supreme court judge and at least two common pleas judges of the district. The district courts had the same limited original jurisdiction as the supreme court, with appellate jurisdiction as provided by law. That might have meant that Ranney would rarely, if ever, preside over a trial. However, the district court was not the "mere paper court, where the suitors never enter" that some delegates to the constitutional convention had fearfully envisioned. In 1852, in accordance with traditional Ohio appellate practice, the General Assembly provided that cases appealed to the district court be retried as though the district court had original jurisdiction. Ranney therefore had occasion to serve as a trial judge.[13]

The legislators and voters who put Ranney on the supreme court surely expected him to issue opinions consistent with his Jacksonian predilections. If so, they were not disappointed. Ranney's jurisprudence reflected the ideas he had expressed as a congressional candidate and constitutional convention delegate. But pinning down the essence of Jacksonian jurisprudence is no easy task. Scholars who try sometimes draw large conclusions from a very small number of U.S. Supreme Court decisions dealing with the Constitution's contracts or interstate commerce clause. A common refrain is that the Supreme Court, under the leadership of Jacksonian chief justice Roger B.

Taney, enhanced the states' police power to adopt regulatory laws for the health, safety, and welfare of the public. In fact, given the limited nature of the Supreme Court's federal-question jurisdiction, it would be more accurate to say that the court refrained from straightjacketing state police power in the few areas where the contracts or interstate commerce clause created the possibility of doing so.[14]

Taking a broader view of the Taney court's work, historian Austin Allen has looked at cases that came to the court through its diversity jurisdiction (the authority of federal courts to hear disputes under state law because the parties are from different states). According to Allen, diversity cases reveal as a key element of Jacksonian jurisprudence a resolve to hold individuals to obligations incurred in the market. This determination stemmed from a revulsion of judicial "elites," both Democratic and Whig, toward the social disorder that characterized Jacksonian America. However, there was nothing peculiarly Jacksonian about this resolve. Furthermore, the diversity cases discussed by Allen were mostly commercial in nature; they disclose nothing about Jacksonian jurisprudence as it relates to negligence, domestic relations, or other areas of law.[15]

Ranney spent a relatively short time on the bench, but he produced enough opinions covering a wide enough range of subjects to enlarge our understanding of Jacksonian jurisprudence. To see what makes his juridical thought Jacksonian, we must keep in mind the web of ideas and attitudes that made up Jacksonian Democracy: equal rights (for white men), limited government, majority rule, suspicion of corporations, states' rights. This is not to say that Ranney or other judges pursued a partisan agenda on the bench. It is simply to acknowledge that they did not change their essential outlook on life when they donned judicial robes. Nor does putting jurisprudence in the context of Jacksonian Democracy mean that there was a direct correspondence between judicial doctrine and party affiliation. Democratic judges disagreed among themselves, and agreed with Whigs, on any number of points. But the general tenor of Ranney's opinions indicates a consistent leaning toward positions that accorded with Jacksonian Democracy.

Democrats tended to harbor less reverence for that tangled accretion of precedents known as the common law, and greater enthusiasm for codification, than did Whigs. Ranney respected the common law, but he did not "venerate" it, as one acquaintance claimed. He warmly endorsed the idea of a simple procedural code that would eliminate "much of useless verbiage, fiction and mystery" from common-law practice. He also insisted that a common-law doctrine that had outlived its usefulness or made no sense under Ohio conditions should not be applied, no matter how old it was or how many jurists had approved it.[16]

One of Ranney's most controversial common-law innovations failed to endure. Ranney recognized the power of a court to dismiss a lawsuit after the plaintiff presented his case, thereby preventing a jury from hearing both sides and rendering a verdict. The question for the court was "whether, as matter of law, each fact indispensable to the right of action has been supported by some evidence." To Ranney, *some* evidence meant *any* evidence, "no matter how slight." This rule, which Ranney established in Ohio, came to be known as the scintilla rule. It ran counter to Ranney's general desire for judicial economy because it merely postponed the day of reckoning for the defendant, possibly at considerable cost of time and expense to both parties. But the scintilla rule may have reflected Ranney's Jacksonian regard for the jury, "the great safeguard of life, liberty, and property." At the constitutional convention Ranney had insisted that compensation for property taken by eminent domain be assessed by a jury; as a judge he expanded the jury's role by rejecting a traditional rule of strict liability and letting the jury decide whether the parties had met their obligations. But after Ranney left the bench for good, the scintilla rule ran into serious opposition from the bar—one opponent of the rule charged his adversaries with invoking "the revered name of Judge Ranney and exclaim[ing] '*ipse dixit*'"—and was eventually thrown out by the Ohio Supreme Court.[17]

Some areas of the common law, such as the emerging law of negligence, required considerable shaping during Ranney's days on the court. In molding Ohio's negligence law Ranney displayed a penchant for finding corporations liable for injuries to persons and property, largely on the ground of corporate obligations to the community. Ranney became a judge during the early days of Ohio's industrialization, with their increasing incidence of injuries among railroad and industrial workers. Liability for negligence required a showing of fault; people were responsible for unintended harm they caused through their own carelessness, unless some special circumstance, such as the contributory negligence of the injured party, absolved the defendant. The fault principle lay at the heart of the fellow-servant rule, a key doctrine in the industrializing world of the nineteenth century. Under the fellow-servant rule, an employer was not liable for injuries suffered by one employee at the hands of another. Established first in England in *Priestly v. Fowler* (1837), the rule swept through the American states, relieving manufacturers, mining companies, and, above all, railroad corporations from liability for harm to employees that could be blamed on the negligence of other employees.

Ohio bucked the trend to some extent by limiting the reach of the new rule.[18] In 1846 two trains owned by the Little Miami Railroad collided, resulting in severe injuries to engineer John Stevens. The fault apparently lay with the conductor on Stevens's train, who had failed to notify Stevens of a change in schedule. The jury found for Stevens, and the railroad company appealed to the supreme court, where the case was heard by the old four-man court. Judge Caldwell's opinion, in which only Ranney concurred, appears confused in retrospect. But the law was in flux, and the judges could hardly be charged with knowledge of the doctrinal distinctions that were then unfolding.

From portions of Caldwell's decision, it is easy to see why some nineteenth-century jurists believed that Ohio initially rejected the fellow-servant rule.[19] Caldwell harshly criticized the leading American case, *Farwell v. Boston & Worcestor Rail Road*—the opinion was written by Massachusetts's Whig chief justice Lemuel Shaw—as "contrary to the general principles of law and justice." Yet Caldwell did not reject the fellow-servant rule altogether. Rather, he created a potentially gaping exception to it by pointing out that the conductor and engineer stood on different levels as employees. The conductor was the "commanding officer" who managed the coming and going of the train on behalf of the railroad. Caldwell therefore found for the plaintiff. Rufus Spalding dissented, relying on both the reasoning and the growing precedential importance of *Priestly* and *Farwell.* Chief Judge Hitchcock concurred only in the judgment without repudiating the fellow-servant rule.[20]

A three-way split on a four-man court was not the happiest way to settle a crucial point of law. A few years later a similar case came before the court, with the defendant arguing that *Little Miami Railroad v. Stevens* had been wrongly decided. *Cleveland, Columbus & Cincinnati Railroad v. Keary* arose when a brakeman for the railroad was injured in a collision allegedly caused by the negligence of the conductor and the superintendent. Ranney, who at the constitutional convention had argued the Radical Democratic case against "special privileges" for corporations, began his opinion for the court by asserting that corporations were subject to the same rights and liabilities as individuals. There followed a paean to the legal maxim that every man may use his own property as he sees fit, subject to "the great social necessity of so using his own, as not to injure others" (*sic utere tuo ut alienum non laedas*). It followed that whoever "puts a force in motion" must "skillfully and carefully control it."[21]

In the case at hand the injured brakeman had not been at fault. By entering the railroad's service he had placed himself under the direction of the conductor and agreed to obey the conductor's orders. But the company had assumed obligations, too. If the servant "was bound to perform with diligence and care the orders of the company given by their substitute, the conductor, were they not bound to govern him with a proper regard to his safety?" Ranney reaffirmed his acceptance of the fellow-servant rule; the servant assumed "all the ordinary risks incident to the business, including liability to injury from the negligence of other servants employed" on the same footing, who "are alone liable for the injuries they inflict." But the situation was different when the careless party was in a superior position, exercising control on behalf of his employer. *Priestly* and *Farwell* were sweeping all before them, but Ranney was undaunted. Those decisions were recent innovations upon the rule of *respondeat superior* (the employer is responsible for the employee's wrongs), a principle "as old as the law itself." The high court of Scotland had firmly rejected *Priestly.* That distinguished company sufficed for Ranney, though no doubt he would have relied on principle and ancient precedent alone if necessary.[22]

In *Stevens* Caldwell had laid the foundation for the "superior servant" or "vice principal" exception to the fellow-servant rule but had carried only Ranney with him. In *Keary* Ranney elaborated on Caldwell's opinion, rooting the exception in the social duty of corporations and venerable common-law doctrine. Together, the two decisions opened the door to what became the major American exception to the fellow-servant rule and to the immunity of railroads and industrial enterprises from liability for on-the-job injuries suffered by their employees.

In both *Stevens* and *Keary* all the parties involved—the employer, the "superior servant," and the injured worker—were, so to speak, in the railroad company's chain of command. But railroads also caused damage to people who neither owned nor worked for the companies, and sometimes the individuals who caused the damage were contractors of the roads rather than employees. Ranney encountered both conditions in *Carman v. Steubenville & Indiana Railroad Company.* The Steubenville & Indiana had hired independent contractors to remove rock from the path of a road being built on land adjacent to the plaintiff's property. The contract called for blasting, the usual method used in railroad construction to remove large masses of solid rock. One explosion threw debris onto the plaintiff's land, damaging his house and fences. There was no evidence of negligence on the part of the contractors and no suggestion that the contractors could have blasted the rock without causing the damage.

In the absence of negligence, on what basis could either the contractors or the railroad company be liable? Ranney again resorted to *sic utere.* The railroad company, said Ranney, "had no right to use their own lands, or authorize others to use them, so as to interfere with the undisturbed possession and lawful enjoyment of adjoining lands." Neither the use of an independent contractor to carry out its express instructions nor the most careful execution of those instructions by the contractor would shield the corporation from liability.[23]

Thus far the only fault Ranney found with the railroad was its nonnegligent use of its property in such a way as to cause damage on a neighboring parcel. If he had stopped there, *Carman* would be simply an early forerunner of *Rylands v. Fletcher,* an English case from 1868 in which the court held that a defendant who engaged in a particularly hazardous activity was liable for resulting harm regardless of negligence. The rule of *Rylands* slowly gained acceptance in the United States. Scholars sometimes imply that the Ohio Supreme Court did not adopt the principle until the 1890s. *Carman* has rarely been recognized as one of the first cases to hold a company strictly liable—that is, liable without proof of negligence or intent—for blasting damage to neighboring property or, indeed, for any damage caused by a company's normal operations.[24]

In fact Ranney did find the defendant in *Carman* at fault, but the fault was not in the manner of blasting. The company, he observed, had given the contractors carte blanche to blast big rocks. It could have insisted that the contractors use a more expensive method of removing the rock, but it chose not to do so. "[H]aving enjoyed the benefits of this cheaper mode of doing the work," he wrote, the defendants "cannot escape the responsibilities attending it. If they reserve no power to prevent injury, where blasting could not be safely employed, they were clearly in fault in giving so unrestricted a license. If they had the power, it is almost equally clear, they should have exerted it."[25] Ranney seemed to be suggesting that the company had been negligent in choosing the method of removing the rock rather than in executing that method. But there was something else at stake: responsibility for the consequences of freely chosen actions. The company had made a choice based on an economic calculation; morality demanded that it bear the burden of its risky decision.

In *Stevens, Keary,* and *Carman,* Ranney came down on the side of those harmed by railroad corporations. Given his Radical background, that is not surprising. The question is, why did he unquestioningly accept the fellow-servant rule, which at the time affected primarily railroad workers? One reason may be that railroad workers, who were the injured parties in almost all of the early fellow-servant cases, enjoyed wages, job security, and other benefits far above those afforded other workers and therefore did not elicit the sympathy of judges. Or the answer may lie in Ranney's anticorporation bias. The Ohio constitutional convention of 1850–51 had denied special privileges to corporations, treating them in most respects the same as individuals. Treatise writers and courts, meanwhile, were holding that corporations could be sued in tort to the same extent as individuals. That meant that where an individual was not liable for harm done to another, neither was a corporation. And if an individual was not liable without fault, neither was a corporation.[26]

Legal scholar Gary T. Schwartz suggested that nineteenth-century judges developed tort liability rules in part to protect persons with whom they could identify and empathize.[27] Perhaps empathy induced Ranney to adopt the fellow-servant rule—empathy not for railroad companies but for the small, noncorporate employers who, without the rule, might be subject to liability for which they were not personally responsible.[28] The ideal Jacksonian was the man who earned his bread, as Democrat William Hawkins declared at the constitutional convention, "through years of toil, industry and economy."[29] Ranney himself was the son and grandson of small farmers and was a self-made man. He may well have identified with the "men of small capital" who had no "superior servants" between themselves and their hired hands and who might suffer inordinately without the fellow-servant rule.

Possibly Ranney saw no danger that the fellow-servant rule would leave large numbers of injured railroad employees without redress. He did, after all, find the railroads liable in *Stevens, Keary,* and *Carman,* in the process opening a big hole in the fellow-servant doctrine, finding fault even in the absence of negligence for the injury-causing act, and imposing on railroads the economic costs of their decisions.[30] Ranney's insistence on the "social duty" of corporations to use their property so as not to injure others was not inconsistent with his advocacy of limited government and private economic development. He simply demanded that corporations, like individuals, exercise their free wills responsibly, and he retained a strong sympathy for society's underdogs, those most likely to be hurt by the irresponsible exercise of will by the powerful.

Whigs as well as Democrats sympathized with society's less fortunate members, but they tended to see solutions in moral uplift rather than equality. For example, Whigs supported public schools in order to mold the character of children, whereas Democrats sought to give poor children the same opportunities as the rich had. Ranney's egalitarian motives can be seen in his opinions dealing with bastards and with children caught up in custody fights. The common-law rule that disinherited illegitimate children offended Ranney's sense of natural justice. A child has no choice in the circumstances of its birth, he wrote; an illegitimate child "has the same right as others, whose origin was more fortunate, to be judged by his own personal conduct." Sitting as a district court judge, Ranney found a common-law marriage to exist on the basis of a promise to marry followed by cohabitation. American courts, he explained, had reached such a result as preferable to rendering the children illegitimate; to do the latter "would be to punish the innocent for the sins of others." Four years later Ranney and all of his Democratic colleagues on the supreme court had been replaced by Republicans, a majority of them ex-Whigs. After a closer examination of English and American authorities, the court reversed Ranney's decision. Evincing no concern for the effect of its holding on the children, the court maintained that Ranney's position would shock the people's "sense of propriety and decency," render the rights of inheritance uncertain, open the door to marriage fraud, "and place honest, God-ordained matrimony, and mere meretricious cohabitations too nearly on a level with each other."[31]

Ranney's most oft-cited opinion relating to children came in *Gishwiler v. Dodez,* a habeas corpus proceeding brought by Louis Dodez to obtain custody of his four-year-old daughter Sophia, who was living with her allegedly dissolute mother and an equally disreputable older couple. All the judges agreed that custody must be determined "with a single reference to [the child's] best interests." But Ranney parted company with his brethren by rejecting the traditional common-law rule that gave the father custody of children who had passed the "tender years" stage but were not yet mature enough to choose between their parents. "I can not believe," wrote Ranney, "that, because [the mother] may have reared [the child] until others can bestow the necessary care and attention, it can be taken from her, and the feelings of both mother and child disregarded, for no better reason than that it is the sovereign will of her husband to do so."[32]

Society's underdogs also included lower-class individuals entangled in the criminal justice system. According to John Marshall, the rule that penal laws had to be strictly construed against the state sprang from "the tenderness of the law for the rights of individuals." But Ranney pointedly asserted the right of impoverished and ignorant criminal defendants to have the prosecution adhere to the letter of the law. In overturning a conviction because of a technical error in the indictment, Ranney observed that to have submitted a bill of exceptions to the court might have exceeded the defendant's resources. "[W]e are to remember," wrote Ranney, "that the ignorant, poor, and unfriended are quite as likely to be charged with the crime, as those who have intelligence, friends, and ability to protect their rights at the trial."[33]

Ranney's jurisprudence in these nonconstitutional cases displayed characteristics that might be thought of as Jacksonian in substance: flexibility in applying the common law, insistence on holding corporations to their "social duties," sympathy for the poor and for victims of railroad activities. To these we might add Ranney's use of simple and direct prose and his habit of getting straight to the heart of a case. "The whole controversy in this case," he began one opinion in typical fashion, "when stripped of extraneous and irrelevant matter is reduced to a single question." Then, stating the question succinctly, he proceeded to a plain-language analysis of the facts and the law, as if he were instructing laymen in legal principles.[34]

It was in constitutional cases, however, where fundamental legal and political principles intersected, that Ranney's Radical Democratic proclivities came through most clearly. Ranney never wrote books or articles articulating his constitutional philosophy, but these cases gave him the opportunity to expound his dearly held notions of limited, popular government and states' rights. Before getting to these doctrines, though, we must consider whether Ranney took a Jacksonian position regarding judicial review—the power of courts to strike down legislation on constitutional grounds.

Larry D. Kramer argues that the majoritarian political philosophy of Jacksonian Democrats conflicted with the concept of judicial review, or at least the version of judicial review that asserted the supremacy of judicial determinations of the constitutionality of legislation. Kramer comments that "[i]nsistence on the supremacy of the people over courts was an important element of Jacksonian democracy." In accordance with their majoritarian political creed, Democrats advocated a "departmental" type of judicial review by which each branch of government was, as one Democratic senator put it, "the agent of the people, doing their business according to the powers conferred; and where there is a disagreement as to the extent of these powers, the people themselves, through the ballot-boxes, must settle it."[35]

But there was a hitch in Democratic majoritarian theory. What if, instead of a wealthy elite lording it over the many, as Democrats often proclaimed was the case, it was the majority that acted undemocratically? What if the many oppressed the few? Most Democrats dismissed the obvious examples of slavery in the South and racial discrimination in the North by restricting the rights of citizenship to whites. But that still left the possibility that the white majority could trample upon the rights of a white minority. Democrats stressed majority rule within the party; dissidents were supposed to yield to the majority on matters of substantive party positions.[36] But that would have been cold comfort to a minority deprived of its rights.

As noted earlier, John L. O'Sullivan, editor of the *Democratic Review*, recognized the problem in 1837 when he pondered "the relation between majorities and minorities, in the frequent case of a collision of sentiments and particular interests." "[T]he absolute government of the majority does not always afford a perfect guarantee against the misuse of its numerical power over the weakness of the minority," wrote O'Sullivan. The problem lay in the word "government." "Understood as a central consolidated power," all government, including democratic government, was evil. Therefore, the best government was "that which governs least."[37]

O'Sullivan's small-government ideas soon became Democratic orthodoxy, an orthodoxy that may have contributed to the belief in judicial supremacy among Radical Democratic judges. Kramer attributes the slowly growing acceptance of judicial supremacy within the legal profession to several factors. One was the tendency of judges to regard constitutions as ordinary law, subject to judicial construction in the same manner as legislatively enacted statutes. Another was the professionalization of the bar; as legal education improved and more and more law reports and legal treatises appeared in print, a general sense arose, at least among lawyers, that law was a science beyond the understanding of untrained laymen.[38]

But popular disgust with legislatures played a role, too. Distrust of legislatures led some Democrats to look to the judiciary to curb unscrupulous lawmakers.[39] Mingled with worries about legislative corruption was a fear among Democratic lawyers and judges of the tyranny of the majority.[40] Ranney expressed concerns at the constitutional convention about abuses of power by the people. In the convention's one brief debate on judicial review, he linked these concerns to his belief in judicial supremacy. Ranney insisted on the need for a court that could "stand between the citizen and the Legislature." He called it "utterly futile" for the convention to bother itself with framing a constitution (a "supreme law") "unless we give to some Court the supremacy necessary to assert and declare what the law is." Suppose, said Ranney, that the state takes away my property in violation of the constitutional guarantee that a citizen's property may be taken only for public use and upon full indemnity. Unless I am strong enough and valiant enough to resort to "club-law," I must seek redress in the courts. "And when I come to the Supreme Court, I say to them, that my property has been taxed against a Constitutional guarantee; the Court interposes, and decides that my property shall not be thus taken away." Is it possible, he asked, that the delegates would deny the court's right to give that redress?[41]

A year after the convention closed, Ranney, as a supreme court judge, reiterated his position on judicial supremacy. The Ohio House of Representatives had once impeached judges for declaring a legislative act void, but it now seemed "to be generally, if not universally conceded, that it is the right, and consequently the duty of the judicial tribunals" to determine whether an act of the legislature that had been challenged in court conflicted with either the United States or Ohio constitution. In the event of a conflict the court had to treat the act as a nullity. Ranney found it astonishing that anyone could ever have doubted the power of judicial review. To adjudicate upon and protect the citizen's rights and interests, he wrote, "constitute the whole business of the judicial department." Every judge takes an oath to support the constitution. When he finds an act of the legislature to be in violation of the constitution, he can either "regard his oath, vindicate the fundamental law, and protect the rights of the individual citizen" or "give effect to an act of usurped authority." To adopt the latter course would be "to nullify all constitutional guaranties, and proclaim the legislative body, like the British Parliament, omnipotent."[42]

Ranney's argument for judicial supremacy was not new. Indeed, it was no different from the arguments that had been made in the early nineteenth century by two Ohio judges who had been impeached for their efforts. But those judges had been criticized as being conservatives who sought to thwart the will of the people, as expressed by their democratically elected representatives. By 1852 circumstances had changed. For one thing, judicial supremacy was by then well established if not often wielded to strike down legislation. For another, the people had come to harbor a deep distrust of their agents, the lawmakers. Now radicals called upon the courts to uphold the constitution from assaults by the legislature.[43]

Ranney acknowledged that the legislature was "in the first instance . . . the judge of its own constitutional powers." Legislators, like judges, took an oath to uphold the constitution, and they could not be presumed to act in violation of that oath. But that did not place the two branches on a par. If a court had doubts about the constitutionality of legislation, it had to sustain the law. Only when an act was clearly incompatible with the constitution could the courts "refuse to execute" the law. This sounds something like the old departmental theory: each branch of government decides for itself whether a legislative act is constitutional. But Ranney made it clear that the question before the court was not whether courts could refuse to enforce an act that the legislature believed was constitutional; it was whether that act was "void," a "nullity." The legislature made its determination "in the first instance"; the final authority rested with the courts.[44]

The *fact* of judicial review was not a topic of debate among Ohio's supreme court judges during Ranney's judicial tenure; *how* the power should be exercised was another matter. Since the eighteenth century jurists had disputed whether a constitution must be construed solely on the basis of its text or also in accordance with its spirit. In 1850 Ohio's Whig chief justice, Peter Hitchcock, warned that when judges appealed to a constitution's spirit, "[t]here is great danger that we shall conclude that spirit to be in accordance with our preconceived opinions or feelings of what it ought to be." On the other hand, Ohio's first constitution declared "[t]hat a frequent recurrence to the fundamental principles of civil government is absolutely necessary to preserve the blessings of liberty." This idea, which seemed to sanction an appeal to something akin to the spirit of the constitution, could be found in a number of other early state constitutions. Although the framers of Ohio's second constitution omitted an express statement of the concept from their handiwork of 1850–51, Ranney embraced it. He saw the adoption of a new constitution as a fundamental act of sovereignty, a new beginning for the people of Ohio.[45]

In *Cass v. Dillon,* a case involving a county stock subscription for the construction of a railroad, Ranney and Allen Thurman engaged in a lively debate over text versus spirit. When the political parties nominated their candidates for the supreme court in 1851, Hitchcock predicted that Thurman, a staunch Democrat, "would be quite as conservative as any one among them."[46] In *Cass* Thurman endorsed Hitchcock's position that spirit had no place in constitutional adjudication. Ranney found himself in the minority in his insistence that the court had to enforce the Radical spirit as well as the letter of the constitution.

Section 6 of Article 8 of the new constitution prohibited the General Assembly from authorizing any political subdivision to become a stockholder in any company. The subscription in *Cass* had been made, and a tax to pay for it levied, after the new constitution took effect on September 1, 1851, but the legislature had passed the law authorizing the subscription on March 1. Thurman, writing for the majority, saw no inconsistency between Section 6 and the act of March 1851. Section 6, wrote Thurman, prohibited future *acts* of the General Assembly, not *subscriptions* made by counties under preexisting laws.[47]

Ranney rejected this narrow reading of Section 6. The provisions of the new constitution, he asserted, had to be read in the light of "a few general principles." If others should regard these principles "as too elementary and radical to be introduced into a judicial opinion, or so old as to have become obsolete and unfashionable in this *fast* age," Ranney pointed out that they had always found "a place among the fundamental laws of the state" and were characterized by Ohio's founding fathers "as the 'great and essential principles of liberty and free government' to which '*a frequent recurrence,*' 'is absolutely necessary, to preserve the blessings of liberty.'"[48]

The first principle, declared Ranney, was that "sovereignty belongs only to the mass of the community," or, as Ohio's bill of rights put it, "all political power is inherent in the people." A government was simply the agent of the people, temporarily entrusted with the exercise of sovereign power, and only to the extent that the people delegated that power in "the instrument of delegation—the constitution." An act of the legislature could be void because it was expressly prohibited by the constitution, but it could also be void because it did not fall within the "general grant of power" to the legislature. Ranney thus rejected the theory that a state government, unlike the federal government, enjoyed plenary power except as explicitly limited by the state or federal constitution. This was a view not shared by prominent Democratic judges in other states, let alone Ranney's Democratic colleagues on the Ohio Supreme Court. It put Ranney among the extreme judicial advocates of limited government.[49]

Second, said Ranney, the people possessed "the absolute right, at any time, to resume any portion or all of the political power they had previously delegated, and to construct their government anew." Finally, from the first two "nearly self-evident" principles derived the conclusion that when the new constitution took effect, "all such power previously given, as is not expressly, or by fair implication, delegated to the present government by that instrument, then returned to its source and now remains with the people." Any doubt on that score was settled by the declaration in the bill of rights that "all powers, not *herein* delegated, remain with the people."[50]

The constitutional convention had been called to correct serious evils that had developed under the first constitution. The evil most pertinent to the issues in *Cass* was "a gross abuse of the taxing power" for the construction of internal improvements. The state's appetite for internal improvements had led to "impaired public credit, wasteful expenditure, and a large state debt; followed by onerous taxation." When the state's credit ran out, "a new and still more dangerous expedient was resorted to, under the influence of the railroad mania, for increasing the public burdens to an unlimited amount, and involving the municipal divisions of the state in all the frauds and disasters of private corporations, by authorizing the counties, cities, and towns to subscribe to the stock of such companies." Ranney observed that the constitutional convention had been called "[w]ith this strong tendency to bankruptcy and ruin" in mind.[51]

Ranney regarded Thurman's construction of Section 6 as contrary to the provision's very purpose. *Cass* demonstrated "the absolute necessity . . . of comprehending, clearly, the *spirit and object* of the provision, and of holding that cases within its *equity* are included within it, and governed by it." No legislator, however wise, could "foresee the infinite variety of circumstantial variation, that may arise in cases to which the reason of the rule extends"; and no legal code, "however voluminous," could precisely describe all such cases. If this was true of statutes, how much more so was it of constitutional provisions, which were "necessarily expressed with brevity, and designed to declare great principles in the fewest possible words." Courts had the difficult job of applying these broad principles to specific cases. In discharging this duty, "the polar star to guide the judicial mind, should be the object intended to be accomplished by the provision; and it should be so construed as to preserve this in full vigor, unimpaired by evasion, although in doing so the letter may not be strictly adhered to."[52] And the "plain, palpable, and undeniable" purpose of the various constitutional provisions that limited state debt, barred the state from aiding private enterprise directly, and prohibited the General Assembly from authorizing local governments to aid private enterprise was "to protect the people of the state from the delusion, embarrassment, and onerous taxation to which they had before been subjected."[53] The act that authorized the stock subscription, Ranney concluded, was clearly inconsistent with the constitution; it was outside the people's delegation of power to the General Assembly. Therefore, the new constitution, which continued in effect all prior laws *not inconsistent with the constitution,* implicitly repealed the act, and no person could be compelled to pay a tax levied to purchase the stock.[54]

Thurman had no sympathy for Ranney's approach to constitutional construction. The debates of the constitutional convention might reinforce the text, he conceded, but the document itself was the only reliable source of the framers' intent. Moreover, Thurman doubted that Ranney correctly understood even the spirit of Section 6.[55] But there can be no doubt that Ranney, who had ardently participated in the convention's proceedings, knew and shared the spirit that took power away from the General Assembly and severely limited the authority of government to incur debt, construct internal improvements, and aid private enterprise. In that spirit Judge Ranney reiterated the laissez-faire ideas he had voiced as a convention delegate. In *Cass* he acknowledged that governments could fund internal improvements on a pay-as-you-go basis, but he insisted that the better course was to leave their construction to private enterprise. History, contended Ranney, "fully demonstrates that they will be built by private enterprise and capital as fast as the investment is safe, and the business of the country will justify." On the other hand, one did not have to be a prophet to foresee that when counties and towns got involved, the projects "will very soon pass into the hands of the preferred creditors, the stock will be sunk, and the counties and towns left to pay up their indebtedness by the most oppressive taxation; or, what is not at all unlikely, to repudiate their obligations, notwithstanding the disgrace, corruption of public morals, and great individual loss sure to result from such a course."[56]

The statute in *Cass* had been passed before the new constitution took effect. In theory the General Assembly could have repealed that law and others like it before the county subscribed to the stock. However, as Ranney pointed out, "[s]ad experience" had taught the people that laws affecting only one locality "seldom commanded the deliberate judgment" of the whole General Assembly. That was why the people had found it necessary to prevent the legislature "from authorizing this evil; and remembering that *minorities were as well entitled to protection as majorities,* they have given each individual citizen a sure guaranty that his right of property shall not be invaded in that manner, or for such purposes."[57]

After the Civil War, protection of the property rights of minorities from attack by majorities became a hallmark of so-called laissez-faire constitutionalism. When governments attempted to use their powers of taxation or eminent domain to promote economic development, courts demanded that the exercise of those powers be justified by some public purpose. Often the economic development project in question was a railroad, so the matter of whether public aid to private railroad corporations fulfilled a public purpose became crucial. Judges of Ranney's age and political background split over the issue.[58]

Before the war, though, it seemed indisputable that railroads satisfied the public purpose requirement. Ranney held that "the construction of public highways" was a legitimate legislative purpose, "inferior to none in its influence upon the comfort, convenience and prosperity of the people, and the security of the state." He used the term "public highways" "in its largest sense, without any restriction as to the character of the structure, or the mode of travel and transportation upon it." In other words, railroads were public highways. A public highway could not be built without the use of private lands, but a landowner might not willingly give up his property for its construction. But because "the necessary functions of government ought not to be paralyzed by the will of a single individual, nor the interests of all be made subservient to the whim or caprice of one," the construction of a public highway "has always presented one of the most clear and unquestionable instances for the exercise of the power of eminent domain."[59]

Ranney saw no constitutional impediment to the exercise of eminent domain powers by private corporations pursuant to law. The General Assembly could choose any apposite means to carry out its objectives "under suitable regulations" and subject to the right of the public to use the improvement. The corporation was "a mere trustee of the interest for their use, with no power to divert it to any other purpose, or to hold it one moment longer than it is made to serve the uses for which it was appropriated."[60]

Ranney regarded the taxing power and the eminent domain power as two versions of the same phenomenon—the taking of private property under the authority of the state—and applied the same principles to both.[61] The taxing power, like the eminent domain power, could be exercised only for public purposes, but those purposes included roads, canals, and other internal improvements "calculated to facilitate the social and business intercourse of the people, and to develop its resources and add to its strength and security." In exercising either power the General Assembly had broad discretion as to the means employed.[62] But taxation, which had been a far more potent issue than eminent domain in bringing about the constitutional convention, induced in Ranney a more cautious approach toward the use of governmental power. It was in a taxation case that he warned against encroachments upon the reserved rights of the people that had not been delegated to any branch of government.[63] Furthermore, a power that the people had delegated to the General Assembly, such as the power to tax for public purposes, remained with that body and subject to democratic control. "The power to tax is one of the highest attributes of sovereignty," said Ranney, and its surrender by the legislature must never be assumed.[64]

Ranney and his brethren on the bench soon found themselves embroiled in controversy over the power of the state to "surrender" any portion of the sovereign power of taxation. One of the great political issues of the Jacksonian era was "banks or no banks." Banks had gotten much of the blame for speculation and financial panics. Suspicion of banks ran wide and deep, especially in the West, and many Democrats wanted to outlaw banks altogether. At the Ohio constitutional convention delegates had twice proposed putting the issue of "banks or no banks" on the ballot along with the constitution.[65]

A standoff between Whigs and Democrats in the 1840s, when the charters of most banks in Ohio were due to expire, threatened to leave Ohio with no banks at all. In 1845 the then-dominant Whigs averted the crisis with the Kelley Law, which overhauled the banking system and allowed new and existing banks to organize under its terms. Section 60 of the Kelley Law required each bank that chose to organize under the statute to set off 6 percent of its net profits to the state in lieu of taxes. In March 1851, however, the General Assembly passed a law taxing banks and corporate stock the same as other taxable property. Many banks argued that any legislation that raised their taxes was an unconstitutional impairment of their "contracts" under Section 60 of the Kelley Law.[66]

The contract argument rested on the *Dartmouth College* case. The contracts clause of the U.S. Constitution prohibits the states from impairing the obligations of contract. In *Dartmouth,* decided in 1819, the United States Supreme Court held that a corporate charter granted by an act of the legislature was a contract protected by the contracts clause.[67] Or at least that was how most people, including judges, had been reading *Dartmouth* for years.[68] Special acts of incorporation often gave to banking, canal, railroad, or other business corporations privileges not available to the general public: the right to issue paper money in the form of bank notes, tax exemptions, eminent domain powers, and so on. Later legislatures might regret the granting of such privileges, but if corporate charters were contracts that the U.S. Constitution protected from impairment by the states, there was nothing the lawmakers could do. *Dartmouth College* therefore stood as a bulwark against legislative interference with corporate privileges.

Andrew Jackson waged a ferocious war against the mightiest corporation of them all, the Second Bank of the United States, and by 1833 had succeeded in "killing the monster." Within a few years the Democratic Party assumed a stance of deep hostility toward corporations in general and banks in particular as bastions of privilege. In the *Charles River Bridge* case,[69] the U.S. Supreme Court, headed by Jackson's former attorney general Roger B. Taney, ruled that corporate charters had to be construed strictly in favor of the public, and that meant no finding of exclusive corporate privileges by inference.

Contemporary critics regarded the *Charles River Bridge* decision as evidence of "agrarian radicalism" on the march and a blow to property rights. However, the decision followed *Dartmouth College* in recognizing corporate charters as constitutionally protected contracts, and Taney turned out not to be the scourge of corporations that Whigs and businessmen feared. By the 1850s corporations and the court had reached an accommodation. Corporations learned to live within the limits set by the court, and the court threw its protective mantle around corporate charters that came within those limits, especially when the charters seemed to protect corporations from taxation.[70]

Some of the Taney court's key decisions on taxation came in cases from Ohio. When the Ohio General Assembly raised the tax on banks in 1851, the banks sought relief in the courts. They did not find a sympathetic ear in their state supreme court. In 1853 the Ohio Supreme Court decided four cases involving the constitutionality of the new tax. A fifth case originated in the federal district court, where it was heard by U.S. Supreme Court justice John McLean sitting on circuit. The state cases appear to have been presented together.[71] A different judge wrote the court's opinion in each case. Ranney, Caldwell, and Corwin wrote unanimous opinions in *Debolt v. Ohio Life Insurance and Trust Company* (*OLI&T*), *Mechanics' and Traders' Branch of the State Bank of Ohio v. Debolt,* and *Knoup v. Piqua Branch of the State Bank of Ohio,* respectively. Bartley wrote the court's lengthy, wide-ranging opinion in *Bank of Toledo v. City of Toledo.* Ranney concurred in *Bank of*

Toledo on the basis of his opinion in *OLI&T,* refusing to add his imprimatur to arguments that he felt were unnecessary to the decision.[72]

All four judges addressed the contentious constitutional issue, but three of them made a point of stating that their remarks on the matter were obiter dicta not essential to the decision. Bartley conceded that *Bank of Toledo* might have been decided on other grounds, but he believed that the constitutional question was too important not to address head-on. The majority of the court, he wrote, "feel no disposition to evade the responsibility of its determination; but deem it a duty to meet it *fully, fairly* and *frankly.*"[73] This was a dig at Ranney, the only judge who concurred separately.

Ranney wrote the most consequential of the four majority opinions. In *OLI&T* Ranney rested his holding primarily on contract law. Rather than plunge into the constitutional question of whether the legislature *could* surrender any part of its sovereign power, he asked whether the legislature, by passing the Kelley Law, had *intended* to part with sovereign power. A grant of sovereign power, he wrote, can never be assumed. As the Supreme Court had declared in *Charles River Bridge,* ambiguities had to be construed in favor of the public. Ranney accurately characterized the Kelley Law as a general law that did not actually grant a corporate charter to anyone. It simply provided the means by which a new or existing bank that wished to take advantage of its provisions, including the tax limitation, could do so. Nor did the Kelley Law expressly incorporate Section 60 into the charters of corporations that organized under the Law—something the lawmakers easily could have done, as Ranney illustrated by examples of previous statutes. In sum, regardless of whether the General Assembly *could* have contracted away a portion of the taxing power via the Kelley Law, Ranney held that the legislature did not *intend* to do so and *did not* do so.[74]

Having found that the General Assembly had not contractually relinquished its power to tax the banks, Ranney thought it unnecessary to discuss whether the legislature had the power to do so. In dicta, however, he explained why it lacked the power. Relying again on the concept of delegation, he asserted that the sovereign power resides in the people. The government has only those powers expressly delegated to it. In the constitution the people delegated to the government the tools necessary to achieve their safety and prosperity, including the powers of eminent domain and taxation. In the hands of the state, eminent domain and taxation were not independent powers to be exercised in any manner, but only means to an end (public safety and prosperity). Any other use of those powers exceeded the delegation of authority.[75]

The company's argument, said Ranney, boiled down to this: the people could have delegated to the government the authority to surrender the taxing power. But in fact, he went on, the people had not done so. They had delegated the power of taxation for public purposes, not the power to surrender any portion of the taxing authority by contract or otherwise. Nor may the government exercise the taxing power in such a way as "to subvert the government, or invade other fundamental rights," including the right to equal protection of the laws. "For every surrender of the right to tax particular property, not only tends to paralyze the government, but involves a direct invasion of the rights of property, of the balance of the community; since the deficiency thus created, must be made up by larger contributions from them, to meet the public demand."[76]

Ranney also argued that the contracts clause had no application to a state's right of taxation. The U.S. Supreme Court, he pointed out, had held that the exercise of sovereign power had to remain subject to the will of the legislature and could never be alienated; that the U.S. Constitution could "by no rational interpretation be brought to conflict with" a state's "right and the duty of guarding its own existence, and of promoting the interests and welfare of the community at large." In short, the contracts clause did not apply to supposed grants of sovereign powers.[77]

Probably everyone involved in the bank cases expected the issue to go to the U.S. Supreme Court. Three of the decisions—four, if we include McLean's federal case—were, in fact, appealed. Only *Bank of Toledo,* in which Bartley insisted that *Dartmouth College* had been either wrongly decided or misconstrued, ended in state court. The Supreme Court handed down decisions in both *Knoup* (or *Knoop,* as the Miami County auditor's name was also spelled) and *OLI&T* on May 24, 1854. The court did not decide *Mechanics' and Traders' Bank* and the federal action, *Dodge v. Woolsey,* until 1856. The opinions in *Knoop* appear to have been written first; there are references to *Knoop* in *OLI&T,* but the only mention of *OLI&T* in *Knoop* is Taney's allusion to his forthcoming opinion in that case. *Knoop* governed the outcomes of *Mechanics' and Traders' Bank* and *Dodge.* The justices, regardless of which side they came down on, ignored Corwin's unanimous opinion in *Knoop* and wrote as if Ranney's dicta in *OLI&T* had been the opinion of the Ohio court. In *OLI&T* itself a splintered court upheld Ranney's judgment because of facts unique to that case.[78]

In *OLI&T* Chief Justice Taney affirmed the state court's judgment despite objections to Ranney's reasoning. The opinion confirmed that Taney posed no threat to corporate enterprise. Taney agreed with Ranney that a legislature could not deprive its successors of a sovereign power that had been delegated to the legislative branch of government unless the surrender of that power was permitted under the state constitution. However, he contended that a string of Ohio precedents had upheld surrenders of sovereign power analogous to the one in Section 60 of the Kelley Law. He refused to be bound by a state court's construction of its own state's constitution that, in his view, flew in the face of well-established state law.[79]

Moreover, Taney ruled that in cases brought under the contracts clause of the U.S. Constitution, the Supreme Court was not bound by a state court's construction of a contract, whether the contract was an ordinary agreement or one in the guise of a law. He made an independent determination that the Ohio Life Insurance & Trust Company had not been organized under the Kelley Law and that Section 60 was therefore not a part of any contract with that corporation.[80]

Only one other justice concurred in Taney's opinion. Three justices dissented on the ground that Section 60 constituted a contract with the company, and another dissented without opinion. Three southern Democrats—Justices Catron, Campbell, and Daniel—upheld the judgment on the basis of their opinions in *Piqua,* to which we will turn in a moment. Daniel added the pointed comment that he could never believe in the "suicidal doctrine, which confers upon one legislature, the creatures and limited agents of the sovereign people, the power, by a breach of duty and by transcending the commission with which they are clothed, to bind forever and irrevocably their creator, for whose benefit and by whose authority alone they are delegated to act, to consequences however mischievous or destructive."[81]

Stanley Kutler remarks that in *OLI&T* "Taney again bowed to the legislature and refused to have the Court judge the wisdom of public policy, even though it might clearly be harmful to the public interest."[82] In fact the conflict between legislative supremacy and community rights was not the only clash of Democratic principles involved in the case. Taney's restraint vis-à-vis the legislature disregarded the opinion of a state court on state law and thereby pitted the Supreme Court against states' rights.

Because of the unusual nature and history of the Ohio Life Insurance & Trust Company, the decision did not bring out in high relief the deep divisions developing among the Supreme Court justices. These differences appeared sharply in *Piqua,* which involved an ordinary bank to which Section 60 unquestionably applied. Writing for the majority, McLean found it incontrovertible that Section 60 was a special law for each corporation that organized under the Kelley Law and not a general law, as maintained by Ranney. Moreover, he had no doubt that the charters of those corporations were true contracts into which the state, by enacting the Kelley Law, had induced the corporations to enter. McLean observed that the highest courts of both the United States and Ohio had long ago determined that a corporate charter was a contract. He denied that a tax exemption (to which, it had been argued, a lower tax rate amounted) was a surrender of sovereignty; rather, it was a matter of policy. Indeed, the making of a contract, even one that offered a lower tax rate to a corporation, was not a surrender but an exercise of sovereignty.[83]

Taney concurred in the judgment, based on his reasoning in *OLI&T* regarding the contractual nature of a corporate charter. Catron, Campbell, and Daniel dissented. Catron lauded Ranney's opinion in *OLI&T* for its "fairness, ability, and learning" and quoted extensively from it. He went on to assert that the decisions of the Ohio Supreme Court on the construction of the Ohio Constitution, including the power or lack of power of one legislature to bind its successors, were binding on the U.S. Supreme Court. Catron insisted that *Piqua* was no different in principle from *West River Bridge,* in which the Supreme Court had recognized the inalienable nature of a state's sovereign powers; that is, that the state's right of self-preservation precluded a legislature from contracting away its sovereign powers in a manner that would forever bind its successors.[84]

Campbell, with whom Daniel concurred, found Section 60 to be a public law, containing no promise that the method of taxation it set forth would be permanent. Section 60 was just one part of a comprehensive scheme to regulate banking and contained no hint of an intent to limit the ability of future General Assemblies to tax banks. The Kelley Law was a matter of public administration, not bargaining. Whatever the corporations might have hoped for when they organized under the Kelley Law, Campbell wrote, hopes and expectations did not amount to a contract. The legislature held its powers in trust for the people who had delegated them, and they had to be returned to the people undiminished.[85]

Several more cases involving the contractual nature of corporate charters reached the Ohio Supreme Court shortly after Ranney left the bench. In each one the majority found the question to have been settled by the U.S. Supreme Court's decision in *Knoop.*[86] But the bank cases had a more significant, and ironic, epilogue. For southerners Campbell, Catron, and Daniel the development of corporate law in the Supreme Court had taken a direction dangerous to the survival of slavery, for it impinged upon the right of a state to manage its internal affairs free from federal interference. "On the eve of *Dred Scott,*" writes Austin Allen, "a majority of justices were invoking the federal Constitution, although grudgingly, against state efforts to abrogate tax exemptions that they had previously granted to corporations." Daniel, Catron, and Campbell "dissented from these rulings because they stripped the states of their inherent right of self-preservation."[87] The irony lay in the high regard with which the three southern justices held Ranney's opinion in *OLI&T* and the contribution Ranney thus made to their cause. Ranney had run for Congress on free-soil principles, had reportedly questioned the constitutionality of the Fugitive Slave Law, and during the Civil War would recruit soldiers for the Union. Daniel, Catron, and Campbell all defended slavery, and Campbell would serve the Confederacy as assistant secretary of war.

The three southerners agreed with Ranney again in 1858, after *Dred Scott.* This time the question had to do with maritime law, which would appear to be at least as distant from the sectional conflict as taxation of corporations. The Ohio case arose in 1849 when one Keating filed a claim in state court against the steamboat *Julius D. Morton* for labor performed in its construction. The sheriff seized the boat, but after entry of judgment he was unable to deliver the vessel to his successor for sale because the U.S. marshal had taken possession of it. The marshal was acting in a federal admiralty proceeding brought by a seaman for wages owed. The question faced by the Ohio Supreme Court was whether the sheriff who had first seized the *Julius D. Morton* was liable for the judgment, or whether the seizure by the U.S. marshal absolved him of liability.[88]

Ranney believed that the seaman's suit was concocted in order to move the steamboat into Lake Erie, beyond the reach of the state court, and he was loath to "place an honest creditor . . . at the mercy of his debtor." However, the legal resolution of the conflict depended on the extent of federal admiralty jurisdiction over internal waters. In his opinion for the court Ranney outlined the history of admiralty jurisdiction, explaining how U.S. Supreme Court decisions had expanded that jurisdiction from its traditional concern with matters on the high seas and noting Justice Daniel's repeated dissents. In the Great Lakes Act of 1845 Congress further extended the admiralty jurisdiction of federal courts to matters of contract and tort involving large vessels engaged in interstate coastal commerce on the lakes and on navigable rivers connecting them. It was on the authority of this statute that the marshal had seized the *Julius D. Morton.*[89]

Without conceding Congress's constitutional power to confer on federal courts exclusive jurisdiction over vessels on internal waters, Ranney observed that the 1845 act expressly preserved concurrent remedies under state common law. But even without the savings clause, he argued, states had concurrent jurisdiction. The U.S. Constitution and acts of Congress were the supreme laws of the land, but they were not "the only supreme laws in the land." The people of the states were the sovereign power before the Constitution came into being, and they remained "the only source and fountain of sovereign authority" in American political theory. In adopting the United States Constitution, the people had delegated to the federal government "certain enumerated and clearly-defined powers" and reserved to themselves or the states all undelegated powers.[90]

The powers delegated to the federal government, Ranney continued, fell far short of all the powers needed for "a complete administration of civil affairs." Therefore the people also delegated certain powers, equally important and more extensive, to the governments of the states. State and federal authority derived from the same sovereign source, the people; and each government, "when acting within its rightful jurisdiction, has supreme control over all the persons and property within the territory covered by its authority." If the federal courts did not have exclusive jurisdiction over a matter—as, in Ranney's opinion, they did not have in the case of the *Julius D. Morton*—then the states had the untrammeled right to provide whatever remedies they chose. Here, the state had authorized the sheriff to take possession of the vessel. Once he had done so, possession was no longer in the owner but the state, and the federal courts could not interfere with that possession. In reaching this conclusion Ranney believed he was preserving the ability of state governments to carry out the important duties for which they had been created.[91]

A case very similar to *Keating v. Spink* came before the U.S. Supreme Court in 1858, and the court came to a similar conclusion. Justice Campbell, writing for a five-man majority that also included Daniel, Catron, and, interestingly, McLean, declared "the duty of this court to give preference to such principles and methods of procedure as shall serve to conciliate the distinct and independent tribunals of the States and of the Union, so that they may co-operate as harmonious members of a judicial system coextensive with the United States." Campbell cited *Keating,* among other cases. Taney wrote the dissenting opinion. He did not take issue with the state-sovereignty implications of Campbell's opinion. Rather, he thought that Campbell had mischaracterized the issue. Campbell, he said, treated the controversy as "a conflict between sovereignties," whereas in fact it really involved "the relative powers and duties of a court of admiralty and a court of common law in the case of an admitted maritime lien." That Campbell deliberately framed the issue as he did to buttress the case for restricting federal power, with slavery in mind, is not clear. But his opinion fit the pattern of thought that he, Catron, and Daniel had displayed in the bank cases. And once again Ranney's opinion lent support to proslavery, disunionist jurisprudence.[92]

Ranney's partial appointive term and full elective term on the supreme court covered a span of just five and a half years. He would sit on the court for another two years during the Civil War, but it was during the 1850s, when men steeped in Jacksonian politics served as state judges all over the country, that Ranney acquired his reputation as an outstanding jurist. "[I]n the short term of five years," wrote one commentator in 1856, Ranney had "given character and tone to the judicial history of the State." With a tenure of ten years or more "his fame as a profound lawyer and judge would extend beyond his own State, and his opinions command a respect, wherever read, equal to those of Chief Justice Shaw."[93] Ranney's body of judicial work was too small to gain him a reputation comparable to Shaw's, but it was enough to indicate the existence of a Jacksonian jurisprudence that included more than a handful of U.S. Supreme Court cases. Ranney insisted on holding corporations to their "social duties" and on preserving the state's taxing power against the claims of banks. He interpreted the law in favor of illegitimate children, mothers seeking custody of their children, and other underdogs. Reading the new state constitution in the spirit of the constitutional convention, Ranney held that governments had only those powers expressly delegated to them by the people. He strictly construed the constitution to limit legislative authority and to protect taxpayers from spendthrift popular majorities. Ranney never developed a judicial philosophy, and he sometimes disagreed with his equally Jacksonian Democratic colleagues; but these positions, taken together, represent a consistent if incomplete jurisprudence derived from Jacksonian political ideals.

FIVE

The Republican Challenge

IN THE penultimate year of Ranney's term on the supreme court, Congress split the federal judicial district of Ohio in two, creating Northern and Southern districts. The incumbent judge for the District of Ohio, Humphrey Howe Leavitt, became the judge for the Southern District. On February 10, 1855, President Franklin Pierce nominated Hiram V. Willson, a prominent Cleveland attorney, for the judgeship of the Northern District. The nomination displeased some of Ohio's congressional delegates, especially Senator George E. Pugh, whose efforts to block confirmation kept the Senate from getting on with other business when it met in executive session. Pugh and his allies wanted Ranney appointed to the court. The Whigs, a small minority in the Senate, had intended to stay out of the Democratic family feud, but the quarrel grew so bitter that they decided to vote as a bloc for whichever aspirant received the approbation of John W. Allen, a Cleveland attorney and former Whig congressman. On Allen's recommendation the Whigs voted for Willson and brought the ten-day fight to a close. The Whig *Toledo Blade* applauded the choice, Willson "being the least rabid and ultra" of the candidates.[1]

Having lost the contest for the federal judgeship, Ranney faced a campaign for reelection to the Ohio Supreme Court in 1856. Politics in Ohio, as in the nation as a whole, had been radically transformed since 1851. The Whig Party, and with it the vibrant, two-party system of Whigs and Democrats, had collapsed. Some historians attribute the demise of the Whigs to their nomination of southern slaveholder Zachary Taylor for president in 1848. The defection of antislavery radicals in 1848, they maintain, "dealt the Whig organization in Ohio a blow from which it never recovered." Other scholars emphasize the fading significance of economic issues that had formed the centerpiece of the Whig program and the rise of the prohibition movement. Prohibition caused headaches for both parties, but more for Whigs, who could not reach out to needed religious and ethnic groups without alienating their "dry" base. Voters disillusioned with Whigs and Democrats could easily form new parties, such as the nativist Know-Nothing Party, which for a time seemed likely to replace the Whigs as the Democrats' chief opposition.[2]

Whatever the part played by prohibition and other ethnocultural issues in the disruption of the second-party system in Ohio, there is no question that the Kansas-Nebraska Act of 1854 helped scuttle that system by rousing the antislavery movement throughout the North and making the extension of slavery the burning national issue of the 1850s. The issue was not new, of course. The United States acquired the vast Louisiana Purchase in 1803, and when Missouri, carved out of the Purchase, applied for admission to the Union as a slave state sixteen years later, northerners raised a howl of protest. That crisis was resolved by the Missouri Compromise, which in part provided that, except in Missouri, the Louisiana Purchase north of the 36°30' parallel would remain free.

The annexation of Texas and the wresting of vast swaths of land from Mexico in the 1840s renewed the fight over slavery in the West. Northern Whigs generally opposed both annexation and the Mexican War. After the war, northern Whigs, with the aid of antislavery Democrats, tried to keep slavery out of the territories seized from Mexico. During the intense fighting over the issue, some southerners threatened secession if they did not get their way. Fear of disunion produced the Compromise of 1850, masterminded by Senators Henry Clay, the Whig elder statesman from Kentucky, and the rising Democratic star Stephen A. Douglas of Illinois. Two features of the compromise would figure prominently in the Ohio gubernatorial race of 1859. One established the principle of popular sovereignty for the territories of New Mexico and Utah; the residents of those territories would decide for themselves whether or not to permit slavery within their borders.

The other was the Fugitive Slave Law, which required U.S. citizens to assist in the capture of runaway slaves and provided for nonjury, one-sided hearings for captured blacks alleged to be fugitive slaves.

The Compromise of 1850 was supposed to have settled the slavery controversy permanently, allaying the threat of disunion, and for a time it seemed to have worked. But Douglas's brainchild, the Kansas-Nebraska Act, destroyed the peace. Douglas wanted to organize the Nebraska Territory, part of the Louisiana Purchase, in order to facilitate the construction of a transcontinental railroad. As the price for southern support for the railroad, Douglas agreed to the repeal of the Missouri Compromise and its replacement with the principle of popular sovereignty. That part of the Louisiana Purchase lying just west of Missouri was organized as the Kansas Territory. Southerners had good reason to hope that Kansas, like Missouri, would permit slavery.

Antislavery northerners raged at the passage of the Kansas-Nebraska Act. In Ohio a "fusion" convention of "Anti-Nebraska men"—Whigs, Democrats, and Free Soilers—met in July 1854 and nominated a Whig and a Democrat for the two state offices to be filled that year. In October the fusionists, often called Republicans, won a rousing victory, taking the two state offices by a wide margin. Anti-Nebraska candidates won all twenty-one congressional districts.

All of this opposition in Ohio to the extension of slavery did not indicate a commitment to the civil rights of African Americans. Racism was deeply ingrained in the Buckeye State. The state constitution and Black Laws restricted suffrage to white males, excluded blacks from the militia and from juries, prohibited blacks from testifying against whites in court, and imposed a variety of other burdens on the education, employment, and immigration of blacks. Even after the repeal of the most notorious of the Black Laws in 1849, blacks remained voteless, politically powerless, deeply disadvantaged, and disdained by most whites.

In 1855 Ohio's Anti-Nebraska fusionists officially became the Republican Party. The Republican state convention nominated Salmon P. Chase for governor and co-opted the nativists by naming Know-Nothings for all other statewide offices. Dissident Know-Nothings and old Whigs who could not stomach Chase held a separate convention and nominated their own candidate for governor, as, of course, did the Democrats. Chase won easily, and the Republicans carried both houses of the General Assembly by a wide margin.

The political upheaval and the new emphasis on slavery and sectionalism in the politics of the 1850s produced new notions of conservatism and radicalism. The conflict between North and South entailed such vehement assertions of rights and such outraged denunciations of adversaries that the country seemed to be coming apart. The threat to the very existence of the Union far outweighed concerns about the issues that had previously separated Whigs from Democrats. Conservatism and radicalism came to be defined primarily in terms of slavery and the Union. Northern and southern politicians and editors indulged in sweeping generalizations about the attitudes of folks on the other side of the Mason-Dixon Line on these matters. They professed their own true conservatism and roundly condemned the radicalism of their adversaries.

The North, wrote one southerner, had gone mad over slavery; the abolitionist steamroller threatened to crush the South. There seemed but one defense. "[T]he superstition—for such alone it is—which found a merit in the Union *per se,* when the Constitution offered no longer any securities—is rapidly dying out in the hearts of the people." The agricultural South, he continued, was "a conservative community; full of veneration, steadfast to old places and habits, suspicious of change." If the Union were to survive, it would have to be brought back to justice, to constitutional guaranties, and to equal treatment for the South.[3] Northerners of all political stripes—and most southerners, too, until the eve of the Civil War—contemplated the rending of the Union with horror and denounced southern "fire-eaters" and secessionists as dangerous radicals. In assigning blame for this existential threat, northerners looked not only to the South but to those in the North who, in their view, encouraged southern extremism or drove southerners to excess. Whoever opposed the aiders and abettors of disunion was, by definition, a conservative.

All the major parties tried to wrap themselves in the mantle of pro-Union conservatism. In 1856 Hamilton Fish of New York, a man of unimpeachably conservative Whig credentials, came out in support of Republican presidential candidate John C. Frémont as the true conservative in the race. In the Republicans, he wrote, "[w]e find no assault upon a single Whig principle—no danger of an unsafe and belligerent foreign policy—no extreme or violent proposition in regard to slavery where it now exists, but only that resistance to its advance and spread over soil long since made free, which we have ever advocated." Supporters of Millard Fillmore, nominated by the remnants of the Whigs and Know-Nothings, trumpeted him as "the only conservative candidate," the only one who would represent the entire nation instead of a section, the man best suited "to restore order out of chaos." Eminent lawyer Rufus Choate, the very embodiment of the conservative Whig, declared it the "first duty" of Whigs to defeat "the new geographical party, calling itself Republican" and announced his intention to vote for Democrat James Buchanan as the candidate most likely to preserve the Union. With the near disappearance of the Whigs and Know-Nothings and the advent of the Republicans, there was, in the view of Democrats, no party but theirs that could even pretend to stand for conservatism. In their own minds they were the only national party, the only party sincerely loyal to the Constitution and the Union, and thus the only real conservatives.[4]

In 1856 the only statewide offices on the ballot in Ohio were attorney general, commissioner of schools, a place on the Board of Public Works, and two supreme court seats, one of them Ranney's. The Democrats renominated Ranney in January.[5] Six months later Ranney attended the Democratic national convention as a delegate. Three men vied for the presidential nomination that year: President Franklin Pierce, Senator Stephen A. Douglas, and the recently returned ambassador to Great Britain, James Buchanan. Pierce's uninspired performance as president, lackluster personality, and southern leanings dissatisfied many northern Democrats. Douglas, who had lost to Pierce at the 1852 Democratic national convention, might have had a clear shot at the nomination had he not carried the Kansas-Nebraska Act to passage in 1854. Northern Democrats who opposed the extension of slavery would not forgive Douglas for this transgression. Buchanan, a Pennsylvanian with a long congressional and diplomatic career, had no better a record on slavery. Indeed, he was the quintessential "northern man with southern principles." But Buchanan had been overseas for the preceding three years and was therefore untainted by the Kansas-Nebraska Act.

At the convention Buchanan led on the first ballot, with Pierce a strong second and Douglas and Lewis Cass, the 1848 Democratic candidate, far in the rear. The Ohio delegation strongly supported Buchanan throughout the contest. Given Ranney's free-soil stance on the extension of slavery and purported condemnation of the Fugitive Slave Law, he could have had little love for Pierce or Douglas. He voted unwaveringly for Buchanan, who finally prevailed on the seventeenth ballot.[6]

The presidential campaign and national issues dominated the political news in 1856. The Republican state platform was devoted entirely to slavery and the sectional conflict. During the campaign Ranney and other

Democratic leaders spoke out on the slavery issue, denying that there was any affinity between "national" Democratic doctrine and slavery. Buchanan won the presidency, but 1856 was a Republican year in Ohio. Ranney stood no chance of reelection. Republican Josiah Scott, a fifty-three-year-old lawyer and former state legislator, received 175,818 votes, to 156,438 for Ranney and 23,868 for Know-Nothing candidate Daniel Peck. The totals were similar for all the statewide offices. Republicans also captured thirteen of twenty-one congressional seats, and Frémont carried the state. Ranney resigned from the court soon after the election, and Governor Chase appointed Scott to fill the vacancy.[7]

Ranney left office with a stellar reputation as a jurist. Even the *Western Reserve Chronicle,* which had no use for Ranney's politics, commented that Ranney had "filled his office in a manner which is highly honorable to himself, as well as to the general satisfaction of both lawyers and clients. As a man, a lawyer, and a jurist, he occupies a deservedly high position."[8]

By early January 1857 word was out that Ranney was about to move to Cleveland and form a law partnership with Franklin T. Backus, a well-known ex-Whig and then Republican who was already practicing in association with Charles W. Noble. In April, following the resignation of the U.S. attorney for the Northern District of Ohio, the freshly inaugurated Buchanan appointed Ranney to fill the vacancy. Federal district attorneys prosecuted crimes under federal law and represented the United States in civil suits in their districts. Just three months after his appointment, Ranney resigned. His whole last year on the Ohio Supreme Court, Ranney wrote to the U.S. attorney general, he had been "afflicted with the chill fever and ague." He thought the illness had disappeared over the winter, but it had returned with the warm weather. Newspaper reports also attributed the resignation to Ranney's inability to meet the demands of both his federal job and his private clients. One paper that supported Ranney's political ambitions asserted that the real reason was inadequate compensation. U.S. attorneys were paid from fees that were taxed as costs in their cases. The *Cleveland Plain Dealer* estimated the district attorney's compensation in 1857 to be three thousand dollars annually. It may be that after five years of a modest salary for his state supreme court service, Ranney found the time spent on his federal position not worth the fees it generated.[9]

Or perhaps Ranney resigned to concentrate on politics. As early as January various Democratic papers were pushing Ranney for the gubernatorial nomination. Joseph W. Gray, editor of the *Plain Dealer,* claimed to have visited Ranney and to have asked him about the endorsements. Ranney, he wrote, disclaimed any interest in the post. In the spring Gray asked him again, and again Ranney disavowed any interest. The *Plain Dealer* then endorsed Cleveland attorney and businessman Henry B. Payne. In April the *Zanesville Aurora* substituted Payne for Ranney as its preferred candidate. On May 4 the *Plain Dealer* noted the widespread support for Payne among Democratic papers and published excerpts from more than half a dozen, giving the impression that a Payne nomination was well-nigh inevitable, although some of the endorsements were based on the assumption that Ranney refused to run.[10]

But Gray did not push Payne's candidacy merely because Ranney had denied any interest in running. Gray had personal and political reasons for favoring Payne. He had studied law in Payne's office, and he, like Payne, was a Douglas Democrat. Shortly before the state Democratic convention met in Columbus, the *Plain Dealer* noted that Ranney would be out of step with the convention if he adhered to the free-soil views expressed in his 1848 letter to B. F. Hoffman.[11]

Gray also criticized Ranney for the timing of his resignation as federal district attorney. On July 27 the *Plain Dealer* implied that Ranney's excuse for resigning, ill health, was disingenuous. Ranney could not very well have given inadequate compensation as a reason, said the paper, in the middle of an important term of court. On August 3, three days before the convention, Gray published Ranney's letter of explanation. Ranney asserted that the poor state of his health at the time was well known. He declared that he could not have resigned until he had wrapped up all outstanding business before the federal court. On July 6, eight days before the opening of the next term of court, he sent his resignation to Washington, leaving no pending matters for his successor. The *Plain Dealer* found Ranney's explanation unacceptable. How could Ranney expect a successor to be appointed in time for the July term when his letter of resignation would probably not even reach Washington before July 14? Ranney's short notice required that cases be postponed for weeks until a new district attorney could be nominated, confirmed, and ready for business.[12]

Although the *Plain Dealer* strove to make Payne's surge toward the nomination unstoppable, on the eve of the convention the state's leading Republican newspaper, the *Ohio State Journal*, believed that Ranney had the edge. According to the *Journal*, "The Ranney men . . . felt sure that their wing of the machine would win." But Payne ran away with the nomination on the first ballot, with 187 votes, to 89 for Ranney and 64 for former congressman Joseph J. McDowell. The hostile *National Era,* an abolitionist newspaper, described the Ohio Democratic convention as a conclave of "contending factions, each bent only on the injury or destruction of the other." Ranney and McDowell headed the Buchanan faction, "while Payne, McLain, and Steadman, led the reckless horde of proslavery Douglasites. The latter were victorious, and returned home congratulating each other that they had buried the affectionate office-seekers and friends of Mr. Buchanan." Salmon P. Chase, running for reelection on the Republican ticket, noted in his diary that Payne's nomination was "a clear triumph of Douglas interest" and probably best for the Republicans.[13]

Racial issues dominated the campaign. Payne advocated white supremacy, while Democratic editors condemned the Republicans' supposed "Congo Creed" of equality, black suffrage, and racial amalgamation. The U.S. Supreme Court, in its *Dred Scott* decision handed down in March, held that slaves did not become free simply because they traveled with their owners' consent onto free soil, and it declared the Missouri Compromise, by which Congress had prohibited slavery in a portion of the Louisiana territory, unconstitutional. The decision appeared again and again in speeches and editorials, as Republicans charged that it threatened "to cover our whole continent with slavery." When the Ohio Supreme Court held in May that a slave became free upon setting foot in Ohio, Republicans lauded the decision, while Democrats denounced it as a willful disregard of the law established by *Dred Scott.* Democrats also decried the Republican-controlled legislature for passing a series of personal liberty laws designed to hamper enforcement of the Fugitive Slave Law in Ohio. In July a federal judge held in a slave rescue case that federal law trumped state law, causing Republicans to demand reforms that would limit the power of the federal judiciary over state law.[14]

But for all the passion aroused by racial issues, they were not the only ones that inflamed political feelings in 1857. The revelation of a huge "defalcation" by the Ohio state treasurer and its cover-up by his successor, together with a nationwide financial crisis that began with the collapse of the mammoth Ohio Life Insurance & Trust Company, kept Jacksonian-era controversies over banking and currency boiling. The embezzlement scandal erupted in June 1857, when the public learned that John G. Breslin, the former Democratic state treasurer, had left office with a half-million dollars unaccounted for. Breslin's Republican successor and brother-in-law William

H. Gibson covered up the shortfall until he was unable to pay interest on the state debt, at which point Breslin ran off to Canada and Governor Chase forced Gibson to resign. Then came the Panic of 1857, with bank failures and fears of depression. Democrats reacted with traditional arguments: increase regulation and taxation of banks, encourage the use of specie, prohibit the circulation of small bank notes, keep public funds in an independent treasury rather than deposit them in private banks.[15]

Chase narrowly defeated Payne in the 1857 gubernatorial contest, but the Democrats, aided by the defalcation and financial panic, recaptured both houses of the General Assembly. Democrats alleged that illegal black and mulatto voters in the Western Reserve had provided Chase's margin of victory. There was an element of truth in the charge. The Ohio Supreme Court had held that men more than half white could vote. According to John Mercer Langston, an African American who had been elected clerk of Brownhelm Township near Oberlin in 1855, the people of that area would let any man vote who swore to being more than half white, no matter how black he looked.[16] But the governor had no veto power in those days, and during the legislative session of 1857–58 the triumphant Democrats passed a law directing the judges of elections to reject the vote of anyone having "a distinct and visible admixture of African blood." They also repealed two of the personal liberty laws and created an "independent treasury" designed to keep all public funds in the hands of public officials.[17]

The Oberlin-Wellington rescue case of 1858–59 raised the partisan fever even further.[18] It began when students and faculty members of Oberlin College, an institution steeped in piety and abolitionism, rushed to the nearby village of Wellington to rescue a fugitive slave from federal custody. After a crowd numbering in the hundreds whisked the fugitive away, an all-Democratic federal grand jury indicted thirty-seven of the rescuers, most of whom were released after being fined ten dollars each. But two of the liberators were tried and convicted under federal law for rescuing a fugitive from service.

During the trials the defense attorneys, who included Ranney's law partner Franklin Backus, repeatedly appealed to a law higher than the constitution and statutes. The defense insisted, declaimed Rufus Spalding, "that by no law, human or divine, did the negro rescued owe service to any man living; that his arrest was kidnapping, procured by the use of the most scandalous and fraudulent deceit, and that, whether the defendant aided to rescue him or not, he was amenable to no criminal statute whatever." Judge Hiram V. Willson, Ranney's rival for the judgeship back in 1855, had warned the grand jury against the "semi-religious" dogma "which arrogates to human conduct a standard of right above, and independent of, human laws" and "makes the CONSCIENCE of each individual in society the TEST of his own ACCOUNTABILITY to the laws of the land."[19]

While in custody the defendants sought from the Ohio Supreme Court a writ of habeas corpus that would free them from federal custody. In seeking the writ they set the stage for a confrontation between federal and state officials. If the court issued a writ for the men's release, Governor Salmon P. Chase told a rally in Cleveland, he was determined to enforce it. However, in a 3–2 decision the all-Republican court found the Fugitive Slave Law constitutional and denied the writ. Chief Justice Joseph R. Swan, who wrote the opinion, was up for election that year. The Republican Party refused to renominate him, and Swan's judicial career was ruined.[20]

In such an inflammatory atmosphere the intensely partisan Ranney could not keep away from electoral politics. In 1859 he became a candidate for governor. One might well wonder why Ranney, or any other ambitious politician, would be interested in being chief magistrate of Ohio. Formally, the governor was little more than a figurehead, having no veto power and little patronage at his disposal.[21] But in such turbulent times the governorship of a large, northern state was a high-profile position. As the highest-ranking statewide official the governor spoke for his party as well as his state, and that meant that a successful gubernatorial campaign might secure the legislature as well. Chase's razor-thin victory in 1857 did not win the General Assembly for the Republicans, but in most years the election of an Ohio governor signaled to the rest of the country the direction of the political winds.

Ohio's proximity to Virginia and Kentucky added to the election's significance. To slaves longing for freedom, the Ohio River, which separated Ohio from its slaveholding neighbors, was the River Jordan. To southerners who had little faith in the North's willingness to respect southern rights, enforcement of the federal Fugitive Slave Law was a litmus test of northern devotion to the Constitution. Slave owners in border states had an economic stake in the recovery of runaways, but the law's more important point from the beginning was the recognition of southern rights. If anything, the law's symbolic importance grew over time. A decade after its passage Senator James Mason of Virginia insisted that southerners felt the loss of honor from northern obstructionism more than the loss of property. "[M]y people are degraded and humiliated," he said, "when they are conscious that they tolerate a Government which is incapable of protecting them, refuses to protect them, and they yet remain in the Government."[22]

Ohio's governor gave southern honor no succor. Chase's longtime legal advocacy for alleged fugitives had gained him a reputation as the "attorney general for fugitive slaves." As governor he not only threatened to execute any order the Ohio Supreme Court might issue to release the Oberlin-Wellington prisoners then in federal custody but also refused a request from the governor of Kentucky for the rendition of a black man indicted in Kentucky for helping a slave escape to Ohio. Would the great state of Ohio continue in the ways of the obdurate Chase and the Republicans, Democrats wondered, or would it demonstrate a desire for comity with the South and perpetuation of the Union?[23]

The Democratic state convention met on May 26, just two days after Chase's address to the prorescue rally in Cleveland. It was clear that slavery and the enforcement of the Fugitive Slave Law, along with the safeguarding of public funds, would dominate the campaign. The Democrats condemned Republican radicalism on issues related to slavery, but they stood no chance of electing their gubernatorial candidate unless he possessed unquestionable antislavery credentials. Ranney, who had received the approbation of Free Soilers in 1848, was the obvious choice. He formally announced his readiness to run in a telegram addressed to allies at the convention. "I do not wish to compete for the nomination," Ranney informed them, "but if pretty unanimously desired, I will not refuse." It was a traditional denial of personal ambition, but there could have been little doubt that Ranney intended to run.[24]

When the time came for gubernatorial nominations, Henry B. Payne, Ranney's rival of 1857, moved that the convention nominate Ranney by acclamation. The motion carried unanimously, followed by the eruption of a spirited demonstration for the candidate. The nomination was "hailed with delight by the Democracy throughout the entire State." Even the abolitionist *Western Reserve Chronicle* praised the selection, saying that Ranney possessed more talent than any other Ohio Democrat and that his personal popularity was deservedly great. "[W]e know of no man belonging to the fugitive law party," said the paper, "whom we should prefer to see in the gubernatorial Chair."[25]

The Democratic platform began with a resolution on slavery in the territories that would cause trouble for Ranney during the campaign. The resolution, which endorsed popular sovereignty and denied the power of

Congress to either establish or prohibit slavery in the territories, conflicted with Ranney's letter to Hoffman of 1848. Another resolution condemned Republicans for flouting the Fugitive Slave Law. Of the remaining ten planks in the platform, all but two addressed race or slavery directly or indirectly. In the only parts of the platform that did not involve those issues, the Democrats favored grants of federal public lands to settlers rather than to railroad corporations and supported the recently passed Independent Treasury Law.[26]

The Republican platform, adopted at the party's convention in June, had far less to say about race and slavery. The Republicans used states'-rights arguments to demand repeal of the Fugitive Slave Law as an unwarranted federal intrusion on both individual liberty and the rights of the states. They commended the course of U.S. senator Ben Wade and the Republican members of Congress for defending freedom in general, but mentioned specifically only the Homestead Bill. Like the Democrats, the Republicans favored grants of federal land to actual settlers, but they blamed proslavery Senate Democrats for defeating the Homestead Bill.[27]

For governor the Republicans nominated forty-five-year-old lawyer and businessman William Dennison Jr. of Columbus. Dennison had served a single term in the Ohio Senate, during which he had vigorously advocated the repeal of the state's Black Laws. The slavery controversy brought the ex-Whig back into politics as an ardent Republican. In 1856 Dennison chaired the Ohio delegation to the Republican national convention. In a letter to the organizers of the Cleveland demonstration following the Oberlin-Wellington case, he denounced the imprisonment of the rescuers as a violent assault on the "sacred principles of freedom, justice and humanity." In June 1859 Dennison received the Republican nomination for governor with little opposition.[28]

A year before Dennison's nomination, Abraham Lincoln warned that "a house divided against itself cannot stand"; the Union would have to become all slave or all free. Now, with a hopelessly divided house careening toward civil war, the great national question of slavery would dominate the campaign for governor as well. Ohio's Republican and Democratic candidates, standing as surrogates for their national parties, offered a fractured state as clear a choice as had Lincoln and Douglas in their senatorial contest in 1858. And, like Lincoln and Douglas, they would take their stands in a series of debates that riveted the voters' attention and would provide twentieth-century students of rhetoric fodder for their theses.

SIX

The Great Debates

THE MOST famous political debates in American history took place in Illinois in 1858, when incumbent Stephen A. Douglas and challenger Abraham Lincoln squared off in a race for the United States Senate. Douglas won reelection, but the disputation continued the next year as both men campaigned in Ohio, ostensibly for the gubernatorial candidates but in reality for the minds of men on the question of slavery and ultimately for the presidency. Lincoln and Douglas never confronted each other face-to-face in Ohio, but the gubernatorial contest featured an extraordinary series of debates between candidates Dennison and Ranney. The campaign had important implications for the fate of the nation. Lincoln's speech in Cincinnati on September 17 brought him to the attention of eastern power brokers and made him a serious contender for the presidential nomination in 1860; but a Dennison defeat would mean a second consecutive failure against Douglas, and that might dampen enthusiasm for his candidacy.

The idea of the Ohio gubernatorial debates may have been in the air from the moment the candidates were nominated. Politics in those days "provided high drama and spirited fun to neighborhoods devoid of activities anywhere near as engaging or exciting." What better entertainment could there be than watching political opponents go at it before a raucous audience? Ohio attorney Roeliff Brinkerhoff recalled in his memoirs that in the 1840s in Tennessee, where he was then living, it was customary for gubernatorial or congressional candidates to engage in public "joint discussions," which Brinkerhoff thought far preferable to "*ex parte* discussions." Abraham Lincoln's future vice president, Hannibal Hamlin, when running for Congress, traveled the district with his adversary, debating the issues before large audiences almost every night for two months. In 1858 the *Chicago Daily Press and Tribune* suggested that Lincoln and Douglas, running for United States senator from Illinois, "canvass the State together, in the old western style." The Illinois debates proved to be great popular entertainment. Notwithstanding the vagaries of the weather, the lack of shelter, and the shortage of seating, thousands of spectators turned out for each event.[1]

The Lincoln-Douglas debates attracted national attention. With the nation rushing toward "the irrepressible conflict" between North and South, the debates were all about slavery. The most important question was whether Congress could or should exclude slavery from the territories. Douglas had staked his career on popular sovereignty. He insisted that, in accordance with the American tradition of self-government, the people of a territory had a right to decide for themselves, without federal interference, whether or not to allow slavery. But the *Dred Scott* decision held that slave owners could take their human chattel with them into the territories and have it protected there by law the same as any other property. The decision threatened to make a mockery of popular sovereignty in the territories. Lincoln repeatedly pressed Douglas on this point. If, as Douglas insisted, a decision of the Supreme Court was binding on all, how could a territory exclude slavery consistently with the Constitution?

Douglas responded by drawing a distinction between an abstract constitutional right and the hard realities of popular demands. If the people of a territory wished to keep out slavery, all they had to do was enact "unfriendly" legislation. "The man who goes there with his slaves," argued Douglas, "finds there is no law to protect him when he has arrived. There are no remedies if his slave runs away to another country." The absence of a slave code, he maintained, excluded slaves "just as positively as a constitutional prohibition would." Douglas's argument appalled Lincoln. "Does Judge Douglas mean to say," he demanded to know, "that a . . . legislature may, by the withholding of laws or by the passing of law, override a constitutional right?" What then became of the legislator's oath to support the Constitution? It was this solemn duty to uphold the Constitution that impelled an antislavery man such as Lincoln to support a fugitive slave law. The Constitution's fugitive slave clause established a right to recapture persons lawfully "held to service or labor" in one state who escaped to another state. "I can not conceive that I do support [the Constitution]," said Lincoln, "if I withhold necessary legislation to enforce the rights guaranteed by it." In Lincoln's mind Douglas's talk of "unfriendly legislation" sanctioned lawlessness and abolitionist defiance of the Fugitive Slave Law.[2]

But Douglas in turn accused Lincoln of fomenting political strife and possibly violence by refusing to accept the binding nature of the *Dred Scott* decision. Invoking the departmental theory of judicial review propounded by Jefferson and Jackson, Lincoln declared that Republicans would not accept the decision as a "political rule" and that they would have it reversed. He hinted that Republicans would reorganize the court if necessary to secure the reversal. But by 1858 the Supreme Court had acquired its sacrosanct status as the final arbiter of constitutional law. "[I]t is the duty of every law abiding man," proclaimed Douglas, "to obey the Constitution, and the law, and the constituted authorities" and not to stir up popular passions against those authorities.[3]

Lincoln saw *Dred Scott* as more than a safeguard for slavery in the territories. He regarded it as a long step toward the nationalization of slavery. The Supreme Court having affirmed "that the right of property in a slave is distinctly and expressly affirmed in the constitution," Lincoln argued, "the conclusion inevitably follows that no State law or constitution can destroy that right." Douglas scoffed at Lincoln's contention, treating the suggestion that the Court would ever issue such a decision as absurd; but, as Lincoln pointedly remarked, a sneer was not an adequate response.[4]

Both candidates viewed the territories as outlets for the energies and ambitions of free white men. For Douglas self-government was the great principle that fostered national prosperity and power. Having prohibited slavery, Illinoisans had "performed our whole duty." Now they must let others govern themselves as they saw fit. In adhering to the "principles of self-government," the United States would grow in greatness, wealth, and extent until it was "one ocean-bound Republic" and "the asylum of the oppressed of the whole world." Lincoln had a similar vision of greatness flowing from settlement of the West, but for him the attractive principle was free soil. Without slavery the territories would attract "free white men," not only from states further east but "from all the world," to "better their condition in life."[5]

For these reasons Lincoln wanted to keep the territories free "irrespective of the moral question." But the moral question was an ever-present undertone that came to the fore in the final debate. It was, said Lincoln, "the real issue." Toward the end of the last speech of the debates, Douglas, with no sense of irony, declared, "I care more for the great principle of self-government—the right of the people to rule themselves—than I do for all the niggers in Christendom." But to Lincoln slavery was simply another version of "the divine right of kings, the same principle that says you work, you toil, you earn bread, and I will eat it."[6]

This distillation of the issues that Lincoln and Douglas debated does not convey the full flavor of the "joint discussions," which at times resembled mutual hissy fits. The candidates charged each other with lying, deceit, and distortion and spent as much time arguing over what one or the other of them had said or what had happened in Congress on a given day as they did debating policy. Douglas accused Lincoln of "conduct[ing] the campaign on personal matters, hunting me down, and making charge after charge, proven to be false by the public records." Lincoln indicted Douglas for engaging in "personal warfare" and "impeach[ing] my honor, truth, and candor." But everyone recognized that matters of grave importance to the nation's survival were at stake.[7]

In 1859 Ohio provided a forum for the continuation of the confrontations. Lincoln and Douglas both came to Ohio during the campaign. In their five combined speeches, they spoke only of slavery and said not a word about the race for governor. But the gubernatorial candidates held their own series of debates. Their confrontations proved more cordial but no less lively than the Illinois discussions. Because the contestants were vying for a state office, the Ohio debates put a different twist on the same subjects and added new ones.

The idea of holding debates seems to have originated in the Ranney camp. On July 13 Ranney proposed that the two men meet for a discussion of the issues in each of the state's congressional districts. Before the debates began the *Cincinnati Enquirer* reported that Ranney's campaign speeches were "said to be the finest efforts on the stump" that had been heard in Ohio for years, and the *Cleveland Plain Dealer* predicted that Ranney would "make such a fortnight's work of it as DENNISON little dreams of." But of course Ranney took a less combative stance in his letter to Dennison. "I am entirely sure," he wrote, "that neither of us could desire to introduce into the discussions anything inconsistent with our standing as gentlemen, or unworthy of the candid consideration of the enlightened and patriotic citizens of the State, who might honor us with a hearing."[8]

Dennison already had a full speaking schedule for August, so he countered Ranney's invitation with a proposal for seven or eight "joint meetings" in September. On July 28, upon his return from a trip out of state, Ranney accepted. Soon the schedule of debates appeared in the papers. The original plan called for seven debates between September 6 and September 20 in Tiffin, Dayton, Cleveland, Canton, Zanesville, Chillicothe, and Columbus, but the order was changed somewhat and at the last minute the final debate at Columbus was postponed to October 4 due to inclement weather. The planners allotted four hours for each debate: one hour for an opening speech, two hours for a reply by the opposing candidate, and one hour for a rebuttal. Dennison and Ranney would take turns going first.[9]

As candidates for governor Dennison and Ranney devoted much of their energy to fixing blame for the state treasury scandal. Lincoln and Douglas, fighting for a seat in the United States Senate, had said nothing about state issues. The Ohio contenders, on the other hand, had a great deal to say about federal issues that were beyond state jurisdiction. Unlike the winner in Illinois, who would have a vote on any legislation relating to slavery in the territories, the victor in Ohio could have no direct say on the matter of free soil. Lincoln and Douglas had said little about the Fugitive Slave Law, another subject on which a U.S. Senator but not a governor might have occasion to vote, but Dennison and Ranney argued over it vociferously. Of course, a state might make the Fugitive Slave Law hard to enforce with personal liberty laws, but in Ohio that was a purely legislative matter, as the governor had no veto. On the other hand, the governor usually spoke for his legislative caucus and, as Chase had shown at the rally in Cleveland, could either facilitate or hamper the recovery of fugitive slaves.

There is little evidence regarding the candidates' preparation for the debates. Dennison, less experienced in political campaigning, sought the advice of more practiced hands. He wrote to United States senator Lyman Trumbull of Illinois for "valuable material" from the Lincoln-Douglas debates that he could use in his face-offs with Ranney. He asked Joshua Giddings for assistance as well. How Ranney readied himself for the debates is unknown.[10]

The public expected a rousing good time. A newspaper report on the Canton debate described the hoopla enjoyed by the "immense crowd." When the speakers arrived on the train from Wooster, a "procession was immediately formed, consisting of a great number of carriages, and the

Democratic and Republican divisions, each preceded by a band, flags, &c. After dinner the procession moved to the county fair grounds, in the midst of which the stand was erected." Notwithstanding the four hours of speeches, "[t]he people remained to the last attentive . . . and dispersed highly pleased with the exercises of the day."[11]

At the opening debate in Tiffin,[12] Dennison spoke first. He reminded his audience of how critical Democrats had been of the General Assembly during the constitutional convention of 1850–51, how they had limited the power of the legislature and demanded a smaller, more efficient, more accountable government. But since 1851, he charged, Democrats had raised taxes unnecessarily and closed their eyes to signs of trouble in the state treasurer's office. Allowing partisanship to override the state's interest, the Democrats had tried to take the power to appoint directors of the penitentiary and statehouse commissioners away from the Republican governor and give it to a three-member board named by the Democrat-controlled legislature;[13] they had refused to appropriate money to repay the state treasury for funds advanced by Republican officials for emergency canal repairs; they had interfered in the municipal affairs of Cincinnati after the voters there elected a Republican mayor.

Dennison contrasted Democratic quiescence and cover-ups concerning the state treasurer's office with Republican responsibility. When the Republicans took office, he declared, they enacted laws to protect the public fisc and forced the Republican treasurer to resign. Dennison attacked the independent treasury system created by the Democrats as an insufficient safeguard of the public interest and an inducement to depression by keeping money out of circulation. Turning to national affairs, Dennison alleged that the South dominated the Democratic Party and especially the United States Senate. Dennison did not accuse northern Democrats, as individuals, of wanting to extend slavery, but he contended that on the question of extension Democrats would always yield to the wishes of their dominant southern wing. In a tone more combative than Lincoln's the year before, Dennison made it clear that the interests of Ohio and those of the South on the matter of slavery were incompatible and that Ohio's Democrats could not be relied on to advance Ohio's interests.

Dennison concluded with a series of questions for Ranney, most of them involving slavery and the independent treasury. They may have been prepared by Giddings, whom Dennison had asked to prepare a "series of interrogatories" that would either force Ranney to back away from the "southern policy" on slavery or put him "hors de combat" in Ohio. Dennison demanded that Ranney deny or affirm the constitutional power of Congress to prohibit slavery in the territories and the right of slaveholders to take slaves into the territories to be held there as property. He called on the Democrat to say whether he was for or against repeal of the Fugitive Slave Law—reports that Ranney had denounced the law as unconstitutional back in 1850 had started appearing in the *Tiffin Weekly Tribune* and other papers in July—and whether he approved or disapproved of Ohio's personal liberty law. Altogether, Dennison posed seven questions related to slavery and several others connected with Ohio finances and patronage. Ranney refused to answer most of the questions directly, perhaps because he did not want to let his opponent dictate the terms of his address. As Dennison repeated the tactic in subsequent debates, though, Ranney adopted a more direct approach; when Dennison presented four questions in the Cleveland debate, Ranney offered straightforward responses, although Dennison insisted that Ranney had again been evasive.[14]

Ranney hit back hard on the handling of public funds, something he could do because the Republicans had provided plenty of ammunition. State expenditures had increased under Democratic administrations through 1855, but they had gone up even more since then, even when Republicans ran the show. As for the treasury mess, there was plenty of blame to go around; the Democrat Breslin was "not the only sinner." However, said Ranney, the real fault lay not with the men involved but with the "faulty system" of keeping public funds. Democrats had voted to keep public money in the hands of public officials, while Republicans had unanimously opposed the plan. Ranney responded briefly to Dennison's charges concerning patronage by noting that in 1855 the Republicans had "remodeled" the laws governing the benevolent institutions and the penitentiary "for the purpose of letting into power a hungry swarm."

Ranney then turned to the burning issue of slavery in the territories. The "true principle," he declared, was "non-intervention by the Federal government." He neither affirmed nor denied that Congress had the constitutional power to prohibit slavery in the territories. Instead he argued that popular sovereignty—letting the people of the territories decide for themselves—had been the policy agreed upon by Democrats and Whigs in 1850 and reaffirmed by the Whigs, including Dennison himself, at the 1852 Whig national convention. "I stand today as I did in 1848 in my strong desire that all the territories should be secured to free labor," Ranney proclaimed. Douglas's "don't care" position of 1858 would not sell well in Ohio, and Ranney wanted to avoid allegations of inconsistency. But Ranney was not prepared to impose his desire in violation of the great principle of the American Revolution that the people of a colony (or territory) should legislate for themselves.

Ranney accused Republicans of advocating nullification of the Fugitive Slave Law, and he chastised them for reviling Judge Swan and replacing him on their ticket for upholding the law in accordance with his constitutional duty. Appealing to the racial prejudice of his audience, Ranney predicted that Ohio's refusal to enforce the law would bring hordes of runaway slaves then in Canada flooding into Ohio. The Republicans, he alleged, wanted "to place the negroes upon an equality with whites." Thanks to Republican tolerance of illegal voting by blacks, "[t]wo hundred negroes will vote against me at Oberlin in October." After more in the same vein, including warnings about the indoctrination of Ohio's young people in the dangerous higher-law doctrines of Oberlin, Ranney concluded with a demand "to know whether Ohio is to be made the asylum for the refugee negroes of the Southern States and of Canada."

In his rebuttal Dennison raised an issue that would haunt Ranney for the rest of the campaign. "The principle which I advocate now," said Dennison, "and which [Ranney] once so ably advocated, is the prohibition of slavery in the territories. Will the gentleman say he did not advocate this doctrine?" According to the report of the debate, Ranney interjected, "It is *not* so, I never did." But there was that public letter to Hoffman back in 1848. As Dennison gleefully observed, the letter fully accorded with the Republican position on the subject.

Dennison admitted that he had supported the Compromise of 1850 at the Whig national convention of 1852. As a member of the Ohio Senate in 1850, he had opposed the compromise, but once it passed and was endorsed by both parties he acquiesced. But then came the *Dred Scott* decision, which Dennison implicitly characterized as a violation of the compromise by the Democrats. (In a subsequent debate Dennison charged that southerners had breached the bargain by trying to force slavery into Kansas.[15]) He would, as governor, obey the odious Fugitive Slave Law, but he was determined to oppose the spread of slavery to the territories. As for *Dred Scott*, Dennison adopted the legally tenable but politically radical position that the Supreme Court's holding regarding slavery in the territories was "extra-judicial" (presumably because the Court could have disposed of the case without addressing the issue) and "not law." And he declared forthrightly that slavery was "a great moral, social and political evil."

The rest of the debates followed more or less the same pattern. The big issues remained slavery and the independent treasury. At the debate in Cleveland on September 15, Dennison asked Ranney point-blank whether he had denied the constitutionality of the Fugitive Slave Law in 1850, to which Ranney replied, "I did not!" In fact, said Ranney in Cleveland, he had merely stated that if the Fugitive Slave Law did away with habeas corpus and the right to trial by jury, then Congress ought to be asked to amend it. As early as mid-July Democratic papers had printed Ranney's version of the Mahoning County "indignation meeting," according to which Ranney just happened to be at the courthouse on legal business when the meeting convened there. His opinion being called for, Ranney had simply stated that the law ought to be carefully examined and, if found objectionable, its amendment or repeal sought through legal means.[16]

But then the *Mahoning Register* dug up and reprinted the original article on the indignation meeting at which Ranney had supposedly spoken out so forcefully against the law. According to that article, published in the Democratic *Mahoning Index,* Ranney had deprecated the manner in which the Fugitive Slave Law had been passed and condemned it as unconstitutional. The *Index* had praised "*the noble and fearless Ranney*" for denouncing the "*outrageous and pestiferous bill.*" Even though Democratic editors had published Ranney's version of the incident two months before the *Register*'s revelation, Republican papers had a field day with the newly discovered report as well as Ranney's 1848 free-soil letter to Hoffman. Ranney constantly had to defend himself against charges of flip-flops. In the Cleveland debate he conceded that in 1848 he had favored congressional legislation to prohibit slavery in the territories, but he accompanied the admission with a reference to human fallibility and to his early "poverty and obscurity" and lack of opportunity for many years to become informed on public affairs. The *Ohio State Journal,* stretching these remarks into an excuse of callow youthfulness for an erroneous position, pointed out that Ranney had not thought himself too young to run for Congress before 1848 or to become a "father of the constitution" or supreme court judge soon afterward. The *Journal* concluded that Ranney, a man of great "eminence and character" and "head and shoulder above any active politician now in the [Democratic] party," had "allowed himself to be used as mere clay to stop the wind out of the Ohio democratic pro-slavery, fugitive slave law platform of 1859." By so doing he had become "a false spectre" and forfeited "any claims to the confidence of the people."[17]

In fact Ranney reiterated his opposition to the extension of slavery, declaring, "God Almighty knows I would not send slavery into your territories, nor to any where else." But in 1850, he said, he abandoned the "extreme ground" he had previously occupied, having concluded "that republican principles, justice, right, and a consistent regard for the rights of the various States were best promoted by leaving the question to the people of the Territories." Ranney approved of the Supreme Court's position in *Dred Scott* that Congress lacked the authority to prohibit slavery in the territories. Moreover, he pointed out that if he had changed his mind once on the subject, Dennison had changed his twice, first by accepting the Compromise of 1850, which removed the question from congressional consideration, and then by demanding a congressional prohibition.[18]

The Ranney of 1848 and 1850 that Republican papers claimed to admire in 1859 was a radical. Of course, what the Republicans esteemed was the Ranney of free-soil, anti–Fugitive Slave Law repute, not the Loco-foco who railed against special corporate privileges and active government and who battled the Whigs, the self-proclaimed champions of order. When word got out that Ranney and Dennison were planning a series of debates, the *Plain Dealer* declared that the "great question" to be decided by the voters was whether or not the "Oberlin Professors" were the "Supreme Judiciary of the land." Ranney, said the paper, was "the advocate of Constitutional law, and the [federal and state] Supreme Courts as expounders of it," while Dennison advocated "the Levitical law and Oberlin Professors and negroes as expounders." If there were any other questions at issue, this one "involving the choice between Order and Anarchy throws them into the shade." Speaking to a crowd in Cincinnati in September, Douglas asserted that the Whigs had been "pre-eminently a conservative party." When that party dissolved and the "sectional men" in its ranks became the "interventionists" of the North or South, "there was nothing left for the conservative Whigs except to join the Democracy, and by our joint efforts, if possible, maintain the peace of the country and the perpetuity of the Union." The northern Democrats had become the self-consciously conservative party.[19]

Ranney embraced this conservatism. In the debates he objected to the "eternal agitation of the subject of slavery," disdaining equally the "wilder Republicans" who wanted Congress to keep slavery out of the territories and the "fire-eaters of the South" who demanded that Congress establish it there. He acknowledged the U.S. Supreme Court as "the sole arbiter in all questions relating to the Federal Constitution." And he excoriated the Oberlin rescuers and Republicans in general for resisting the Fugitive Slave Law. Judge Swan had courageously stood up against nullification of the law, and so, Ranney said, the Republicans "took off his head." Ranney's obeisance to the Supreme Court and homage to Swan were not mere cant. We have seen how, at the constitutional convention and during his time on the bench, Ranney had held up the judiciary as the ultimate authority on the constitution and the guarantor of liberty. The Republican decapitation of Swan presented the people of Ohio with the great challenge of whether they would "stand by the side of an honest and upright and independent judge or by the proceedings of such a party. The moment you decide on the latter alternative your property and your rights and your liberties are pretty near ruined."[20]

Ranney was also conservative in adhering to the tried and true. During the war Democrats would insist that they were fighting for "the Constitution as it is, the Union as it was." That was a conciliatory attitude that Ranney displayed during the debates. For Dennison the conflict between North and South was, as Republican William Henry Seward proclaimed the year before, irrepressible. Dennison did not use the term, but he insisted that southern Democrats and northern Republicans, the controlling powers in the two sections, had incompatible aims. Northern Democrats had become "the mere instrument of the slave power of the South," the "great end and object" of which was "to strengthen and extend slavery over the Territories." Republicans meant to keep the territories free. Their "great leading, control[l]ing purpose" was "to defend the interest of freedom in the States and in the Territories, against the assaults of slavery, come in whatever form they may, and from whatever source they may."[21]

Ranney demanded that Republicans stop agitating the slavery question. The territories, he asserted, had been fought for by, and belonged to, the whole country. In the Compromise of 1850 northerners and southerners had given up their "extreme pretentions" and taken "common ground" by allowing the people of the territories to decide the slavery question for themselves. Ranney saw no danger in that. "[W]here in the name of God," he asked, "have the people ever extended slavery one inch?" Virginia herself, by surrendering her claims to western territories in 1787 on condition that slavery be prohibited there, had extended the domain of freedom more than antislavery "shrieking" ever would. "The truth is," Ranney warned Republicans, "that if we propose to maintain a free government at all, we must maintain it by allowing all the people to have those rights that we claim for ourselves." If Republicans refused to accept popular sovereignty, "the very foundation of free government," they risked destroying "that fraternity which ought to exist between the sister States of our confederacy." Denouncing the "fanatics" of the South and the North who demanded federal intervention on the slavery question, Ranney claimed to stand with the Revolutionary patriots and their constitution, which gave to the people of each state—and, by extension, to the people of the territories—"the right to frame their institutions in their own way." "We fought that principle out then," he declared, and the Democrats "will fight it out now." At the end of his last speech in the debates Ranney "thank[ed] God that our fathers framed a government that has brought us so many blessings; and we must look to it, as the only sure guaranty of them."[22]

The debates revealed both Dennison and Ranney to be faithful to the general tendencies of their parties as expounded by Lincoln and Douglas in 1858. Dennison was strongly antislavery as a matter of policy and principle; Ranney espoused popular sovereignty as true Americanism and a boon to white men. But there were differences, too, apart from the fact that the Ohioans spent so much time on the state treasury debacle. Dennison was more radical than Lincoln, his tone toward the South more condemnatory. The old Whig-Republican warhorse Tom Corwin, with an effective speaking tour in the southern part of the state, largely relieved Dennison of appeasing conservatives. (With both Corwin and abolitionist Joshua Giddings campaigning for the Republicans, Ranney repeatedly queried Dennison as to which of them represented the Republican Party.) Dennison openly advocated a reorganization of the Supreme Court so that it would no longer be "bound hand and foot to the slave power," and he characterized *Dred Scott* as "not law," without fussing over departmental theories of judicial review or the need to reverse the decision. He called for the territories to be cut up into "quarter sections of land, where every man can go and live and enjoy the fruits of his own labor," without ever expressing a purpose to exclude slavery there solely for the benefit of whites. And while Dennison denied that Republicans sought to nullify (which he took to mean forcibly resist) the Fugitive Slave Law, to Lincoln's chagrin he demanded the law's repeal.[23]

Ranney, too, departed from the script of his party's candidate in Illinois. Douglas had carefully avoided any suggestion that popular sovereignty would result in free territories, professing indifference on the subject. Ranney voiced what Douglas believed but would not say for fear of further alienating the South: that the result of popular sovereignty in Kansas had been to create a free state in territory that had been open to slavery since the repeal of the Missouri Compromise. Ranney also censured southern fire-eaters as no less a threat to the Union than the abolitionists, something that Douglas had refrained from doing. *Dred Scott* presented Douglas with a grave challenge because it undermined popular sovereignty by holding that territorial legislatures could not exclude slavery—so, at least, Taney's opinion seemed to say and both Douglas and Lincoln acknowledged. But when Dennison asked Ranney whether the latter agreed with the Supreme Court's holding "that the Territorial Legislature has no power to exclude Slavery from the Territory," Ranney rejected Dennison's premise. According to Ranney the Court's only holdings were that *Congress* could not prohibit slavery in the territories and that blacks could not be U.S. citizens having the right to sue in federal court. Whether or not to allow slavery, he averred, was a "domestic question" that each state or territory could decide for itself.[24] This view, and Dennison's failure to press him on it, allowed Ranney to avoid the bog of "unfriendly legislation" argumentation. Ranney's stance was a minority one then and still is now, but he was not alone. At the time of the decision the Democratic *Pittsburgh Post* editorialized that *Dred Scott* had "approved, affirmed and established" popular sovereignty for the states and territories. Even Taney's opinion has been understood as leaving the question open. But whatever its technical validity, Ranney's position offended southerners as much as Douglas's.[25]

The Ohio debates also differed from the Illinois discussions in their degree of cordiality. At the outset the newspapers expected a well-mannered contest. "Both candidates are gentlemen," wrote one, "and, personally, the debate between them can not be otherwise than pleasant." Ranney's attempt to tarnish Republicans by brandishing a rather innocuous letter from Chase to Breslin—that is, to establish guilt by association—prompted the *Ohio State Journal* to caution Ranney against risking his "reputation for decency and decorum" in a long-shot run for the governorship. Nevertheless, after two debates the *Journal* remarked that both Dennison and Ranney, if not Ranney's minions, were "carrying on the debate in a manner and spirit honorable to themselves and to the State." Another paper subsequently commented on the "perfect decorum and good feeling" that characterized the discussions. When Dennison denied a story claiming that he had promised to resist enforcement of the Fugitive Slave Law with the militia's bayonets,

Ranney took him at his word. In the last speech of the debates Dennison praised Ranney as "a very able lawyer" and "an accomplished gentleman." "In the course of the discussion between us," Dennison continued, "I am happy to say that nothing has occurred to disturb those relations of friendship, or to mar that courteous consideration which has characterized all our meetings."[26]

How well Ranney performed in the debates is an unanswerable question. Historian Daniel J. Ryan wrote that Ranney did not live up to the expectations of his party, but he gave no source for this conclusion.[27] The openly partisan newspapers of the day almost always claimed victory for their own candidates. After the Dayton meeting the *Plain Dealer,* in typical fashion, concluded that Ranney had "completely swept the boards," leaving the Republicans "terribly discomfited," and the *Dayton Daily Empire* claimed that Ranney had proved himself a clear, logical, and witty "intellectual giant." The Republican *Dayton Gazette,* on the other hand, while conceding that Ranney was "a shrewd, adroit and able debater," observed that Dennison's supporters thought their candidate was "an overmatch for Mr. Ranney, both as an orator and logician." Following the Tiffin debate, though, a correspondent for the Democratic *Plain Dealer* acknowledged that Dennison had "raised considerable enthusiasm and noise, and his friends claim a right to call it a drawn game." And at Canton, wrote the *Ohio State Journal,* "[t]he efforts of both speakers excited the admiration of their friends, and commanded the respect of their opponents." As for style, one Democratic paper declared Ranney "in point of real animating, enlivening and thrilling eloquence . . . vastly Mr. DENNISON's superior," while a Republican paper claimed that Ranney lacked "vivacity, versatility, and copiousness." To some extent Republican critics disagreed among themselves. One asserted that Ranney was "a fast speaker with a good voice" and an impressive "sledge-hammer sort of gesticulation," but another opined that his "voice and manner" were "not very favorable for out-door speaking."[28]

Probably neither candidate was up to the task of addressing a large crowd without a microphone. Campaign demands took their toll on both men. During a thirteen-day swing through southeastern Ohio in August, Ranney was scheduled to speak in nine different counties. In late September and early October he had engagements in seven counties in the southwestern and northeastern portions of the state. When the candidates arrived at the debate locales, their partisans called for additional speeches. The turnout for the debates themselves was impressive, with the *Plain Dealer* reporting an attendance of five thousand for the Cleveland meeting. Dennison and Ranney, both of whom complained of hoarseness throughout the debates, worried about not being heard by the far reaches of the audience.[29]

Neither Douglas nor Lincoln seems to have attended any of the debates. Douglas was in Dayton when Ranney and Dennison met there on September 8, but he had a bad cold and was forced to rest. He spoke at length in Wooster on September 16 with Ranney by his side but did not linger to accompany Ranney to the next debate in Canton. But high officeholders of both parties, from in and out of the state, showed up in support of their candidates. Republican editors harped on the fact that Democratic politicians accompanied Ranney to the debates. The *Ohio State Journal* labeled the entourage "a self constituted committee of seconds and bottle holders to train, cram, rub-down, prompt and sponge their champion and bring him up to scratch." According to the *Journal* Ranney's deficiencies required the presence of less scrupulous Democrats to provide him with notes, to hiss or clap at appropriate times, to interrupt Dennison with shouted questions, and to help Ranney address crowds before the formal debates. The Democratic *Plain Dealer* retorted that the Republicans were also importing backers and asserted that Republican politicians attending the debates, including Governor Chase, picked verbal fights with their adversaries and came out on the losing end.[30]

Ranney once again had the misfortune to run in a Republican year. On the eve of the election Democratic papers urged white men to turn out early and by their votes condemn "negro equality." The election, ranted the *Plain Dealer,* would decide whether "the Nigger question" would become "national, not sectional, for all time" or popular sovereignty would let each community manage the matter for itself. The appeal to racial prejudice failed to sway the majority. Dennison won the election with 51.9 percent of the vote. The Republicans triumphed in all the other statewide races as well and won control of both houses of the legislature. Ranney carried Franklin County, where Dennison lived, but the entire Western Reserve, Ranney's home territory, went for Dennison.[31]

While Ranney and Dennison debated, the Union teetered on the verge of catastrophe. Historian Kenneth Stampp called 1857 the "political point of no return," the year when violent conflict between North and South became inevitable. However, a case can also be made for 1859 as the tipping point. Allen C. Guelzo writes that southerners saw John Brown's ill-fated attempt to incite a slave revolt in October of that year at Harpers Ferry, Virginia, as "argument-clinching proof" that the North was bent on forcibly destroying the South. After Harpers Ferry, southerners finally concluded that they could no longer trust northerners and demanded ironclad (and to northern Democrats, unacceptable) protections for slavery and southern interests in the national Democratic Party platform.[32]

Brown's raid on Harpers Ferry followed the Ohio elections by just five days. Would it have been the point of no return if Ranney had defeated Dennison? Ohio in 1859 was a large and influential state that by virtue of its long borders with the slave states of Virginia and Kentucky sat at the center of the fugitive slave controversy. The home of fiery abolitionist politicians Joshua Giddings and Ben Wade, Ohio had the "attorney general for fugitive slaves" as its governor. But Ohio also had a Democratic legislature that had repealed the personal liberty laws and enacted the Visible Admixture Law. Dennison defeated Ranney by 13,331 votes. A swing of 6,666 votes, less than 2 percent of the total cast, would have given Ranney the election. The celebration of Brown's raid in the North bolstered southern extremists who had been warning that the North could not be trusted. The episode "would have been a very trivial affair to the Southern people, but for the manner in which it was regarded by the people of the North," wrote one Virginian. But if Ranney had won—if the important state of Ohio, with its long southern border, had been in Democratic hands—perhaps Brown's raid would not have tipped the scales toward disunion. Maybe an Ohio governor who had asked "why should we be continually day after day, and year after year, denouncing the South," and who announced that he would rather lose his arm than "violate our faith to the other States of the Union," could have allayed southern fears just enough to give sectional compromise a chance. As it was, the conflict could no longer be repressed.[33]

SEVEN

Constitution and Union

THE REPUBLICAN victory in the 1860 presidential election was followed by the secession of seven states before Lincoln's inauguration and four more afterward. Leading secessionists defended their action as true conservatism. "*We* are not revolutionists," they proclaimed. Rather, they had been driven to secede in order "to preserve their old institutions" from "a revolution [that] threatened to destroy their social system." Most northern Democrats rallied to the flag, putting country above partisan politics, at least for the moment. Their insistence that the rebellion must be suppressed did not signal a political conversion but merely a postponement of the settling of accounts with Republicans. Clinging to their time-honored, states'-rights conviction that the Constitution created an unbreakable Union with a federal government of strictly limited powers, northern Democrats adopted the motto, "The Constitution as it is, the Union as it was." It was an eminently conservative slogan.[1]

Ranney, the Radical of 1850, had become a conservative by 1860. His views, except perhaps with regard to free soil, had not changed in the interim. The notions that had made him a Jeffersonian liberal—limited, popular government, states' rights, abolition of special corporate privileges—remained essential to his political philosophy. What had changed was the context of American politics. Democrats who shared Ranney's orthodox party values saw the Republicans as radicals bent on destroying traditional relations between the federal and state governments and between whites and blacks. These Democrats deliberately described themselves as conservatives. As the Civil War progressed, the sense that they were fighting a revolutionary tide intensified. The Republican Congress and administration, made up largely of former Whigs, created a national banking system, issued paper money, ran up a huge public debt, subsidized railroad construction with federal largesse, and enacted a protective tariff. Lincoln enhanced executive power, ordered the arrest of opposition editors, suspended habeas corpus, and emancipated slaves. Congress conscripted men into military service and tore a huge chunk out of Virginia to create a new state.

It was no wonder that leading Ohio Democrats blasted the Republicans as revolutionaries. State representative Otto Dresel captured their spirit when he offered a series of resolutions in the Ohio House of Representatives avowing that "the liberties of the people are menaced by Congressional and Federal usurpations," that the national banking system was "covertly designed to establish a vast central money power," and that the Emancipation Proclamation, the result of "pandering to the insane fanaticism of the Abolition faction," threatened to "carry lust, rapine and murder into every house in the slaveholding States." The proposed resolutions charged the government with establishing a "military despotism," creating a system of secret police to spy on the people, arbitrarily arresting and detaining citizens without charge, depriving them of trial by jury, transporting them to faraway places, answering their petitions for redress with "repeated injury and insult," suppressing freedom of speech, and otherwise violating constitutional rights.[2]

Dresel belonged to the Peace Democrats, the wing of the Democratic Party that objected to the war even if attempts to restore the Union peacefully could not succeed. Another Democratic faction agreed to cooperate with Republicans as the Union Party for the duration of the conflict. In 1861 the Union Party in Ohio, dominated by Republicans, chose as its gubernatorial candidate David Tod, a two-time Democratic nominee in the 1840s and former minister to Brazil. With Tod and other Democrats running under their banner, the Unionists won a huge victory at the polls that fall. Most Democrats, however, even those who supported the war effort, remained loyal to their separate party identity. They blamed Republican fanatics no less than southern fire-eaters for bringing on the conflict. Indeed, they regarded themselves, with their willingness to conciliate the South, as the true Unionists. Ranney belonged to this group. Loyal to the party whose standard he had so recently borne, he never wavered in his support of the war effort.[3]

Ranney demonstrated his devotion to the Union, the law, and the Democratic Party in 1861 when he assisted in the prosecution of one Frederick Court, charged with conspiracy to drive Lincoln from office and overthrow the government. Fears of conspiracy abounded during the war. Peace Democrats routinely charged the Lincoln administration with conspiring to establish a military despotism. Republicans accustomed to thinking of a "slave power conspiracy" to control the United States government readily saw in opposition to the war plots to overthrow the government. In July 1861 Congress passed a seditious conspiracy act under which persons suspected of disloyalty could be detained without the difficulties of alleging and proving treason. Frederick Court had supposedly gotten mixed up with subversives in Marion County. He and John M. Christian, a leading Marion County Democrat, were arrested, charged under the conspiracy act, and brought before U.S. commissioner Bushnel White in Cleveland for a preliminary examination of witnesses.

For both political and professional reasons, federal district attorney Robert F. Paine urgently desired Ranney's assistance in the prosecutions of Court, Christian, and others, and he sought approval from U.S. attorney general Edward Bates to retain the Democrat. However, Bates balked at the compensation Ranney requested. The attorney general preferred Rufus Spalding, the Republican former Ohio Supreme Court judge. But Spalding was out of town, and when Ranney agreed to work on the cases as long as his services were desired for whatever compensation Bates would fix, Paine hired him without waiting for formal approval.[4]

In a closing argument against Court, Ranney denounced the notion that Democrats needed the help of secret societies, such as the Knights of the Golden Circle, to which Court allegedly belonged. "The Democratic party," he declared, "is not to be aided by such underhanded measures." Abraham Lincoln was nothing by himself, but as president he represented "the majority of the law." A Republican paper praised Ranney's "powerful speech," and Commissioner White sent the case to the federal court for trial. It turned out, though, that the evidence was too flimsy to justify further proceedings, and Paine dropped the prosecution. Neither Court nor anyone else was convicted under the conspiracy act during the Civil War. But Ranney had done his best to dissociate the Democrats from secret societies and to demonstrate their loyalty to the Union.[5]

The depressing military situation gave the Peace Democrats a strong hand at the Ohio Democratic state convention in July 1862, but they could not disregard the War Democrats if they hoped to win the state elections that fall. Ranney represented the War Democrats on the committee that drafted the party platform. The platform began with a declaration of loyalty to the Constitution and the Union and the need for an "unbroken front" in the struggle "for the preservation of the Government." However, it quickly moved on to a denunciation of abolitionism and of schemes to convert the conflict into a war for emancipation of the slaves. The party condemned "the contemplated sweeping and indiscriminate acts of confiscation and emancipation" for many reasons, including the likelihood that blacks would flock to Ohio and "underwork" white laborers during the war and returning soldiers afterwards. The Democrats proclaimed at length their devotion to the Constitution, especially the bill of rights, and rebuked the Lincoln administration for its "repeated and gross violation" of freedom of speech and the rights of criminal defendants. One resolution about which Ranney might have had reservations, to judge by his most significant wartime judicial opinion, regretted the General Assembly's refusal "to permit our gallant soldiers in the field the right to vote."[6]

There was no gubernatorial contest in 1862, but several state offices were up for grabs, including a judgeship of the supreme court. Ranney, an outspoken defender of the Union and supporter of the war, claimed that he did not want the nomination. To deny an interest in high office was still conventional practice in 1862, but Ranney may have been sincere; he would resign less than halfway through his term. On the other hand he may have felt that during the nation's great travail, when constitutional questions of the utmost importance might reach the court, it was crucial to have men of the right stamp on the bench. Since his resignation in 1856, the only Democrat on the supreme court had been the extremist Bartley, who failed of reelection in 1858. Ranney received the nomination over token opposition; after the first ballot, his only rival withdrew and the delegates made the nomination unanimous.[7]

After being nominated Ranney addressed the convention, reminding his listeners that three years earlier, as candidate for governor, he had warned "that fanaticism at both ends of the Union was dragging you on to civil war." Now that the war had come, all the sacrifices of blood and treasure were tolerable if they were made "for the sole purpose of upholding that glorious fabric of government to which Washington put his name." The Democrats had not supported Lincoln, but, said Ranney, "he is none the less our Executive; he wields the power of Government, and it is our Government, thank God." But if Democrats had a duty to help put down the rebellion, they also had a right to demand that the government uphold the Constitution as it had been handed down by the founding fathers and not fight a war "for the purpose of overturning the institutions of the States [or] annulling [constitutional] guarantees of liberty." Furthermore, Democrats had the duty to tell Lincoln and the Congress that they were fighting for "the proud race descended from the freemen of Runny Meade" that had built America and spread across the continent. "[W]e are not prepared," he roared, "to divide this goodly land with the cannibals that have been imported from the coast of Africa." Ranney concluded with a ringing call to leave a proud legacy for future generations. When "our children . . . read the history of this day," he predicted, they "will rejoice to see that their fathers could stand up in their country's hour of peril, not despairing or giving up for a moment, but rallying to the last for the prosperity and security of their common country."[8]

Despite reports of political harmony at the convention, the campaign brought out the divisions in the party. Governor Tod asked Ranney and other prominent Democrats to speak out in support of the war and to help raise the three hundred thousand troops recently called for by Lincoln. Ranney set out on a four-day, four-city speaking tour with Republicans Samuel Galloway and Thomas Ewing. The tenor of his speeches no doubt mirrored that of his address at the Democratic state convention on July 4. Hugh J. Jewett, the party's nominee for governor in 1861, made a similar speech in Zanesville, declaring that suppression of the rebellion was not a party matter and that Democrats must abide by the will of the majority until the public will could be reconsidered at the ballot box.[9]

On July 23, at a "large and enthusiastic" rally in Lancaster, Ranney urged an energetic prosecution of the war. He supported the president's call for troops as necessary to enforce the laws of a democracy. "We are not called upon to uphold this dynasty or that privileged class," he asserted, "but we are calling upon the American citizen to defend the laws he himself has made." Ranney hoped that men would readily enlist so as to avoid a draft, which would drain the cause of much of its moral force, and to put down the rebellion before foreign nations recognized and offered aid to the Confederacy. Failure to suppress insurrection would be tantamount to an admission that Americans were incapable of self-government. Ranney appealed to all men to enlist if their circumstances allowed, and not to look to others to fill the quota. The United States was "peculiarly the country of the poor man, and of the foreigner, who was oppressed in his native land. It stretches its protecting ægis over them—diffuses its blessings over all alike, offers its rewards to rich and poor. . . . No other Government on earth has done so much for the people, and if it fails the principle of free government dies with it." Ranney dismissed any notion of compromise. After careful reflection he had concluded that "we can reach the haven of peace only through war." He ended his speech with a paean to "the glory of the great West"—and an appeal to its sectional interests. The West's prosperity depended on maintaining control over its great natural outlet, the Mississippi River. Before he "would allow the Mississippi to be closed," he thundered "with great earnestness," he would "rather bury the last man in the West." The speech received "tremendous applause."[10]

Many Democrats reacted angrily to Ranney's address. One, as he was leaving the rally, called it "the d—dest, dirtiest, Black Republican speech of all." Edson B. Olds, a former Speaker of the Ohio House and ex-congressman who would soon be arrested by military authorities for his inflammatory antiwar speeches, denounced Ranney as an abolitionist. The *Lancaster Eagle* dropped Ranney's name from the slate of Democratic candidates it had been carrying since the convention.[11]

Ranney's public pronouncements on the war were sufficiently patriotic to win him the support of some Republicans for the supreme court. The *Cincinnati Enquirer* reported rumors that the Republicans might even nominate Ranney themselves. But "An Earnest Republican" would have no truck with a man who refused to join the Union movement and who, at the recent Democratic state convention, had avowed that "if the war was carried on by the General Government for some other purpose than the maintenance of the 'Constitution as it is and the Union as it was' [the cant phrase of all Northern rebels], then the people would be forging chains for themselves by contributing men and money for its support."[12]

The Unionist state convention, held on August 21, did not consider endorsing Ranney. To run against him the Unionists nominated his law partner, Franklin T. Backus. Backus had run for a supreme court seat once before, as a Whig. He had been a Whig member of both branches of the Ohio legislature. Before the war was over, though, he would switch to the Democratic Party, and in 1868 he would be the Democratic nominee for Congress in Cuyahoga County. In his memorial tribute to Ranney, Samuel E. Williamson wrote that Ranney had not sought nomination because he wanted Backus to have the position, but this seems highly unlikely. After all, Ranney could have declined to run.[13]

On August 28, after it had become obvious that Ranney and the Republicans remained as distant from each other as ever—the *Ohio State Journal* had called Ranney politically unfit and of dubious loyalty to the Union—the *Eagle* restored Ranney to its list of Democratic candidates. Governor Tod, fed up with what he saw as the *Eagle's* disloyal, obstructionist stance, had called editor Charles Roland to Columbus and threatened to suppress the paper if he did not change his ways, but it is not clear that pressure from Tod accounted for Ranney's restoration to the *Eagle's* good graces. The paper denied that it had dropped Ranney because of his recruiting speeches. Rather, it had objected to his speechmaking in the company of the "blackguard abolitionist" Galloway. "Judge R. was caught in bad company," explained the *Eagle,* "and to some extent he was judged by that company." And the paper remained vehemently antiadministration.[14]

The military situation by itself might have sufficed to give victory to the Democrats in October, but Lincoln's preliminary Emancipation Proclamation in September, promising to free the slaves in those areas still in rebellion on January 1, 1863, sealed the deal. The Democrats won every statewide contest—for secretary of state, attorney general, supreme court judge, member of the board of public works, commissioner of common schools—and fourteen of nineteen congressional seats. A historian of the Ohio Republican Party blamed the Unionist debacle on the inability of soldiers to vote,[15] but military defeats and squabbling between Republicans and Democrats within the Unionist coalition were the real culprits. The Democratic margin of victory was similar in all the statewide races, but Ranney won more votes and triumphed by a larger margin than any other Democrat.

Eighteen sixty-three promised to be another disastrous year for the Union Party. Olds, while still a federal prisoner, had been elected to fill a vacancy in the Ohio House. On January 3, 1863, he took his oath of office. With the war still going badly Democrats boldly assailed the Lincoln administration. Dresel introduced his antiadministration resolutions in the House, and arrests of editors failed to stem violent attacks on the administration by Democratic newspapers. In some rural areas citizens forcibly resisted attempts to arrest deserters or to enforce the draft.[16]

On May 5 General Ambrose E. Burnside, at the instance of Governor Tod, arrested Clement Vallandigham, who, having lost his bid for reelection to the Ohio House thanks to a gerrymander, had decided to run for governor in 1863. In an overheated political atmosphere and in violation of Burnside's order against expressions of "sympathy for the enemy," Vallandigham made a series of incendiary speeches. Convicted by a military court, denied a writ of habeas corpus by a civilian court, Vallandigham quickly became a martyr in the eyes of Peace Democrats. Rather than have Vallandigham imprisoned and perhaps set off a civil war within Ohio, Lincoln shipped him to the Confederacy and forbade him to return. On June 11 the Democratic state convention chose the absent Vallandigham as its candidate for governor.[17]

The Union Party, burdened with the horrific costs of the war and riven by dissent, carefully avoided giving the Democrats any additional ammunition for the campaign. At their state convention in June the Unionists chose former Democrats as their candidates for governor and state treasurer and adopted a cautious platform that stressed prosecution of the war and avoided any mention of emancipation or other inflammatory issues. Democratic stalwarts such as Thurman, William Allen, and Samuel Medary worked hard on Vallandigham's behalf, but others, including Ranney and Payne, remained conspicuously silent. Vallandigham had campaigned for Ranney in 1859, but that was before the Union's survival had been put to the test. On July 4 Union arms triumphed at the decisive battles of Gettysburg and Vicksburg, crushing Democratic claims that the war could not be won and fortifying Unionist morale. The two great victories, coupled with prosperity based on wartime demand, gave the Unionists a smashing win.[18]

Ranney took his seat on the supreme court in February 1863, when Unionist fortunes were at low tide, and resigned on February 20, 1865,[19] when victory was in sight. During this second term he remained true to the Democratic principles of his first-term opinions. It will be recalled that in *Cass v. Dillon* the supreme court had upheld a county subscription to the stock of a railroad company based on a statute enacted before the constitution of 1851 took effect, even though the proceedings pursuant to the statute occurred after the constitution took effect. Ranney had dissented in *Cass,* and he continued to dissent now over the majority's insistence that overruling *Cass* "would involve consequences too serious to be contemplated."[20] Ranney would not sacrifice constitutional principle to practicality.

In the stock subscription cases Ranney fought a lonely and losing battle to prevent the kind of public aid to private enterprise that had so agitated

Radical Democrats at the 1850–51 constitutional convention. But Ranney had the unanimous support of the justices in other cases in which corporations coaxed the General Assembly into passing special legislation or infringed on the property rights of ordinary citizens.

One important case arose out of the wreckage of the Marietta & Cincinnati Railroad. The road's backers had high hopes that the Marietta & Cincinnati would turn the Queen City into a great metropolis by linking it to the east coast via a connection with the Baltimore & Ohio Railroad. Hard times, though, forced the "hopelessly insolvent" company to reorganize under a law passed specifically for the relief of its creditors and stockholders. When the bill passed the House a group of seventeen lawmakers, most of them Democrats, protested that the legislation was unconstitutional on several grounds, one of which was that the legislation had created a new corporation in violation of the constitutional prohibition against the conferral of corporate powers by a special act.[21]

Pursuant to the statute the company's mortgagees purchased the railroad's property at a judicial sale and proceeded to reorganize. Subsequently, the Marietta & Cincinnati sought to appropriate real property belonging to various landowners to put down tracks. The railroad claimed authority to condemn private property under a statute of 1852 that granted eminent domain privileges to corporations. The plaintiffs contended that if the reorganization act of 1860 was unconstitutional, the reorganized railroad was not a corporation and therefore had no legal authority to appropriate property. The company argued that the reorganization act did not "confer" corporate powers but merely declared that the effect of the "transfer" of corporate powers, as the result of the judicial sale of the railroad's property to the mortgagees, was to transfer its franchise and charter. The reorganized company was still a corporation and therefore could exercise eminent domain powers under the 1852 statute.

Ranney, writing for the court, rejected such hairsplitting. Whatever the form of the transaction, he held, its constitutionality must be determined by its substance. The constitution must be construed to "preserve its great leading objects intact," including the abolition of special legislation and the equal treatment of all corporations. What would the creditors of the Marietta & Cincinnati have acquired at the judicial sale without the benefit of the act? asked Ranney. They would have obtained the property of the railroad and the right to operate it, but not its charter. The company's corporate existence, he wrote, "survives the wreck." Neither the mortgage nor the judicial decree of sale transferred the corporate franchise and powers from the old stockholders to the purchasers at the sale. If anything effected the transfer, it could only have been the act of the legislature. "If, then, the act alone, either directly or indirectly, has been *legally operative* to take this franchise from the stockholders and vest it in the purchasers, what is this but *conferring* upon them, by 'special act,' not only corporate existence, but very important 'corporate powers?'" Although the supreme court would not always be so scrupulous regarding the prohibition against special legislation, in this case of special legislation for the benefit of a railroad corporation the court enforced the constitution.[22]

The Marietta & Cincinnati case arose when the railroad tried to take property under a statute that granted eminent domain powers to corporations. At the constitutional convention and during his first full term on the bench, Ranney had acknowledged the propriety of allowing corporations to exercise such powers, but he had insisted on protecting the rights of the landowners and on securing to them adequate compensation. In *Cincinnati and Spring Grove Avenue Street Railway Company v. Incorporated Village of Cumminsville,* Ranney protected property owners when the legitimate use of a corporate franchise impaired the value of their property.[23]

In *Cumminsville* the Ohio court continued on an independent path marked out during the interval between Ranney's terms on the bench. Ohio was the only state to dissent from the mid-nineteenth-century consensus that if certain acts, most notably street grading that impaired a lot owner's access to a public street, could not support a trespass action, then the legislature could authorize those acts without requiring compensation.[24] Ohio continued on its separate course after Ranney rejoined the court. In 1862 several individual property owners in the Village of Cumminsville sought to force the Cincinnati & Spring Grove Avenue Street Railway Company to remove track it had laid on a public highway and to enjoin it from putting down additional track. The owners of the lots asserted that the tracks were being constructed too close to their side of the street, effectively preventing wagon access to their homes and improvements and thus constituting a nuisance. The trial court restrained the company from extending its tracks.

As Ranney noted in his opinion for the supreme court, street railways were quickly spreading to cities and towns throughout the state, so that an understanding of what they could and could not do under the law was imperative. Although street railroads were a new mode of travel, Ranney thought that their use of public roads presented no new principles of law.

The owner of a street-front lot, he wrote, had an easement in the street that was "as much property as the lot itself." Even if a street railroad had the statutory authority to invade the property rights of the lot owners, for the public purpose of improving public transportation, by obstructing access to their land, it could not do so without compensating the owners. "[T]he justice of the constitution," wrote Ranney, "has provided that what the [public] thus gains, and the [lot owner] loses, shall be paid for, before the property is taken or invaded."[25]

Cumminsville reflects Ranney's continued commitment to property rights. At the time of the midcentury constitutional convention, Democrats sometimes felt compelled to defend themselves against the imputation that they were agrarians or revolutionary socialists having no regard for property rights. One convention delegate declared his pride in having been a Jeffersonian Democrat from his youth and a believer that all citizens were entitled "to the same privileges and the same blessings." But, he continued, "I never was, and never can be an agrarian. . . . Agrarianism is calculated to dry up every source of individual and national prosperity . . . and would as certainly prove the destruction of all public property, as it would the demolition of every private right or interest." Another Democrat complained that he had been denounced as an agrarian for insisting upon the individual liability of stockholders for obligations of the corporation.[26]

Ranney came in for his share of abuse on this score. Democrat Lucius Case, believing that a power in the General Assembly to repeal corporate charters would be nothing but "plunder," implied that Ranney and other proponents of the power were "agrarians."[27] But Jacksonian Democrats such as Ranney were sincere in their protestations of devotion to property rights. It was on Ranney's motion that the constitutional convention required that damages for property taken by eminent domain be assessed by a jury without deduction for benefits to any of the owner's property.[28] Without the amendment the commissioners who appraised property taken by eminent domain might calculate the amount by which the landowner's remaining property benefited from the road or other improvement for which the property had been taken and then deduct that amount from the award to the owner. Ranney regarded this deduction as inherently unfair and the so-called benefits as usually illusory. He gave the example of a farm cut in two by a canal. If the canal raised the value of the property left to the owner after the condemnation by an amount that exceeded the value of the property taken for the canal, the owner would get nothing for his land. His farm would be reduced by a third, and he would be left with the expense of building and maintaining bridges and fences. Landowners rarely got justice under the commissioner system, said Ranney, and it was a "mockery" of the constitutional guarantee of the inviolability of private property "to pay for it in moonshine."[29] Ranney's *Cumminsville* opinion was a logical extension of his arguments at the convention. It was meant to protect the fruits of man's labor, his home or shop, built in reliance on things as they were, from being appropriated without compensation in the name of new public needs.

In other respects, too, Ranney, during his truncated second elective term on the bench, remained attached to the ideas that had animated his arguments at the constitutional convention and his decisions during his first term on the court. Ranney retained his sympathy for the underdog. For example, he construed a will to ensure that a widow would not be left destitute. One Silas Pruden had left a will giving his wife Mary all his property "for her benefit and support, and for her to have and hold during the term of her natural life." The will also directed that all the proceeds from the sale of Silas Pruden's real or personal estate be paid over to Mary. Mary claimed a right to have the entire estate converted into money and to use it for her own benefit as she saw fit. The executor thought another construction possible: that Mary was entitled only to a life estate in the property, so that she could take the annual income it produced but had to leave the property itself intact for Silas's children by former wives and their descendants. "The amount of money in dispute is small," wrote Ranney, "but it is all that one of the parties, at least, has, and it is very important to her that it should be secured to her, if it can be done consistently with the rules of law, and the intention of her deceased husband."[30]

Holding that the language of the will could be construed to support either argument, Ranney ruled that the court could look at extrinsic circumstances to help it arrive at a proper construction. At the time of Silas's death, Mary was old, infirm, and without any means of support other than Silas's small estate. Silas had clearly intended to carry out his "high moral duty" to provide for Mary's support after his death. That intention could not be fulfilled with just the annual income. Ranney recognized that the will used language that defined a life estate, but he stretched the inferences of other phrases to do equity for an underdog.[31]

Ranney served only two years on the supreme court during the Civil War. In that time the court decided few cases occasioned by the conflict, the most important of which involved the constitutionality of a law passed in

April 1863 to enable soldiers to vote in the field. The law probably impressed many citizens as a matter of simple fairness: men who otherwise were qualified to vote, and who were risking their lives in defense of their country, should not be denied the opportunity to vote. But there was also a political motive behind the law. The war was going badly for the Union, and popular discontent with the administration threatened to sweep the Democrats back into power in Columbus and in Washington. The army leaned Republican, and Republicans needed all the help they could get.[32]

After the state and county elections of October 1863, Henry Lehman, the Republican candidate for probate judge in Wayne County, defeated Democrat John K. McBride on the strength of votes cast outside the state. McBride challenged the constitutionality of the soldier-vote law in court. Republican justice Josiah Scott, writing for the court, upheld the statute. Scott posited as his fundamental premise that the General Assembly had plenary power to enact legislation; that is, the legislature's authority was limited only by prohibitions found in "express terms" in the constitution or by "necessary implication" from the language of the constitution. Scott thus flatly contradicted Ranney's cherished constitutional principle that the legislature had only those powers expressly delegated to it by the constitution. Scott then examined every constitutional provision that in any way bore on the time, place, or manner of holding elections and found nothing to preclude the General Assembly from authorizing balloting outside the state. Indeed, he noted that the 1802 constitution expressly prohibited voters from voting "except in the county and district in which he shall actually reside at the time of the election," a condition omitted from the 1851 constitution.[33]

The *Lehman* majority opinion rested on a "volitional" concept of suffrage, which was coming to replace the longstanding "consensual" concept. As historian Kenneth J. Winkle has explained, certain important rights, most notably suffrage and poor relief, had traditionally rested on residence in a community. In Ohio, as in New England since colonial days, that community was the township. The consensus of the community decided who was a resident and could therefore exercise the rights and privileges of residence.[34] Even when statutes or court decisions set down the qualifications for voting, community members who served as judges of election applied the law in accordance with community standards. The Ohio Supreme Court having decided that the constitutional limitation of suffrage to whites meant that a would-be voter just had to be more white than black, the people of the Republican-leaning Western Reserve would let any man vote who swore to being more than half white, regardless of how dark he was. In some places, especially where Democrats predominated, non-naturalized immigrants voted with the tacit acquiescence of the populace.[35]

However, the trend of the law was toward suffrage based on the will of the individual voter rather than the consensus of the community. Ohio had a highly mobile population. People were constantly moving through and around the state, weakening the idea of community that underlay the consensus theory. If people were not to be disenfranchised, "residence" had to be defined by something other than acceptance by the community. In 1841 the General Assembly passed an election law that for the most part allowed the voter to choose his own residence by establishing a physical presence in a town and showing an intent to stay there. Judges of election still had considerable latitude when poll-watchers challenged would-be voters, and they might bend or even break the law, but the theoretical basis for residence, and therefore voting, had shifted.[36]

Democrats at the constitutional convention of 1850–51 had found themselves badly divided over the definition of residence for electoral purposes. The committee on the elective franchise proposed to give the vote to every white male citizen of the United States who had been a resident of Ohio for one year and of the county, township, or ward in which he resided for such time as might be provided by law. Ranney objected to giving the General Assembly the power to establish the length of the local residency requirement. He proposed instead that the citizen be a bona fide resident of the township or ward at the time of the election. Poverty or other circumstances might compel a man to move from one township to another every year. A probationary period for an immigrant from another state to learn about Ohio's laws and institutions made sense, but Ranney could see no reason to give the legislature the power to deprive a man of a "previously acquired franchise." Democrats William Hawkins and Lucius Case, pointing to abuses resulting from "loose rules" and the transience of canal workers and other laborers, thought some fixed period of residence necessary to forestall corruption. On Ranney's motion, the convention amended his amendment to require a residence of twenty days before the election.[37]

Winkle interprets Ranney's position as a defense of the traditional consensual basis of voting. He contrasts Ranney's views with those of another Democrat, G. Volney Dorsey, who declared flatly that a citizen should be allowed to vote in the county "where he is on the day of election." Dorsey's position would not do in a closely divided township or county, retorted

Ranney. "Would the gentleman permit him, under such circumstances, to vote where he might choose to be?" Dorsey said he was aware of the abuse but that it would be a greater abuse to bind a man to a residence and thereby deprive him of the right to vote. Winkle correctly characterizes Dorsey's position as "completely volitional," but he goes too far in saying that Ranney, notwithstanding his professed concern for in-state migrants, "was really defending the community." Ranney insisted on actual residence because, like Hawkins and Case, he wanted to prevent voter fraud. The twenty-day period of residence that he suggested would have placed only a mild burden on migrants while still demonstrating the voter's good faith; it was hardly enough for a new man to gain general acceptance in the community.[38]

Ranney's real objection to the committee's report had nothing to do with consensual or volitional ideas of suffrage. It was, rather, that the report gave to the General Assembly yet another power with which it could not be trusted. The legislature might keep changing the residency requirement, producing "a constant state of incertitude and fluctuation." He declared himself "not tenacious" on the wording of the constitution, provided that it did not leave such an important right as the elective franchise to the General Assembly. Ranney's amendment lost, and the constitution followed the committee report.[39]

Although Winkle misconstrues Ranney's position at the convention, he seems on surer ground when he casts Ranney's opinion in *Lehman v. McBride* as a defense of tradition. Responding to Scott's opinion of twenty-six pages in the official reports, Ranney wrote a forty-page dissent. Notwithstanding the obvious political implications of the soldier-vote law, Ranney claimed, no doubt sincerely, that he would have preferred to agree with the nearly unanimous General Assembly on the validity of the statute. He warmly supported the Union cause and must have sympathized with soldiers who wanted to vote on matters that affected their very lives. But Ranney could not uphold a law that violated his most basic constitutional premises. Reiterating his argument that the legislature enjoyed only such powers as the constitution expressly delegated to it, he pointed out that the bill of rights declared in no uncertain terms that "all powers not herein delegated remain with the people."[40]

But beyond that, Ranney founded his case on a deeply conservative historical argument. The principle that voters could cast their ballots only in the districts in which they lived, he wrote, "is older than this constitution, and has been adhered to with unyielding tenacity down to the passage of the act of 1863." The current constitutional provisions on voting could be understood only in light of the history of election laws and practices going back to the days of the Northwest Territory. General, undefined terms used in the constitution, such as habeas corpus and trial by jury, had to be construed with their traditional usage in mind. Every voter in Ohio knew what "election" meant. "Twice in each year at least [the voters] had been accustomed to resort to the polls, and there witness the practical workings of an election, until its essential features, and the time when and the place where the elective franchise was to be exercised had become as familiar as household words." The right to vote was not a "*mere* personal privilege, carried by the elector wherever he may go," but "a *public franchise,* belonging to the whole community . . . to be exercised for the common benefit of the whole."[41]

An election, then, was democratic in the profoundest sense. It was a civic activity through which the people exercised their sovereignty in a public, community setting. The local setting also provided safeguards against abuse. Under the old constitution, noted Ranney, many people who did not reside in a given township or ward would show up at the polling place, claim to be residents, vote, and then skedaddle, thus defrauding the legitimate residents. To address this abuse the framers of the 1851 constitution required that every voter be a resident of the county, township, or ward for a legislatively prescribed period in order to vote there. They adopted this provision to enable "the *bona fide* electors of counties to know, before the elections, who were entitled to vote, and at the elections, through the officers charged with the duty of conducting them, *to protect themselves from fraud.*"[42]

In *Lehman* Ranney explicitly adopted a conservative approach to constitutional construction. Reaffirming his distrust of the legislature, Ranney insisted that the framers had not intended to leave the essential features of the ballot box "to the control of fluctuating majorities in the general assembly." The constitution "is to-day what is was the day it took effect, and requires the construction now, which would have been given it then." Ranney based his conclusions on "the language of the constitution itself, construed in the light of principles approved by time and experience." Acknowledging at last the political purpose of authorizing the soldier vote, he lamented, "It will be a sad day for constitutional government, when legislative enactments are either sustained or overthrown, upon mere considerations of temporary policy or expediency."[43]

As for the specific issue at hand, Ranney read his own position at the convention into the constitution as it had been adopted. Under Ohio's first constitution, he observed, the voter had only to be an actual resident of the county or district at the time of the election. Such abuses had grown up under this provision that the convention had insisted upon a period of residence prior to the election. The purpose of the new wording was to enable "the *bona fide* electors of counties to know, before the elections, who were entitled to vote." Any construction that permitted the General Assembly to allow voters to remove themselves from local scrutiny "completely annihilates the means, and the only means, relied upon to make this provision practically operative."[44]

According to Winkle, the *Lehman* majority was "looking to the future" of a "rapidly changing society" in which voting was an individual rather than a community right, while Ranney was "committed to the past."[45] There is an element of truth in this assertion, but perhaps not the one that Winkle had in mind. As we have seen, Ranney did not approve of the constitutional convention's decision to leave the residency requirement to the General Assembly. But the convention had still insisted on *some* residency requirement, and Ranney was determined to enforce what he believed to be the letter and spirit of the constitution. The past to which Ranney was committed was not the past of community consensus but of strict constitutional construction and limited legislative power. It was the same Radical Democratic constitutionalism Ranney had espoused at the convention and during his early years on the court.

EIGHT

Conserving Democracy

RANNEY REMAINED active in Democratic politics during and after the Civil War. Recognized as one of the leaders of the War Democrats, he sat out the gubernatorial campaign of 1863, when his party, in a fit of antiwar fervor, chose the exiled Clement Vallandigham as its candidate. In March of the following year, the Democratic state convention had to select four at-large delegates to the presidential nominating convention in Chicago. Major General George B. McClellan, who despised Lincoln and his policies but who insisted on pursuing the war to preserve the Union, was the leading Democratic candidate for president. In the voting for delegates-at-large, William Allen, Allen G. Thurman, and George H. Pendleton, outspoken critics of the Lincoln administration who nevertheless feared that the nomination of an extreme Peace Democrat would lead to defeat in the fall, secured majorities on the first ballot. Ranney, too, worried that Vallandigham's "dead weight" would drag the party down. Ranney finished fourth in the voting, followed closely by Vallandigham and then Samuel Medary, but he lacked a majority. General George W. Morgan, who had recently resigned his commission in the Union army, moved that the fourth-place finisher be unanimously elected, but Vallandigham's supporters refused to concede. Medary threw his support to Vallandigham, but on the second ballot Ranney won by five votes. Outraged Vallandigham men raised a storm of protest, some of them even threatening to fight. After a recount confirmed the result, most of Vallandigham's supporters yielded to pleas for party unity and agreed to a motion to make the election of all four delegates-at-large unanimous, although a few diehards dissented.[1] The *Plain Dealer* predicted that Ranney would have a "leading position" at the convention, where his "good sense" and "uprightness of character" would help harmonize the discordant interests in the party. The published record does not indicate that Ranney took an active part in the proceedings; perhaps he exerted influence behind the scenes. But Ranney was chosen as Ohio's representative on the National Democratic Committee and a member of that committee's executive committee.[2]

As election day approached Ohio congressman Samuel S. Cox sought Ranney's assistance in his reelection campaign. Cox was one of the less extreme Peace Democrats, but Republican editors classed him with the Copperheads, those antiwar Democrats likened by Republicans to poisonous snakes. Historians of the Copperheads contend that Copperheads were conservatives who "thought that the wheel of revolution turned too fast and too far. . . . [T]hey looked toward the past and feared the changes which the war foisted upon the country."[3] But one did not have to be a Peace Democrat to share that conservative outlook. Ranney had a well-earned reputation as a War Democrat, but there was little difference between his political views and Cox's. And as the war ground on, even that little diminished.

Ranney politely rebuffed Cox's request for campaign assistance on two grounds: that the people would not approve of a supreme court judge going on the stump and that Ranney's as-yet unreported opinion in the soldier voting case, when it became public, would provoke vituperation in the press, to the injury of both Cox and McClellan. The judge's excuses seem disingenuous. The fact that he had dissented in *Lehman v. McBride* had been announced by the court in April. He had supported McClellan's successful bid for the presidential nomination in August, and he spoke at Democratic rallies both before and after refusing Cox's request. Although Cox also had supported McClellan's candidacy at the Democratic national convention, at the cost of being accused by Peace Democrats of selling out, it may be that Cox was too closely associated with Vallandigham for Ranney's taste.[4]

Ranney grew so disenchanted with the war, though, that he began to sound like a Copperhead himself. At campaign rallies, he described Lincoln as a purveyor of filthy jokes who was unfit to sit in the chair once occupied by Washington, Jefferson, and Jackson. He blamed the president for conducting an endless war for the sake of abolition and "negro superiority" while imposing a ruinous debt on the nation, shredding the Constitution, and squandering America's patrimony of "light and easy government" that had produced unprecedented wealth and liberty. As long as Lincoln, with his policy of subjugating the South, remained in power, preached Ranney, peace was a forlorn hope. But McClellan knew both how to fight and "when fighting is no longer useful." With McClellan in the White House, thought Ranney, many of the southern states would leave the Confederacy and rejoin the Union. A Republican paper charged that Ranney had revealed the thinking of Copperhead leaders by "hint[ing] at revolution" should McClellan lose the election.[5]

Ranney resigned his supreme court seat in February 1865 with three years left to his term. Although he would never again hold a major public office, he was not through with politics. In August Ranney presided over the Democratic state convention. Until four years before, he told the delegates, there was no other place on Earth where men's rights were "so well and so perfectly respected" as in the United States. Now the disunited country, wallowing in blood, had lost all security of persons and property; all its "guarantees of liberty"—habeas corpus, freedom of speech, freedom of the press—had "been broken down." Invoking Jefferson, Ranney declared that Ohio's Democrats had assembled not to create a new political system but "to go back again to the chart of our own great principles as recorded by our fathers, and place ourselves upon the ground they occupied." Their first duty, though, was to restore the country. Ranney did not say how that was to be accomplished.[6]

In 1866 Ranney took part in the National Union movement, launched by the murdered Lincoln's successor, President Andrew Johnson, for the purpose of galvanizing support for Johnson's Reconstruction program and ensuring that Radical Republicans would not get control of Congress in the fall elections. The chief feature of Johnson's plan of Reconstruction was the immediate and unqualified readmission of southern states into the Union. Once those states regained their seats in Congress, any hope of Radical measures, such as congressional approval of the proposed Fourteenth Amendment, would be doomed. Johnson hoped that the National Union movement would unite Democrats and conservative Republicans behind his program and isolate the Radicals.[7]

In June the leaders of the National Union movement called for a convention to be held in Philadelphia. Each state was to send a delegation twice the size of its full congressional delegation, equally divided between former Lincoln and McClellan supporters from 1864. On July 11, the *Cleveland Plain Dealer* published a notice to the electors of the Eighteenth Congressional District that a meeting would be held in Cleveland on July 21 to choose delegates to the Philadelphia convention. The notice was subscribed by Ranney, Backus, Payne, and Moses Kelly, a prominent lawyer. By taking the lead, the four men essentially elected themselves delegates. The Cleveland meeting ratified the self-selection.[8]

Backus, Payne, and Ranney all addressed the meeting. Ranney gave a short speech in which he accused Congress of treating one-third of the country (the conquered South) like an Ireland or Hungary, solely to keep the dominant party in power. The Republicans, he maintained, had resolved to "put down" the president for trying to restore the country, a state of affairs to which, in Ranney's view, the people would not submit.[9]

Many Democrats saw the call for a National Union convention as an invitation to abandon their old party organization. The party's parlous political prospects generated considerable public comment about the desirability and even the inevitability of dissolution. The Democratic state central committee, though, would not even consider such a possibility, insisting upon the need to "hold fast" to the party's organization and principles. Only after much squabbling did the committee agree to participate in the National Union convention. The committeemen need not have worried. Radical Republicans would have no truck with the Philadelphia convention, and, notwithstanding the dramatic arm-in-arm entrance of Democrats and Republicans into the convention hall, the convention failed to persuade even conservative Republicans to join hands with the Democrats. Despite the best efforts of the movement's leaders to keep extreme Copperheads from tainting their unification scheme, the Ohio delegation included Vallandigham, whose presence in Philadelphia the Republicans in attendance could not stomach and even some Democrats regretted. The *New York Times* reported that the "more prominent members" of the Ohio delegation were "bound and determined" that Vallandigham would not be seated, a sentiment they conveyed to Vallandigham "in no very complimentary terms." Under intense pressure, Vallandigham withdrew.[10]

What part Ranney played in the Vallandigham brouhaha or other proceedings of the convention is unknown. Within the Ohio delegation, when one member proposed that the delegation recognize Vallandigham's right to a seat but that Vallandigham withdraw for the sake of harmony, the resolution was referred to a committee of five that included Ranney. The committee endorsed the proposal, Vallandigham consented, and on that basis the contretemps was resolved. In the convention itself, Ranney served as vice president for Ohio, but that may have been an honorary post with no substance. In any event, Ranney's efforts went for naught. By election day the convention and the National Union movement as a whole had faded into insignificance.[11]

Democrats called the Philadelphia meeting the "conservative convention,"[12] an apt characterization for an event meant to halt the advance of the Radical Republicans. Although the National Union movement failed, Ranney continued his quest to defeat the Republicans and bring the nation back to its roots. By August 1866, when the National Union convention met, it had become obvious that southerners intended to reduce the freedmen to a state as near to slavery as possible and that President Johnson would do little to thwart that plan. Johnson had vetoed measures to extend the life of the Freedmen's Bureau and to protect the civil rights of blacks, both of which had broad support among Republicans. He rejected all attempts to give even limited suffrage to the freedmen and sought the quick restoration of the South to Congress. Had he had his way, a South ruled by whites and dominated by Democrats would have joined with northern Democrats to overwhelm even a moderate Republican Reconstruction.

When moderate Republicans finally decided that they could not work with the president, Congress forged ahead with its own plan of Reconstruction. It overrode Johnson's vetoes of the Freedmen's Bureau and Civil Rights Acts and sent the Fourteenth Amendment, which penalized states that refused to grant black suffrage by reducing their representation in Congress, to the states for ratification. The Republicans won a smashing victory in the 1866 congressional elections. When Congress reconvened, the Republicans pushed through the Reconstruction Act of 1867, which divided the South into five military districts, placed supreme political authority over the states within those districts in the hands of the army, and required black suffrage and ratification of the Fourteenth Amendment as prerequisites for the resumption of those states' representation in Congress.

Democrats denounced Radical Reconstruction as the unconstitutional imposition of military rule on American civilians and a trampling of states' rights. But Reconstruction hardly exhausted their list of complaints. The

Civil War was a big event that called forth big government and big business. Congress created the Bureau of Internal Revenue, the forerunner of the Internal Revenue Service; imposed a host of taxes, including a federal income tax, excise taxes, and stamp taxes; established a national banking system that, thanks to a tax on the notes of state-chartered banks, eventually drove state banknotes out of circulation; and raised the tariff. The federal government issued hundreds of millions of dollars in war bonds and in paper money ("greenbacks") not backed by gold or silver. The public debt soared from $65 million in 1860 to $2.7 billion in 1865. Federal fiscal policy, together with new tariffs and the huge demand for war matériel, stimulated industrial production and laid the foundation for the rise of great corporations. Congress gave enormous tracts of public land to railroad corporations to help them finance the construction of lines to the Pacific.

To combat what he saw as revolutionary challenges to American constitutionalism—as massive accretions of governmental power and threats to the liberties of the people—Ranney eagerly took to the election campaign trail. The party's state executive committee arranged arduous speaking tours for Ranney, Thurman, Vallandigham, and other leading Democrats. Ranney's initial schedule for August included engagements in thirteen cities and towns in seventeen days. A revised scheduled eased the burden a bit, but it was still demanding. Many of the speakers maintained a similar pace throughout the campaign, but Ranney seems to have made only spot appearances in September and early October.[13]

On August 6, 1867, at his first scheduled stop, Ranney delivered a long, impassioned speech in Mansfield. The *Ohio Statesman* thought it "a brilliant effort" from one of Ohio's "ablest minds" and published it in its entirety. The party had the speech printed as a pamphlet for distribution.[14] Ranney began by noting the extraordinary nature of the current campaign. It was not a mere contest over policy but involved fundamental questions of civil liberty and constitutional government. Citing the examples of ancient Rome, revolutionary France, and modern Mexico among others, he warned that once liberty is lost, it is lost forever. Before the advent of the Republican Party, the United States had been a free, prosperous, and growing nation. Now, said Ranney, one-third of the country was politically disconnected from the rest, and the tax-gatherers were everywhere. The annual federal revenue exceeded $500 million, a sum so vast that it could not be kept track of. It was a situation ripe for corruption. So much money could not be disposed of, he said, "without some little portion of it sticking to the fingers of the gentlemen who greased the wheels to get it through."

Ohio's own experience showed that when government loaned its credit to private corporations, "some loyal patriot" got the work and the public ended up paying the debt. Now there were great eastern manufacturers and nationally chartered banks dependent on the federal government for profits. Speculators were buying up public land granted to the states to support agricultural colleges, while the federal government gave huge swaths of western land to giant railroad corporations and political favorites instead of making it available to poor but industrious settlers. Washington was also guaranteeing the payment of railroad bonds, which threatened to drive up the already enormous federal debt. Ranney recalled the great consternation over Ohio's $16 million state debt at the 1850–51 constitutional convention. At least Ohio had something to show for all that debt: its "magnificent" canals. But, on a per capita basis, Ohio's share of the current national debt was a staggering $300 million, and all that money had produced nothing with which to bring the debt down. All the tariffs and taxes on manufacturers that the government imposed simply got passed on to the people.

As if all the economic shenanigans were not enough, Ranney accused Republicans of "partisan violence." The damning indictment: The Republican majority in Congress was keeping ten states in the political wilderness. Congress had expelled Democrats from the loyal states of Kentucky and Maryland without justification. The House had launched inquiries into whether Kentucky, Maryland, and Delaware, all controlled by Democrats, had republican forms of government as required by the United States Constitution. The Republican governor of Tennessee had used the militia to secure victory for his party at the polls. Congress had run roughshod over the president, reducing Johnson to the "merest nothing," and Republicans had attacked the independence of the judiciary by threatening to impeach Supreme Court justices for rendering an "honest opinion."

On their face, the Republican offenses reeled off by Ranney constituted a frightening assault on democracy and states' rights. But Ranney's one-sided condemnation was not entirely accurate, and it provided only half the context. No one from Maryland had been expelled from Congress. One representative and one senator from Kentucky had been thrown out in the months before the war for disloyalty to the Union.[15] The House inquiries into the nature of the state governments in Delaware, Maryland, and Kentucky rested largely on the denial of black suffrage in those states and on the political influence there of men who "went South" during the war.[16] Political and racial violence in Tennessee required a military presence at the polls.[17] President Johnson listed so far to the South that even moderate Republicans gave up on him. After the Supreme Court disallowed the use of military tribunals to try civilians in places where the civil courts were open, some Republicans did bandy about the word "impeachment," but there was no serious effort to remove any of the justices.[18]

However one-sided his specific charges may have been, Ranney justifiably felt betrayed by the transformation of Republican policy during and after the war. He pointed out that he and thousands of others had supported the war effort because Republicans had pledged to restore the Union and respect the rights of the states. Now, however, claimed Ranney, Congress had established a military despotism in the South, treating ten states as conquered provinces. Furthermore, the federal government's arrogation of power defied the Tenth Amendment, which reserved to the states or the people all powers not expressly granted to the federal government.

Ranney's denunciation of corporate-government coziness, fear of corruption, concern about public debt, anxiety over legislative encroachments on the other branches of government, respect for states' rights, and insistence that government be restricted to its expressly delegated powers all had their roots in Jacksonian Democracy. So, too, did his ugly appeal to racism. Radical Reconstruction had disenfranchised many southern whites, and the military authorities in the occupied states were registering blacks to vote in order to aid the Republican Party. According to Ranney, the disenfranchised included "nearly all the intelligence" of the conquered region, while "negroes who are not able to take care of themselves" now made up a majority of the registered voters in some of the southern states. Everyone's taxes went to support these Negroes (through the Freedmen's Bureau) and to maintain a great standing army, but one party reaped all the benefit of such policies. Referring to Charles Sumner's remark that Congress would soon be welcoming black members, Ranney asked his Mansfield audience, "Won't you feel proud when that happens?" Negro suffrage was upon Ohio, Ranney warned, but he refused to "slander" the people by supposing that they would not vote it down.

Ranney wound up his efforts on behalf of the party with an address before a large crowd in Delaware, Ohio, on October 5. The *Statesman* estimated the "vast assemblage" at six thousand to eight thousand strong, a guess that must be viewed with suspicion because the partisan newspapers always gave high numbers for the crowds at their own parties' events and disparaged the turnout for their opponents. "[N]ever was an audience better entertained or more delighted," crowed the *Statesman*. Ranney's "cogent reasoning, strong argument and forcible array of FACTS . . . swept like a plowshare through the rotten schemes of rotten Radicals and their whole course of disunion and negro policy."[19]

Ohio's voters did not disappoint Ranney. After a vituperative campaign during which Democrats promised to free Ohio "from the thralldom of niggerism," the voters gave Republican Rutherford B. Hayes a narrow victory in the gubernatorial race. But they rejected a state constitutional amendment to grant suffrage to blacks, and they elected a Democratic legislature. The new General Assembly rescinded the previous legislature's ratification of the Fourteenth Amendment, investigated charges of illegal voting by blacks and mulattoes, overturned a senatorial election on the grounds that only men who were "pure white, unmixed" could vote, and enacted a new Visible Admixture Law to replace one that had been repealed during the war. (The supreme court, still in Republican hands, declared the new statute unconstitutional.) The legislature also refused to ratify the Fifteenth Amendment to the U.S. Constitution, which prohibited racial discrimination in voting laws.[20]

Despite his antiblack rhetoric, Ranney's views on race do not seem to have been based on pure bigotry. Beginning in 1860 and for years afterward, Republican newspapers delighted in printing a "catechism" asserting that Ranney had voted at the 1850–51 constitutional convention to permit black children to go to the same schools as white children and to defeat a proposal to block the immigration of blacks into Ohio. The latter charge was disingenuous. The main question before the convention was whether to require appropriations for the colonization of Ohio's blacks in Africa. Ranney voted against the proposal, but so did most of the other delegates. Ranney belonged to a small minority whose position on a procedural motion could have been seen as an attempt to prevent a vote on an amendment to prohibit black immigration into the state. However, the amendment probably had little support; the sponsor had already offered and withdrawn the amendment once, and he would withdraw it again.[21]

As noted in chapter 2, Ranney voted at the convention not to enshrine school segregation in the constitution. He would later explain his votes as an effort to leave the question of school segregation to the legislature to adjust "from time to time" in accordance with the "feelings of the white race, as to what was practicable to elevate and enlighten all classes of the population."[22] After the Civil War, it would become common for northern Democrats to say, or at least imply, that they opposed Negro suffrage not on racial grounds but because blacks were too ignorant to vote. That may have been a sentiment Ranney, to whom education was so important, sincerely held. He complained in his Mansfield speech that Republican Reconstruction policy gave the vote to Negroes who could not even take care of themselves while disenfranchising whites who included "nearly all the intelligence" of the southern states. A few years later, an educated African American who encountered racial discrimination in Cleveland found Ranney to be genuinely sympathetic.

John P. Green, who would become Ohio's first black state senator, had dropped out of school to support his family. He returned to high school as an adult, attended law school, and from 1873 to 1882 served as a justice of the peace in Cleveland. When a local restaurant refused him service, Green went for advice to the office of Judge Daniel R. Tilden, an old abolitionist Whig and Republican. There, finding Ranney sitting with the judge, he related his experience. Both men, recalled Green, were "greatly surprised and chagrined." "Why Dan," Ranney exclaimed, "Green and my Charlie used to go to school together!" Neither Ranney nor Tilden seems to have done anything to assist Green, who went back to the restaurant the next day in the company of another sympathetic lawyer and was duly seated. But Green believed that Ranney understood his plight. And Ranney apparently sent his son to a school that admitted black pupils.[23]

In 1868 Ranney, a Democratic presidential elector at large, campaigned for candidate Horatio Seymour, meeting him at the train station on October 24 when Seymour swung through Ohio. His own last grasp for a major public office occurred the next year. At the Democratic state convention of 1869, A. V. Rice, a Union general, businessman, and future congressman from Putnam County, nominated Ranney for governor. Ranney's 156 votes put him ahead on the first ballot, but with eight men in the running he had nowhere near the 295 votes needed to win. General William S. Rosecrans stood second with 107 votes. Ranney's lead was deceptive. He picked up 14½ votes on the second ballot, but Rosencrans, with 302 votes, finished far out in front. When Rosencrans declined the nomination, the Democratic state central committee unanimously chose as its candidate George H. Pendleton, McClellan's running mate in the 1864 presidential election, even though Pendleton had firmly refused to be considered before the convention.[24]

One Democrat thought Ranney had lost the nomination by asserting in a speech that Congress would ignore a congressional redistricting bill favored by the General Assembly's Democratic caucus. Another blamed the combined influence of Ohio's U.S. senators, Democrat Allen G. Thurman and Republican John Sherman, who each had his own reasons for desiring Ranney's defeat. Ranney was "distasteful to the Columbus Regency," wrote "A Disgusted Democrat," because he was honest as a Democrat and consistent as a politician." Whatever the cause of his loss, Ranney's day as an office-seeking politician was just about done. One Democratic paper, seeking a leader to save Ohio from the Fifteenth Amendment, wrote that Ranney "has no qualifications for any thing but the *routine* of the Governorship; and we are long since past the age of *routine.*" Ranney had run for popular election to federal or statewide office seven times since 1842 and won just twice. Both of his victories had come in races for the supreme court. His reputation was as a jurist, not a politician. But, as we will see, Ranney continued to play a role in Ohio's political life.[25]

NINE

Conservative Reform in the Gilded Age

IN 1873 Mark Twain and Charles Dudley Warner published *The Gilded Age,* a novel that mocked the superficiality and corruption of the day's politics and pursuit of wealth. Historians later attached the epithet "Gilded Age" to the next quarter-century, during which America experienced enormous growth and social disruption through the rise of giant railroad and industrial corporations, technological innovation, mass immigration, the rapid growth of cities, labor organization, and violence. The social and economic dislocations of the era, including the depression of the 1870s and the decline of traditional small-town life, led people to search for the root causes of their troubles. That search in turn gave rise to popular reform movements that sought to capture one or the other of the two major parties or to break their hold on the political system.

The conservative tone that characterized the calls for reform, with their demand for a return to traditional virtues, was foreshadowed by Democratic critiques of the Lincoln administration during the Civil War. Northern Democrats assailed the administration for its centralizing tendencies, aggrandizement of federal power, and assaults on civil liberty. "Essentially Jeffersonian in outlook," mainstream Democrats "harkened back to a lost past, to a decentralized, agrarian, pre-industrial America." They remained attached to "an older, federalized American Union that was passing from the scene forever, unable to withstand the irresistible and irreversible forces of modernization and the exigencies of a massive civil war."[1]

Clinton Rossiter claimed that postbellum capitalist conservatives pulled off the "Great Train Robbery of our intellectual history" by appropriating Jeffersonian, small-government liberalism for their own purposes. Democrats who allegedly clung to Jeffersonian laissez-faire notions with the interests of big business in mind came to be called Bourbons after the French royal house that supposedly had "learned nothing and forgotten nothing." In the United States "Bourbon" originally referred to "Southern Democrats of the old school," mostly former Confederate officials and soldiers who resisted Reconstruction and sought to ensure white supremacy. By the 1880s, though, a Bourbon Democrat, at least in the North, had come to mean a small-government, free-market Democrat like Grover Cleveland. Bourbon Democrats seemed less hostile than their Jacksonian predecessors toward corporations. One historian describes Bourbon Democrats as "wealthy, self-esteemed, self-appointed guardians of an already fixed pattern for living and making a living" who favored the industrial revolution then taking place and tried to protect it from the assaults of "restless farmers and wage earners." Another notes less pejoratively that the free-trade, hard-money, limited-government Bourbons "had close ties to business and commercial interests."[2]

But Democratic true believers in laissez faire regarded themselves as conservatives precisely because they *opposed* governmental aid to corporate enterprise. Bourbons such as Cleveland rejected the Republicans' most cherished big-business policy, a protective tariff. John G. Carlisle, one of the most powerful Democrats of the Gilded Age, denounced the Republicans' "radical and revolutionary policy," including "the tariff . . . subsidies to steamship companies, bounties to the manufacturers of sugar, [and] extravagant appropriations of the public money." Republican advocacy of "extreme measures," wrote Carlisle, had alienated the "great body of conservative voters." Democratic congressman Samuel S. Cox declared that his party was still Jeffersonian, resting its faith on the Tenth Amendment and the old maxim "the world is governed too much." The only "impregnable barrier against excesses," asserted Cox in good Jacksonian fashion, was government at every level strictly limited to its express constitutional duties. "As the function of government . . . is limited to the prescript, the conservatism of the country will rally upon the frontier of written and granted powers."[3]

If Democrats such as Cleveland, Carlisle, and Cox were conservative, it was not because they were in thrall to corporations but because they retained venerable Democratic ideas about the proper role of government. Some Democrats, along with many Republicans, may have allied themselves with big business, either to advance their political careers or because they feared that the popular movements of farmers, industrial workers, and reformers might gain power and endanger corporate interests. But that fear, too, when not based solely on self-interest, had roots in Jacksonian thought, for there had been good, consistent Jacksonians who opposed majoritarian threats to the property of minorities.[4]

In their commitment to small government and free trade, Democrats resembled British liberals. However, the first American political party with "liberal" in its name grew out of a split among Republicans in Missouri in 1870. An early historian of the dispute, focusing on fights within the party over Reconstruction and black suffrage, noted the rise of a "moderate" or "liberal" group within the party's Radical wing. These moderates became the Liberal Republican Party when they walked out of the Republican state convention in September 1870 and held their own convention.[5]

But the Liberal Republicans stood for more than moderation on Reconstruction. Many of them were Republicans of Democratic or Free Soil background.[6] Of the seven Ohioans identified by one scholar as leaders of the Liberal Republican Party, all but one had been Democrats.[7] Liberal Republicans, for all their demands for reform, sounded the theme of restoration. Just as Jacksonian Democrats had invoked Jeffersonian republicanism as their political ideal, the Liberal Republicans sought to purge republicanism of the dross that had accumulated during and after the Civil War. The centralization of power in the federal government, military rule in the South, the disenfranchisement of many southern citizens, the protective tariff and other economic measures that favored special classes, abuses of the patronage power: all, in the Liberal Republican mind, threatened to destroy republican government in America. And all had been fostered by the Republican Party. Control of that party had to be wrested away from machine politicians and returned to true republicans. Except perhaps for the Liberal Republicans' commitment to the rights of blacks, which Radical Republicans considered insufficiently ardent, the first Americans to wear "liberal" as a party label were conservatives.

Ranney shared the concerns of the Liberal Republicans. In his Mansfield speech of 1867, he had warned of the corruption that would come from the federal government's connections with big business and complained of the centralization of power in Washington. In 1871 Ranney lent his name to a "People's ticket" in Cuyahoga County, a mixed slate of Democrats and disaffected Republicans who were intent on "breaking down the most corrupt and unblushing gang of office seekers that have ever attempted to control a county of 130,000 inhabitants." Endorsed for the Ohio Senate by a temperance convention that opposed repeal of the state liquor laws, Ranney refused to give pledges one way or the other and was branded a "whiskeyite" (as well as a Copperhead) by regular Republicans. Ranney seems to have been genuinely reluctant to run. He initially declined the People's nomination, reportedly because of poor health, but reconsidered a few days later. The *Cleveland Daily Leader* claimed that the real aim of the People's coalition was to get Ranney into the state senate to ensure that the next legislature would replace John Sherman in the U.S. Senate, perhaps with Ranney himself. The Democratic county convention endorsed the People's ticket, but the Republicans won in a landslide.[8]

As demonstrated by his willingness to run for office on a ticket that included reform-minded Republicans, Ranney was deeply concerned about the political condition of the country. When on January 24, 1872, the Missouri state Liberal Republican convention called for a national convention of like-minded men to meet in Cincinnati on May 1, Ranney must have been interested. The Liberal Republicans disdained President Ulysses S. Grant, but they knew they could not oust him without Democratic support. And perspicacious Democrats knew that they had to accept the fundamental changes wrought by the Civil War, including constitutional guarantees of civil and voting rights for blacks, if they were to emerge from the political wilderness. Democrats in Montgomery County, Ohio, led by Clement Vallandigham, had already launched a "new departure" in May 1871 by accepting the Fourteenth and Fifteenth Amendments and emphasizing economic and class issues and civil service reform.

Although some sort of cooperation between Liberal Republicans and Democrats seemed necessary to both, it did not come easily. Leading Liberal Republicans distrusted Democrats as longtime adversaries who had hindered the war effort and shown scant regard for the rights of the freedmen. Democrats disagreed among themselves over the prospects for their survival as a party and the desirability of a merger with a Republican faction. Some Liberal Republicans wanted to allow Democrats into local Liberal Republican organizations. Others, fearing contamination of their movement through the admission of Democrats, instead urged the creation of separate Reunion and Reform Associations as political vehicles for "liberal Democrats." The Cincinnati Reunion and Reform Association issued a call for a nonpartisan, national Reunion and Reform convention to meet in the Queen City simultaneously with the Liberal Republican convention in the expectation that it would endorse the Liberal Republican ticket. Two hundred delegates from eleven states met at Mozart Hall for the Reunion and Reform convention on May 2 and elected Ranney presiding officer.[9]

Although not in his "accustomed health," Ranney delivered a vigorous opening address.[10] The delegates had not assembled, he asserted, to promote the interests of one party or to turn out one set of officeholders in favor of another. Rather, they had come together to reform the administration of the government. No existing political party had "the disposition and the power to stay this tendency toward centralization and corruption." The consolidation of power in the federal government threatened "to sink not only the individual sovereignty of the State" but also "the individual manhood of the citizen." The people had approved the Constitution in the first place because it had strictly limited the authority of the national government. They had been "entirely unwilling" to impair the great republican principle that made the representatives subject to the supervision of the people and readily accountable to them. Blasting the program of Radical Reconstruction, Ranney accused Radical Republicans of using secession as a pretext for "swallow[ing] up the original sovereignty of the States." As sovereignty resided in the people, and governments had only such powers as the people delegated to them, any assault on the theory of state sovereignty was in fact an attack on the power of the people to regulate their own affairs.

Ranney did not use the phrase "power corrupts," but he expressed the sentiment in no uncertain terms. "What are we most in danger of?" he asked. "That inordinate party spirit and that ungodly thirst for gain which is everywhere manifest—a thirst for gold and power." Notwithstanding the enormous cost of the war, the administration continued to burden the nation with onerous debt and taxes. No one suffered more than "the terribly governed States of the South." "Their fault was great," Ranney conceded, "but, pray heaven, have they not expiated it most sadly?" In the North legislatures had been bought, public officers had stolen public money, and corruption had found its way into every level and branch of government. Elections everywhere had been corrupted and senatorships purchased. Generals Washington, Jackson, and Harrison had put aside their military personas upon becoming president, but Grant seemed to regard government as a military matter.

Ranney did not aim his barbs solely at Republicans. The Republicans, as the dominant party, had more opportunities to pursue corrupt activities, but where the Democrats had spots worth cultivating, they "cultivate[d] those spots pretty well." Ranney called on "all honest men of all parties" to provide "purification" and "reform." Upon the conclusion of his speech, a delegate offered a resolution praising Liberal Republican Charles Francis Adams and supporting his election to the presidency should the Liberal Republican convention nominate him.

The Liberal Republican and Reunion and Reform conventions adopted very similar platforms. Both called for equal protection of the law for all citizens, universal amnesty for participants in the rebellion, local self-government by the states, opposition to centralized authority, civil service reform, reduced federal taxation, and a return to specie as the national currency. The chief difference was a vital one. The Liberal Republicans had two major goals, civil service reform and free trade. However, protectionist Republicans of Whig provenance succeeded in gaining control of the convention, securing the presidential nomination for Horace Greeley, an old Whig and persistent advocate of protective tariffs, and forcing a noncommittal tariff plank into the platform. But the Reunion and Reform convention refused to fudge. Opposing any duties that were "unnecessary for the purposes of revenue," the delegates demanded "a thorough revision . . . of the present iniquitous tariff."[11]

The Reunion and Reform position on the tariff recalled the party battles of the Jacksonian era. In other ways, too, the platform looked back to old Democratic values. Demanding "for the individual the largest liberty consistent with public order," the convention affirmed "that that people is best governed which is governed least" and called for a return "to the constitutional limitations of power." Even the civil service plank sounded the theme of restoration, insisting upon "a return to the early practice under our government" of appointing and retaining public officers solely on the basis of merit.[12]

When the Liberal Republicans nominated Greeley, convention delegates George Hoadly and Roeliff Brinkerhoff stalked out of Exposition Hall, "fully determined to have nothing more to do with" the convention. Brinkerhoff suggested that they go to the Reunion and Reform convention and get it to nominate Adams. But Hoadly decided to go back to Exposition Hall to check on the Liberal Republican nomination for vice president, and

Brinkerhoff went on alone. By the time Brinkerhoff reached Mozart Hall, the Reunion and Reform convention had already learned of Greeley's nomination and was "redhot with indignation." Brinkerhoff wanted the Reunion and Reform convention to nominate Adams and appeal to the Democratic Party for support, which he thought Hoadly could have persuaded it to do. Instead, in Hoadly's absence, the convention appointed a national executive committee headed by Ranney, authorized it to call a national convention in the hope that more states would send delegates, and adjourned.[13]

Notwithstanding his condemnation of "corruptionists" of all parties, Ranney showed up at the Ohio state Democratic convention in June, but not as a delegate. In their desire to defeat Grant, Ohio's Democrats, like Democrats across the country, leaned toward endorsing Greeley and the Liberal Republican platform. There was considerable talk about dissolving the Democratic Party altogether in favor of the formation of a new entity comprising liberals of both parties. But Ranney, no doubt riled by the outcome of the Liberal Republican convention, urged Ohio's Democrats to maintain their party organization and to nominate "straight" Democratic candidates. However, with no realistic hope of defeating Grant on their own, the Democrats endorsed Greeley and the Liberal Republican platform. Someone placed Ranney's name in nomination as a delegate-at-large to the Democratic national convention in Baltimore, but it was withdrawn in favor of Henry B. Payne.[14]

The Reunion and Reform associations never held a national convention. The Democratic national convention endorsed Greeley, who carried just six states in the presidential contest. After the election, about 150 prominent Liberal Republicans and Democrats met in Columbus to discuss a future course of action. Ranney does not appear to have been among them. In June 1873 the Allen County Democratic convention castigated both major parties for their inability to meet the needs of the nation or to eliminate corruption. It called for a mass meeting in Columbus on July 30 to push for reform. At the Columbus convention, Democrats from the Reunion and Reform movement, Liberal Republicans, and assorted others joined forces as a third party that would come to be called the People's Party, adopted a platform, and nominated a candidate for governor.[15]

The Allen County movement and formation of the People's Party frightened Allen Thurman and other longtime Democratic leaders who had no intention of abandoning their party. In response the Democratic state convention in early August nominated an old Jacksonian, William Allen, for governor, and adopted a platform that incorporated most of the positions of the People's Party agenda, sounding the same small-government, laissez-faire theme. The convention also condemned military rule in Louisiana and demanded that the public lands be reserved for actual settlers. More significantly in light of the widespread pro-greenback sentiment in the state, the platform endorsed a careful return to a specie-based money supply, thereby adhering to the traditional Democratic position on the currency but allowing some wiggle room for soft money in the short run. The Republican *Ohio State Journal* noted the backward-looking character of the Democratic platform and its gubernatorial candidate. The Democratic Party, it said, "falls back on its ancient prestige and time-worn traditions, hoping they will be a sufficient covering and apology for its later follies. We are now to have a revival, if such a thing can be in this progressive period, of what is known as Jacksonian Democracy."[16]

Newspaper reports of the People's Party convention make no mention of Ranney. By this time Ranney may have given up on the idea of a new party and begun trying to work his way back into the Democrats' good graces. At the 1873 Democratic convention, some delegates considered the possibility of nominating Ranney for the supreme court. The *Cincinnati Commercial* reported that a dispatch had been sent to him and that his nomination hinged on his answer. Perhaps the delegates wanted to hear of Ranney's willingness to run. In view of his recent antiparty activities, however, it seems more likely that they needed assurances of Ranney's party regularity. How Ranney responded is not known, but the many "old wheel-horses" at the convention may not have been ready to readmit him to good standing. No one placed his name in nomination.[17]

Notwithstanding Ranney's prominent role in the Reunion and Reform movement and his rebuff at the 1872 and 1873 Democratic state conventions, Ohio Democrats soon embraced him again. After the Greeley catastrophe, they must have realized that they had gained nothing by sacrificing principle and siding with renegade Republicans. Buoyed by a great financial panic and the scandals of the Grant administration, the Democrats triumphed in the 1873 elections, winning control of both houses of the General Assembly and electing Allen governor. If Ranney still harbored political ambitions, he had nothing to gain by participating in fruitless, third-party movements.

Democratic Party leaders apparently felt that they had nothing to gain by further estrangement, either. At their state convention in 1875, Democrats signaled Ranney's return to favor by electing him chairman. The selection accorded with the return to Democratic orthodoxy. One reporter noted the "flavor in the air of the old-time Democracy Conventions," with many established party leaders in attendance. In his opening address to the delegates, Ranney stressed the greatness and historical continuity of the Democratic Party and the need to return the nation to its fundamental principles. Acknowledging that he might be an "old fogy," Ranney "advise[d] all men to come back to these principles, to the pure and better days of the Republic."[18]

Two issues dominated the delegates' deliberations, school funding and the currency. The school funding issue stemmed from the desire of Catholic schools for a share of the public funds raised for educational purposes. Catholics, mostly of Irish and German descent, tended to support the Democrats; Republican editors claimed that Catholics "owned the Democratic party." Ranney bristled at the implication that he and other Democrats had gone back on their great principle of separation of church and state. He characterized the Republican attack as the start of "another crusade on religion and nationality." The purposes of the Democratic Party, proclaimed Ranney, had always been to ensure equal rights, to see that the proceeds of every man's labor went to his own benefit, to perpetuate the Union, and to protect conscience from encroachments by the state. Recalling his part in the constitutional convention of 1850–51, he pointed out that the Democrat-dominated convention had enshrined the inviolability of the public school fund in the constitution.[19]

Ranney devoted less of his speech to the currency question, which badly divided the party. The convention adopted a soft-money platform the next day, but Ranney made his hard-money proclivities clear, denouncing the Grant administration for furnishing a depreciating currency and noting the gap in value between greenbacks and coins. He also assailed the administration for creating a huge public debt, establishing carpetbag rule in the South at bayonet-point, and generally aggrandizing the Republican Party at the expense of the American people.[20]

Democratic papers naturally applauded Ranney's speech. The *Cleveland Plain Dealer* called it "strong," and the *Stark County Democrat,* which acknowledged Ranney's weakness as presiding officer of a boisterous convention and his lack of "lung power," thought it "splendid, able and sensible." The Republican *Ohio State Journal,* though, called the speech "a long and tedious harangue." Ranney's "dry thin voice," said the *Journal,* did not even reach the front-row seats, and Ranney drove the delegates to distraction by repeating every motion "with the amplitude and verbosity of a petition in chancery." The *Cincinnati Commercial,* an independent paper that would soon become a Republican organ, agreed that the address had lost much of its force because of the "low tone" in which it was delivered. The *Commercial* also noted the hypocrisy of lauding legal equality and the rights of labor as Democratic principles when the party had a proslavery history. The Democratic Party, editorialized the *Commercial,* should send out younger people to canvass among blacks during the campaign; they would be able to "enlarge upon the Democratic application of the preamble to the Declaration of Independence to the rights of all men, without blushing for the inconsistencies of record that would embarrass" Ranney and Allen.[21]

However deficient Ranney's performance as president of the convention might have been, it did not prevent his selection as a delegate from his congressional district to the party's national convention to be held in St. Louis in 1876. But Ranney was tied up with a big railroad case in Cleveland that year, and the judge would not grant a continuance to allow him to attend. Ranney's absence may have affected the outcome of a "protracted fight" within the Ohio delegation. Thomas Ewing Jr.—Civil War general, lawyer, defender of Andrew Johnson, prominent participant in the People's Party in 1873, and advocate of greenbacks and an inflationary monetary policy—was determined to represent Ohio on the platform committee. Most of the Ohio delegates, supporters of Allen Thurman and hard money, were equally determined not to have Ewing forced upon them. But according to the reporter for the Republican *Cincinnati Times,* Ewing and his allies "monopolize[d] all the brains in the delegation. The rest are boys and old women." Had Ranney been there, he might have resisted the Ewing assault, but without him the Thurman men had no leader. Threats, promises, and booze, wrote the *Times* reporter, gave Ewing his victory.[22]

Ranney still had admirers among Ohio Democrats in 1876, some of whom tried to organize a movement to put him on the national ticket. In a letter to the *Plain Dealer,* "Lisle," noting the importance of Ohio to the outcome of the presidential election, argued for Ranney's nomination to counter the Republicans' selection of Rutherford B. Hayes as their presidential candidate. Ranney, wrote "Lisle," had practically "carried the party in this section on his shoulders for years." He might not have "[t]he enthusiasm of the corner grocery and the hustings," but he stood "in the front rank of that profession, which, above all others, says Edmund Burke, disciplines the faculties and ennobles the mind." The tenor of the letter suggests that Ranney was, as he had conceded in his address to the state Democratic convention the year before, an "old fogy," a man respected as an elder statesman of the party but with little popular recognition. Ranney still enjoyed enough local regard to receive the congressional nomination that year from the Cuyahoga County Democratic convention, but he declined to run, giving as his excuse his recent recovery from "a long illness" and the "labor and responsibilities" of his profession.[23]

Except for a brief but vigorous reappearance during the presidential election year of 1880, the 1876 state convention marked the end of Ranney's political career. A sixty-three-year-old Jacksonian was indeed an old fogy in politics. On the vital issue of currency, he adhered to his hard-money views even as greenbackism became the preferred position of most Ohio Democrats. His law practice, which now included representation of great corporations, demanded his time and energy. And it may be that, at a time of labor restiveness, violent strikes, and destruction of property, he was souring on democracy, if that term meant majority (or mob) rule at the expense of social order and property rights.[24]

Between 1876 and 1880 Ranney made only one speech to a political gathering. In the latter year, though, Ranney reappeared as a delegate to the state Democratic convention, which chose him as a presidential elector at large. After the convention Ranney presided over a mass rally in Cleveland called to "ratify" the party's nominations and platform. He defended the Democratic presidential nominee, Major General Winfield Scott Hancock, as a military hero who had demonstrated his executive ability by managing armies and commanding military departments. (He said nothing about Grant's similar qualifications for the presidency, even though Grant was a leading contender for the Republican nomination.) Ranney also decried the theft of the presidency by the Republicans in 1877 after the Democrats had won a majority in the popular vote, alleging that the "miserable instruments" used to steal electoral votes had all been given public offices. And, as usual, he called for a "restor[ation of] constitutional and honest government" and denounced Republicans for "belittl[ing] and degrad[ing] the states."[25]

Ranney continued to campaign for the Democratic Party. On October 4 he made what may have been his last major political speech at a rally at the Cleveland Armory. He stepped forward, reported the *Plain Dealer*, "amid deafening cheers," a description confirmed by the Republican *Cleveland Leader*.[26] Ranney told the crowd that he felt compelled to return to the political fray by the lies and deceits of the "shoddyites," a label originally applied during the Civil War to contractors who grew rich by defrauding the government and used afterward by Democrats as a term of opprobrium for Republicans.

Ranney accused Republicans of violating the Constitution by dividing the Union instead of bringing about a more perfect union, by fomenting discord instead of ensuring domestic tranquility, and by strangling liberty. His speech had two main themes: a defense of the South and an attack on corruption in government. Fifteen years after the end of the war, declared Ranney, voting was still taking place under the watchful eyes of commissioners and soldiers. Since 1860, a new generation had grown up in the South that was not responsible for the war. A majority of southern voters were struggling under difficult conditions. It was time to stop whipping up enmity toward the southern states.

A few days before Ranney's speech, Republican United States senator Roscoe Conkling had addressed a political rally in Warren. There he had asserted that Virginia and her child, Ohio, had created two opposing civilizations, one based on slavery and the other on the dignity of labor.[27] Ranney slammed Conkling's assertion as a libel not only against Virginia but also against all those Ohioans who traced their ancestry to that state. Virginia, he reminded his audience, was the home of Washington, Jefferson, Madison, and even, indirectly, Lincoln, who hailed from Virginia's "first daughter," Kentucky. Virginians had done more than the people of any other state to create the Union, proclaimed Ranney, and even though he had opposed them during the rebellion, he now sought to better their condition and bring them comfort.

Ranney attributed to Conkling and John Sherman the "damnable lie" that Democrats had played no part in suppressing the rebellion. He was exaggerating. At Warren, Conkling acknowledged the patriotism of individual Democrats but claimed that the Democratic organization had hindered the war effort. Without noting the distinction, Ranney asserted that he had traveled the state to plead for recruits while Conkling and Sherman sat in Congress nursing their political careers.

In tackling his second theme, corruption in government, Ranney again invoked Lincoln, who in 1880 had his political uses. The Republican Party, said Ranney, was no longer Lincoln's party. Lincoln's Republicans "had great objects in view, great purposes to perform . . . Their first assault was against slavery—not by violence but by carrying such influences against its continuance in the South as would tend to its ultimate abrogation." But after Lincoln's death, the shoddyites took over the party, gaining offices and threatening the very existence of the republic with their corruption. Money ruled in the party's councils. In the past the political conventions of all parties had always advocated selling the nation's western lands to actual settlers, but now Republican administrations were handing over to railroad corporations tracts larger than most European kingdoms.

Corruption took other forms as well. When it came to civil service reform, President Hayes talked a good game but failed to follow through. Instead, said Ranney, he accepted a salary double that of previous presidents (a reference to the federal "salary grab" law of 1873) and spent his time junketing with railroad tycoon Jay Gould. Americans supported swarms of revenue officers and other federal employees by paying taxes on everything from beer to imported goods, while the party in power levied political assessments on public officials. In effect the taxpayers were subsidizing the Republican Party. Ranney adverted briefly to that den of patronage abuse, the New York Customs House, which Hayes had in fact cleaned up against Conkling's resistance, and to the notorious Whiskey Ring bribery scandal under Grant. These episodes were in the past but recent enough to remind voters of Republican corruption.

Ranney spoke for a long time, perhaps too long. The *Leader*, hardly an objective source, reported that by the time Ranney got to civil service reform, the audience "began to leave in large numbers." The speaker's closing jabs at John Sherman, said the paper, "were properly laughed at by the decimated audience." The fault was not all Ranney's. Music by Fay's Cornet Band and speeches by Harvey Rice and Henry B. Payne preceded Ranney's address. The meeting did not end until after eleven o'clock. Still, if Ranney had ever been a crowd-pleasing orator, he may have been losing his touch.

Ranney had come out of political retirement for the 1880 campaign. After the election, he withdrew from the arena once again. He was sixty-seven years old, his health seems to have been impaired, and he had other things to occupy his time: the Ohio State Bar Association, the Case School of Applied Science, and the Standard Oil Company.

TEN

Corporate Lawyer

ON MARCH 10, 1851, the day Ohio's second constitutional convention adjourned *sine die,* the General Assembly granted a corporate charter to fifteen individuals, including Rufus P. Ranney, for the Franklin & Warren Railroad Company.[1] Although Ranney said harsh things about corporations at the convention, he also remarked that corporations organized for "proper purposes" were unobjectionable. As a judge a few years later, he treated railroads as public highways and railroad corporations as trustees for the public. With these views in mind, there was nothing inconsistent in a Radical Democrat holding an interest in a railroad corporation. Charles Reemelin was president of the Dayton & Cincinnati Railroad Company in 1855 and secretary of the Cincinnati & Zanesville in 1867, yet in 1875 he was still warning of the dangers of railroad and other corporations.[2] But Ranney's interest in the Franklin & Warren would lead to his involvement with the large, monopolistic, "corrupting" corporations that he had once decried.

Construction of the Franklin & Warren began in July 1853. After changing its name to the Atlantic & Great Western, the railroad would become part of a chain of roads running from New York State through Pennsylvania and Ohio, all the way to St. Louis. During the Civil War, the company became the country's leading carrier of oil. In 1863 three railroads named the Atlantic & Great Western but incorporated separately in Ohio, Pennsylvania, and New York extended their reach to Cleveland by jointly leasing the Cleveland & Mahoning Railroad. The lease not only benefited the Atlantic & Great Western Railway Line, as the three corporations called their joint venture, but also brought a bonanza to the many refineries that had sprung up in Cleveland after the discovery of oil in northwestern Pennsylvania in 1859. In 1865 the three Atlantic & Great Western corporations merged. The next year, an analyst wrote that the company "carries oil extensively to Cleveland for the refineries" and that its "prospect as regards oil traffic is even more promising than at any former period." Cleveland's largest refiner in 1866 was Rockefeller & Andrews, incorporated four years later as the Standard Oil Company.[3]

Ranney, meanwhile, resigned from the supreme court in 1865 to accept an offer of partnership from Joel W. Tyler, a "stanch Republican" from Cleveland and one of Ohio's leading railroad lawyers. Ranney had three years left to his term and his reasons for quitting are unclear. Perhaps he felt that with the war just about won, he could attend once again to his personal business and make up pecuniarily for lost time. Ranney no doubt knew Tyler well. Tyler had been a law student in the office of Ranney's brother John and from the 1850s an attorney and officer of the Atlantic & Great Western Railway in Ohio.[4]

When Ranney and Tyler joined forces, the latter was secretary of and general counsel for the Atlantic & Great Western. The partnership lasted about four years. The railroad's financial difficulties may have contributed to the breakup. In 1867 creditors sought to foreclose their mortgages, and the company's property was put into receivership. Three years later, under a second receivership, the receiver leased the entire line to the Erie Railway pending foreclosure, which occurred on July 1, 1871. Until then, Tyler remained the attorney for the Atlantic & Great Western.[5]

Ranney, too, stayed involved with railroad affairs. He was "legal counsellor" for the Cleveland & Pittsburgh Railroad Company for about twenty years beginning in 1869, with a seat on the board of directors for two decades. He also served on the board of the New York, Pennsylvania & Ohio Railroad, organized in 1880 to purchase the assets of the defunct Atlantic & Great Western, and represented the new road in federal court in Pennsylvania. In the 1870s Ranney appeared in Ohio and New York in cases brought by creditors of the Atlantic & Great Western. In the 1880s he was on the team of eminent lawyers who represented the Vanderbilt railroad empire in its unsuccessful attempt to consolidate two Ohio railroad companies as part of its westward march, and in 1886 he and his associates faced off against his old partner Tyler in a right-of-way dispute between the Cleveland & Pittsburgh and the Cleveland, Loraine, & Wheeling Railway Company.[6]

In 1874 Ranney entered into a law partnership with his nephew Henry C. Ranney that endured until 1890. Rufus's son John joined the firm in 1876.[7] A bit more about Ranney's postbellum legal career can be gleaned from the reported cases in which he or his firm appeared. They indicate that he had a varied civil practice covering everything from actions on promissory notes to the validity of assessments on real property to the construction of wills. Ranney teamed with several other lawyers to represent the plaintiff in a long-running slander action that, ironically for so staunch an advocate of judicial economy, became a swollen "theatrical exhibition" long before it ran its course.[8] He made a "masterly" but unsuccessful argument to uphold the Scott Law, a politically explosive Republican measure to tax saloonkeepers.[9] Ranney had a substantial corporate practice at both the state and federal levels, acting both for and against railroads and appearing in several cases before the United States Supreme Court. (Whether he actually went to Washington for the Supreme Court cases or just submitted briefs is not clear.) Occasionally a case in which Ranney prevailed became an important precedent.[10]

Sometimes Ranney represented criminal defendants. In 1858 the Geauga County Court of Common Pleas assigned Ranney and A. H. Thrasher to represent Hiram Cole, an indigent defendant accused of murdering his wife by poisoning. Thrasher handled the trial, but the two lawyers, after securing an acquittal, jointly sued the county for additional fees. Perhaps it was Ranney's experience in the Cole case that led to his participation on the defense team in one of Ohio's most sensational murder cases of the nineteenth century. Sarah M. Victor was convicted of poisoning her brother in order to collect on a life insurance policy and was sentenced to death. Governor Rutherford B. Hayes commuted the sentence to life in prison, and in 1887 Governor Joseph B. Foraker pardoned Victor. The commutation led to a landmark decision on the nature of commutations.[11]

While the reported decisions of cases in which Ranney is listed as counsel shed some light on his practice, their usefulness for that purpose is limited. Ranney frequently cooperated with other attorneys on a party's behalf. The reports in such cases rarely indicate what each lawyer contributed to the representation. Similarly, a statement that "Ranney, Backus and Noble" or

"Ranney and Ranney" represented a party does not tell which of the partners handled the case. And, of course, much of a lawyer's practice takes place outside the litigation process. Ranney no doubt spent much of his time drawing up contracts, deeds, and other instruments and advising clients on business and personal affairs. When George Fessler, the Stark County auditor, absconded with public funds in 1878, the dispute over the liability of Fessler's sureties seems to have hinged on Ranney's opinion. The county eventually filed suit against the bondsmen, who retained Ranney as their counsel, but the parties reached a compromise and no evidence of the whole affair shows up in any reported case.[12]

According to Edwin Blandin, Ranney was more likely to take on the case of "a meritorious man or woman in distress" than one that promised a large fee. But another source wrote in 1886, when Ranney was well into his seventies, that Ranney's law practice was "chiefly confined to great cases" and was "both lucrative and extensive." The official reports of Ohio cases show that Ranney remained very active until the mid-1880s. Toward the end of his life, he gradually reduced his practice, but a good challenge could bring him, and an appreciative audience, back to the courtroom. Young lawyers who had not seen Ranney in action discounted him at their peril. When one such attorney told an associate, "I can concede all of Ranney's premises and then overwhelm him with authorities," the older and wiser man informed the tyro that "no man can concede Ranney's premises, and win. Conceding his premises no man can withstand his logic."[13]

By the late 1870s Ranney was associating, both personally and professionally, with men of wealth. He had become Standard Oil's "ablest lawyer," was well-acquainted with Cleveland philanthropist Leonard Case Jr., and vacationed with Case's nephew, Levi Kerr. Kerr had sold his oil-refining interests to Standard Oil and become part owner of a line of steamships plying the waters between New York, Havana, and Brazil.[14]

Ranney may have played a key role in the development of Standard Oil's pioneering industrial trust. Brutal competition and a severe depression in the 1870s induced Standard Oil and other corporations to try to control prices and production in their industries through cartels (pools) or stock purchases by the shareholders in each other's companies. But pooling agreements were legally unenforceable and mutual stock purchases did not place day-to-day management of the companies in one set of hands. What companies needed was some form of merger. Some railroads had effected mergers through the device of the holding company, a corporation formed to hold the stock of other corporations. At that time, though, it was generally illegal for one corporation to own stock in another corporation except as expressly authorized by statute or corporate charter.[15] A holding company could be created only by a special act of a state legislature, and legislative support for a law that would effectively legalize cartels was unlikely. For Standard Oil, which wanted to create an entity that controlled corporations in different states, the problem was especially acute. Rockefeller and his associates needed a legal form of consolidation that would stand up everywhere.[16]

For several years, Standard Oil addressed the problem through the instrument of the trust. Well-known in other contexts, the trust was a device by which a person transferred property to another party, the trustee, for the benefit of a third person. Standard Oil shareholders would buy stock in another corporation and give it in trust to one of their associates. The arrangement worked at first, and it allowed Rockefeller to deny that Standard Oil controlled the corporation whose stock he or his partners had purchased. But the numerous trusts became cumbersome and did not really unify management. They also raised the possibility that a trustee would someday refuse to cooperate with Standard Oil.[17]

According to Rockefeller biographer Allan Nevins, three men came up with a new type of trust to strengthen Standard Oil's control of the companies whose stock its shareholders acquired. One was Henry Flagler, an early partner of Rockefeller and secretary of the corporation. Another, Cleveland attorney Myron Keith, had been Rockefeller's chief legal adviser for years. The third man was Ranney. How or when Ranney came to be legal counsel for Standard Oil is a mystery. None of the biographical essays or obituaries on Ranney so much as mentions his Standard Oil connection. However, the Atlantic & Great Western Railway had carried Standard Oil petroleum, and it may have been the railroad that brought Ranney and Rockefeller together. By 1878 Ranney was representing Rockefeller in the latter's battle with oil producers in Pennsylvania.[18]

The respective contributions of Flagler, Keith, and Ranney to the new form of trust are unknown, but, according to Nevins, Ranney put Flagler's draft of the trust agreement into proper form in April 1879 and revised it in November.[19] In place of an individual trustee for each company purchased, the new trust named the same group of three trustees for all of them. The shareholders of the subsidiary corporations and the trustees of the original trusts transferred their interests to the three new trustees. The new trustees still held the stock for the benefit of the Standard Oil stockholders rather than for Standard Oil itself, and they were still theoretically independent of Standard Oil. But this new type of trust was a legally plausible if not foolproof method of consolidation,[20] and, as Nevins remarked, the "trustees were merely dummies, behind whom stood the real managers."[21]

Notwithstanding Nevins's account of the origin of the Standard Oil trust, Samuel C. T. Dodd is almost universally credited with the invention of the industrial trust. There are several possible explanations for the persistence of Dodd's preeminence. First, Dodd wrote a new trust agreement for Standard Oil in 1882, and that is the one that became the subject of legislative and journalistic investigations and the model for trusts in other industries. Second, Dodd's work came to light first. From Rockefeller's vantage point, one of the trust's great advantages was its secrecy. The industrial trust was a new phenomenon, and no one yet knew whether it would survive legal challenges based on common-law or statutory prohibitions of combinations in restraint of trade. As long as the Standard Oil trust remained secret, it was safe. That there existed a trust into which Standard Oil shareholders had placed their stock was already known in 1882, but the public first learned the details of Dodd's trust agreement during a New York State Senate investigation in 1888. Ranney's 1879 agreement remained unknown until the commencement of the federal government's great antitrust suit against Standard Oil in 1906.[22]

A third possible reason for Dodd's reputation as the inventor of the industrial trust may be Ranney's reluctance to travel. Dodd joined Standard Oil's legal team in the spring of 1879, as the company was planning to move its headquarters to New York. Nevins writes that the company wanted "to retain Ranney as chief counsel, [but] they found him difficult and somewhat undependable, for he had other clients, was frequently ill, and greatly disliked travel."[23] As a result, Dodd became chief counsel, and he rather than Ranney had the opportunity to observe the workings of the original trust and to modify it. As the attorney who prepared the trust agreement of 1882, Dodd has received the credit for one of the great legal developments in American industrial organization.[24]

Finally, Nevins might have been mistaken. As an eminent historian who immersed himself in the Rockefeller and Standard Oil papers, Nevins is entitled to the benefit of the doubt. However, the only evidence he cites for Ranney's role in creating the Standard Oil Trust is a letter from Rockefeller to Oliver H. Payne dated December 8, 1879, indicating that Rockefeller wanted Ranney to "complete a trust paper; probably to bring a new company under the trust agreement." Nevins provides no other documentation for Ranney's preparation of the original trust agreement, the company's desire to keep Ranney on as chief counsel, or Ranney's illness or disinclination to go east. Dodd's own brief memoirs do not mention Ranney and in fact suggest that Dodd came up with the idea of the Standard Oil trust on his own.[25]

Ranney's dislike of travel in 1879 might have been a recent, temporary development due to the poor health noted by Nevins. He enjoyed travel before then and afterward. In 1864 Ranney attended the Democratic national convention in Chicago and in 1866 the National Union convention in Philadelphia. Only pressing legal business kept him from going to the 1876 Democratic national convention in St. Louis. A newspaper reported that year that Ranney's ill health prevented him from running for office, but the illness may not have been serious; all the "good" Democrats seemed to be conveniently sick. Illness sometimes *induced* Ranney to travel. One year he went south "in hope of recruiting his health." Around 1880 Frederick T. Wallace, describing Ranney as "no older apparently to-day than [in 1854], and good for twenty years more," asserted that Ranney and other Clevelanders "have ranged the interior of the Continent for pleasant recreation and vivifying airs, from the valley of the Saskatchawan [*sic*] and the waters of the Winnipeg in the Dominion of Canada to the City of Mexico." In 1881 Standard Oil treasurer Oliver H. Payne, in need of Ranney's legal expertise, was anxiously awaiting the voyager's return from the South. Ranney continued to work for Standard Oil for a time, appearing with Dodd and four other attorneys as counsel for the corporation in a case before the Pennsylvania Supreme Court in 1882. But the arrival of Dodd and the company's move to New York must soon have brought his connection with Standard Oil to a close.[26]

There was no shame for an old Jacksonian Democrat in fostering such useful enterprises as railroads; as we have seen, Radical Democrats had held railroad directorships before the Civil War. Still, Ranney's representation of railroad corporations and Standard Oil is surprising at first glance. At the constitutional convention of 1850–51, Ranney had spoken forcefully against corporations, making allowances for corporations formed for "proper purposes" but insisting on the personal liability of shareholders for corporate obligations and the right of the legislature to repeal corporate charters. His postwar activities might indicate a change of heart. Unfortunately, Ranney appears to have left no letters, diaries, articles, or other material explaining his position. Perhaps he regarded the right of repeal as irrelevant in light of the constitutional ban on special acts of incorporation and gave up shareholder liability as a lost cause or as unnecessary in an age of insurance.[27] The new economic landscape of postwar America included huge industrial, commercial, and transportation corporations as permanent features; there was no point in tilting at windmills. For Ranney personally, the allure of wealth and social standing after years of futile politicking and relatively unremunerative judicial labor may have been irresistible.

We may never know if Ranney had trouble squaring his Jacksonian principles with his corporate activities in the Gilded Age. It might not have been that hard. Dodd was a Democratic delegate to the 1872–73 Pennsylvania constitutional convention who sought like an old Jacksonian to curb corporate abuses; six years later he went to work for Standard Oil. Perhaps Ranney satisfied himself with the knowledge that however monopolistic Standard Oil might have been, it did not get that way through a special act of incorporation, governmental subsidies or stock subscriptions, grants of eminent domain authority, or other special privileges of the kind Jacksonians had railed against before the constitutional convention of 1850–51.[28]

The Jacksonian legacy has been called a two-sided coin, with libertarianism on one side and populism on the other, but the latter side gets most of the attention. Vernon L. Parrington asserted that the "democratic movement" of the late nineteenth century "was determined to carry forward and supplement the Jacksonian movement" by "strengthen[ing] the political state to enable it to cope with corporate wealth and constrain the ambitions of the plutocracy." Similarly, Chester McArthur Destler called Populism "a re-elaboration of the Jeffersonian tradition" (and the Jacksonian tradition exemplified by William Leggett) that "re-oriented" radical opposition to "the money power" from "political negation to positive but limited state intervention in the economic field." Gilded Age populists did indeed echo Jacksonians in flaying "the money power" as parasites who accumulated fortunes through speculation and exploitation of the producers of tangible wealth. On the basis of this populist Jacksonian heritage, one scholar argues that conservative judges of the late nineteenth century who opposed class legislation (legislation that "benefited one segment of society at the expense of another") "turned the [Jacksonian] tradition on its head." These conservatives, unlike the Jacksonians, believed "that wage earners, farmers, artisans, and laborers represented the entrenched forces of political privilege and that corporations and powerful business interests were the oppressed."[29]

But the link between the limited-government side of Jacksonian ideology and Gilded Age "laissez-faire conservatism" was direct and right-side-up.[30] In the late 1820s and 1830s, when men of Ranney's generation were coming of age, libertarian writers such as William Leggett and Condy Raguet boldly expounded laissez faire as a philosophy of liberty and the best guarantor of equality. Leggett, editor of the *New York Post,* even attacked New York City's attempts to regulate auctions, securities, and weights. He decried the appointment of weighmasters as nothing more than a way for politicians to reward their supporters. "The weighing of merchandise," he declared, "is a matter with which legislation has nothing to do: the laws of trade would arrange that business much more to the satisfaction of all parties concerned than the laws of the state can ever do." We have seen that John O'Sullivan launched the *Democratic Review* in 1837 with the declaration that the "best government is that which governs least." At the Indiana constitutional convention, held at the same time as Ohio's, Democrat Daniel Read insisted that "individual sagacity and enterprise" could manage internal improvements and banking better than the state, and he characterized state monopolies and partnerships as robbery.[31]

At the Ohio constitutional convention, Democratic delegates repeatedly demanded that government be restricted to a few basic tasks and otherwise leave people to take care of their own affairs. Their slogan was, as Ranney proclaimed, "the world is governed too much." The call for less-active government was not just a matter of political principle. It was also a matter of economic sense. Who, asked Ranney, was responsible for the transformation of Ohio from a wilderness to a land of "cultivated farms" and "thriving cities and towns"? It was not by actions of the legislature that "forests were cleared, railroads were built and our vast system of canals constructed." Rather, "it was by the hard industry of the people that it was effected, without any aid from the Legislature; it was their energy, their industry, and their stern enterprise that made the State as it was, without Legislative aid."[32]

Because Ranney was a jurist, it is especially pertinent to examine the connection between Jacksonian ideas on limited government and the phenomenon known as laissez-faire constitutionalism. Laissez-faire constitutionalism is a concept usually associated with the late nineteenth and early twentieth centuries, when, according to a long-held view, conservative judges strove to protect property rights and corporate enterprise from governmental regulation by incorporating laissez-faire economic ideas into constitutional law. An alternative understanding, once labeled revisionist but now generally accepted, locates the roots of laissez-faire constitutionalism partly in Jacksonian Democracy, with its deep suspicion of corruptible legislatures and its belief that equality would be better served if government stayed out of economic affairs.[33]

Ranney neither served on the bench nor left any evidence of his jurisprudential thought after the Civil War, so it is impossible to say for certain how, from a constitutional perspective, he viewed governmental attempts to promote or regulate business in the late nineteenth century. However, there may be a hint in one of his early opinions. In 1846, when the General Assembly was still passing local laws for the benefit of particular enterprises, the legislators enacted a statute that prohibited the sale of liquor within three miles of any iron foundry in Scioto, Lawrence, or Jackson County, except any foundry located in Portsmouth. Foundry owners in the iron-producing region of southeastern Ohio probably sought the law in an effort to ensure a sober labor force. In 1848 the owner of a grocery store was convicted of selling a quart of whiskey less than three miles from a foundry. Why, asked Ranney, did the statute affect only three counties? And why only iron manufacturing? And why did it make an exception for Portsmouth?[34]

Ranney threw out these hints at an equal-protection argument without pursuing them further. He also ignored the contention of the defendant's attorney that the state statute conflicted with a federal law passed under the commerce clause of the U.S. Constitution. That argument might have offended his Democratic, states'-rights sensibilities. Instead, Ranney relied on a strict construction of "this highly penal law" to reverse the conviction. Before the law was passed and for two years afterward, noted Ranney, the defendant had been engaged in a lawful business. Then the iron manufacturers built a plant within three miles of the defendant's store. Ranney construed the statute as applying only to foundries that existed at the time it was passed. The law was not "migratory," he said; it does not go out seeking people to punish. "It is only when Mahomet goes to the mountain, and not when the mountain comes to Mahomet, that its penalties can be invoked." Ranney refused to put the mom-and-pop grocery store at the mercy of the iron foundry. The grocery store had been there first, and Ranney favored its longstanding commerce over the needs of the foundry.[35]

Ranney's opinion has often been cited for the principle that a criminal statute must be strictly construed against the state, but it also foreshadows Judge Robert Earl's opinion in *In re Jacobs,* one of the best-known cases in the historiography of laissez-faire constitutionalism. Earl, a one-time

Democratic newspaper publisher who served for a quarter-century on the New York Court of Appeals, was one of the old Jacksonian Democrats still active after the Civil War as judges or treatise writers. A generation-long controversy that has not yet completely died out raged over the contributions of these old Jacksonians to postbellum laissez-faire constitutionalism. Thomas M. Cooley was exhibit number one in the dispute. Until 1967 historians portrayed him as a disciple of Herbert Spencer and capitalism's answer to Karl Marx. Then Alan Jones, in a path-breaking article, demonstrated that Cooley's jurisprudence sprang from Jacksonian notions of equality and a belief that state interference in economic affairs invariably ended up favoring the rich and powerful.[36]

Historians have ignored Earl, which is puzzling in view of the importance they attach to his opinion in *Jacobs.* One of the most widely cited cases in which "state power over individual liberty rights and property was challenged," *Jacobs* has been seen as "one of the most extreme judicial statements of laissez faire ever made by an American tribunal," "a landmark in the history of 'laissez-faire constitutionalism,'" and the beginning of the era of "classical legal thought." In *Jacobs* the New York Court of Appeals struck down a law that prohibited the manufacture of cigars in tenement houses in cities having more than five hundred thousand inhabitants (meaning New York and Brooklyn, which were then separate cities). The significance of the decision lay in Earl's use of due process of law to invalidate regulatory statutes, which, scholars have asserted, derived from his laissez-faire economic views. Earl's references to "the fierce competition of trade and the inexorable laws of supply and demand" and "the unceasing struggle for success and existence which pervades all societies of men," wrote one commentator, demonstrated the judge's knowledge of "the teachings of Spencer and the classical economists."[37]

Both large cigar manufacturers who had abandoned the tenement system and the Cigar-Makers International Union, which represented factory workers, supported the New York law—and both wanted to put the tenement cigar makers out of business. Under the statute, said Earl, the independent cigar maker "must either abandon the trade by which he earns a livelihood for himself and family, or, if able, procure a room elsewhere, or hire himself out to one who has a room upon such terms as, under the fierce competition of trade and the inexorable laws of supply and demand, he may be able to obtain from his employer." Earl was not endorsing "fierce competition" and "unceasing struggle." He was lamenting that the law, by depriving tenement cigar makers of the right to pursue their trade in their homes, would throw them into that struggle and make them dependents of the unions and manufacturers. He dismissed the contention of the statute's defenders that the act had been passed with the health of the cigar makers in mind. If that were so, he wrote, its operation would not have been limited to two cities.[38]

William E. Forbath has called Earl's opinion "an unconscious parody of the values and fears of mid-nineteenth-century artisans" that ignored the true, and truly horrific, conditions under which tenement cigar makers labored. But most likely the opinion was neither unconscious nor a parody. When Earl, an ardent young Democrat, acquired the *Herkimer County Democrat* in 1848, he declared "uncompromising warfare" against the Whigs. Below the masthead he printed a quotation from Andrew Jackson opposing "a splendid Government, supported by powerful monopolies and aristocratical establishments," and favoring "a plain system, void of pomp, PROTECTING ALL AND GRANTING FAVORS TO NONE." Fifty years later, Earl condemned the constant meddling of legislatures in the affairs of men, recurring to Jefferson's dictum that a good government was "one that would restrain men from injuring one another and leave them otherwise free to regulate their own pursuits of industry and improvement." Whatever may have been the effect of *Jacobs* on the lives of tenement cigar makers, Earl probably saw his opinion as a blow against special privilege and class legislation and for the same small businessmen and artisans that Ranney had championed at Ohio's mid-century constitutional convention and seemed to be protecting in the iron foundry case.[39]

The postbellum laissez-faire constitutionalism of Cooley and Earl was conservative in that it continued the laissez-faire constitutionalism of the midcentury state conventions. It was an attempt to preserve Jacksonian ideals in the realm of law, much as Grover Cleveland sought to preserve them in the world of politics. Ranney, notwithstanding his representation of railroad corporations and Standard Oil, could well have believed that he remained conservatively faithful to the radical views of his youth.

ELEVEN

Elder Statesman

IN 1876 Philadelphia celebrated the centennial of American independence by hosting a great international exposition. Officially named the International Exhibition of Arts, Manufactures, and Products of the Soil and Mine was more than a world's fair. Like London's Crystal Palace Exhibition of 1851 and subsequent European expositions, it brought together scholars and educators as well as inventors, industrialists, and agriculturalists. As a Canadian commissioner for the Philadelphia event commented, these international exhibitions "were the first grand levers which were used to uplift the nations to a higher plane of intellectual life, and to demonstrate to them . . . the great practical truth . . . that 'knowledge is indeed power.'"[1]

In 1874, the year after President Grant officially announced the dates for the Philadelphia exposition, Governor William Allen appointed Ranney and four other prominent citizens to the board of managers for Ohio's exhibit. The board oversaw the construction of the Ohio building on the Exhibition grounds and the exhibits displaying the Buckeye State's archaeology, natural resources, agriculture, industry, art, and education. Ranney, who served as the board's president, had great expectations for Ohio at the Exhibition. Addressing the Ohio State Agricultural Convention in January

1876, Ranney noted that the General Assembly had provided generous funding for Ohio's exhibits and that many Buckeyes who had never been more than thirty or forty miles from home intended to go. He believed that the exposition would offer an "immense display of every thing which interests the people, which advances civilization, which makes the people of one part of the world acquainted with the very best efforts of the people of another," and he wanted Ohio to be "conspicuous" among the states for its contributions to "the best of every thing that the civilized world produces." Ranney exhorted his audience of agriculturalists to "make the very best showing of that great, overwhelming interest of our State."[2]

In its final report the board expressed great satisfaction with Ohio's showing in Philadelphia. Unfortunately, it had to acknowledge shortcomings in the agricultural exhibits. The wool-producing counties were well represented and the fruit exhibition won a medal, but the cereals fell far short of expectations due to an overly rainy growing season, and stock breeders refused to bear the expense and risk of loss entailed in shipping prize animals to the exposition. But the board lauded Ohio's geological, archaeological, and educational exhibits, the artwork displayed at the Women's Pavilion, and the proof of Ohio's industrial prowess.[3]

The Philadelphia Exhibition was an exercise in public education. As the board observed in its report to the legislature, a major purpose of the great exposition was to mark the progress of the American people "in education and its practical results, as evidenced in the application of intellectual and inventive power, skilled labor, and scientific knowledge" to industry, agriculture, and the development of natural resources. Poverty had compelled the young Ranney to give up his own dream of a formal education, but later in life he helped found or expand libraries and served on a school board. After acquiring status as an elder statesman of Ohio law—a position recognized by Western Reserve University in 1871 when it awarded Ranney its first-ever honorary degree, a doctorate of laws—Ranney sought to promote higher education both within and outside the legal profession.[4]

One of Ranney's close personal friends was Leonard Case Jr., a Cleveland philanthropist with a keen interest in the natural sciences. A believer in practical education that could be used to develop the nation's resources, Case donated valuable real estate to a trust, created with Ranney's assistance, for the endowment of a new school of engineering. When Case died in 1880 the trustee organized a corporation and secured a charter for the Case School of Applied Science. Ranney, one of the school's fifteen incorporators, served as chairman of the school's board of trustees for its first decade. It was an ideal situation for a Bourbon Democrat. Wealthy benefactors who had made their fortunes in the world of corporate capitalism, men such as John D. Rockefeller and Andrew Carnegie, were then endowing universities to train the scientists, engineers, and business managers needed by America's burgeoning industries. The governing bodies of these institutions differed from the college boards of the past. Western Reserve College, briefly attended by Ranney in the 1830s, had been founded and dominated in its early days by Protestant clerics and their religion-minded neighbors. The board of trustees of the Case School of Applied Science consisted mostly of bankers and lawyers.[5]

In the fall of 1880 the board sent Ranney and the minister who had officiated at Case's funeral on an expedition to the east coast to gather information that would help in the organization of the new school. The trip proved fruitless, however, and it quickly became apparent that someone better qualified in the sciences would have to carry out the mission. The board sent an astronomer to do the job.[6] Notwithstanding the failure of his eastern excursion, Ranney remained attached to the school and to the applied sciences.

Ranney was deeply impressed by the technological advances he had witnessed in his own lifetime. "The last half century," he enthused in 1881, "has been most wonderfully distinguished for the eager efforts of civilized man to subject additional elements of nature to his uses, which has been accomplished by such an advance in the physical sciences as far surpasses any other equal period in the world's history." Nothing better illustrated the wondrous application of science than the recent "triumphal march" of electricity, thanks to which news and correspondence traveled almost instantaneously and the night was illuminated. And the future held the promise of even more astounding accomplishments. Electricity would soon "furnish the light, heat and power of the world." "[A]pplied to supply these indispensable needs of mankind," Ranney rhapsodized, "what a revolution in the business and social condition of the race must ensue!"[7]

Ranney soon carried his interest in applied science to the Ohio bar. He had always taken pride in being a lawyer. Populists who viewed the bench and bar as conspirators bent on keeping the law's mysteries secret for their own benefit had sought to break the power of the lawyers by simplifying the law, reducing or even eliminating educational qualifications for admission to the bar, electing rather than appointing judges, and quashing ideas of judicial supremacy.[8] Ranney had shared the populist program to the extent of advocating the election of judges, keeping the courts close to the people, and codifying legal procedure, but he had no use for an uneducated bar or for a judiciary without the power of judicial review. He regarded the law as a learned profession—"a novel, a scientific profession," he called it in 1850[9]—and he wanted it to have the public esteem that learned professions deserved.

But the bar as a whole did not live up to Ranney's ideal. The standards for admission to the Ohio bar in 1880 had not changed since Ranney's initiation in 1836.[10] Lawyers, no less than men of other professions, succumbed to the temptations of Gilded Age politics. Given the traditional involvement of lawyers in politics, they may have wallowed even more in the tawdriness. Lawyers made up a quarter or more of the Ohio General Assembly at a time when legislatures all over the country were falling into disrepute. The corruption of the bench and bar in Boss Tweed's New York City induced the "decent part" of Gotham's legal profession in 1870 to organize the Association of the Bar of the City of New York for the purposes of cleaning up the administration of justice and "maintaining the honour and dignity of the profession."[11]

The formation of the New York City bar association spawned imitators all over the country. In Ohio the Franklin County Bar Association, established in 1869 as a law library society, adopted the lofty goals of its New York brethren. Within the next few years, other local bar associations sprang up in Ohio. On March 22, 1873, a group of attorneys organized the Cleveland Bar Association "to maintain the honor and dignity of the profession of the law, to cultivate social intercourse and acquaintance among the members of the bar, to increase [their] usefulness in aiding the administration of justice, and in promoting legal and judicial reform."[12]

To the members of the Cleveland Bar Association, "social intercourse" may have been as important as improving the administration of justice or promoting reform. The American Bar Association, formed in 1878 and joined by Ranney the next year, "exuded the genial tone of a social club," while the bar associations of the major metropolises tried to restrict their membership to the "better elements" of the profession. State bar associations, which began appearing in the late nineteenth century, included small-town lawyers and general practitioners and so were less exclusive; but they, too, along with city and county bar associations, often began primarily as social organizations. At their annual meetings in 1881, the Columbus Bar

Association and the Ohio State Bar Association hosted sumptuous banquets, with entertainment provided by bands. Many of the wives and daughters of members attended the state bar meeting, together with "a large number of ladies and gentlemen, who were drawn by the name and fame of Judge Ranney." The state bar festivities closed with an excursion to Put-in-Bay and other Lake Erie islands. Ranney reveled in such galas. His speech at the Cleveland Bar Association's banquet in 1881 elicited many bursts of laughter, and Judge Tilden claimed credit for turning Ranney from a somber young man into "one of the most genial, social fellows in the world."[13]

The Ohio State Bar Association got its start in 1880 when the Cleveland Bar Association invited other bar groups in Ohio to send representatives to a meeting for the purpose of organizing a state bar association. The delegates convened at Case Hall, Cleveland's cultural center, on July 8, 1880. Ranney, named temporary chairman of the convention, gave the welcoming address. In it he emphasized the need for better education of attorneys. The law, said the chairman of the board of the Case School of Applied Science, was "an applied science—applied a thousand times every day to the concerns of men in society." The natural sciences were then enjoying unprecedented prestige. As Ranney pointed out, science had "astonished the world" with discoveries ranging from microscopic life to the composition of the sun, discoveries that were regularly taught in the great institutions of higher learning. The science of law was advancing, too, and it was the bar's obligation to ensure that the lawyer of the future would "stand upon a science applied to man in society, and understand the great principles which underlie his profession." The future lawyer must not be a "man who is familiar with forms only, and has a very poor appreciation of the principles of the science which he is called upon to administer."[14]

The idea that law was a science akin to the natural sciences had been gaining ground since the early nineteenth century. Although not universally accepted, by the 1870s it was the rage among philosophically minded jurists. According to the author of *The Science of Law* (1887), "A science . . . is a definite department of immutable principles, or laws of nature—as Chemistry, Mechanics, Mathematics, Mental and Moral Philosophy. Our claim is that the principles of justice are such a definite body of immutable principles, and hence constitute a true science." This type of thinking blossomed into full flower with the educational reforms of Dean Christopher Columbus Langdell at the Harvard Law School in the 1870s. That Langdell's methods were genuinely scientific is debatable, but he sought to classify legal doctrines, as expressed in leading cases, in an orderly fashion. The best way to train young lawyers, thought Langdell, was to have them derive legal principles from the analysis of great decisions. And because such analytical thinking required both intelligence and effort, Langdell tightened the standards for admission to and progress within the law school. At the Cleveland meeting, Stanley Matthews told the assembled attorneys that "[a]s a science [jurisprudence] classifies into system the body of our knowledge acquired by a study of its actual development and history, and traces the principles which connect its various results." It may be that a classification of legal doctrines and the mental effort need to comprehend them were all Ranney had in mind when he called for a scientific understanding of legal principles rather than a rote reliance on forms. As his failed trip to the East on behalf of the Case School of Applied Science demonstrated, he had a limited knowledge of true science.[15]

In his speech at the Cleveland convention, Ranney did not discuss the "great principles" of the law, except to say that they were "the laws of nature—the voice of God." To Ranney, natural law seems to have encompassed individual rights of person, property, reputation, and whatever else the individual "holds dear."[16] Beyond that, Ranney did not venture. Perhaps his audience shared his understanding, making further explication unnecessary.

In any event, Ranney insisted that the bar had a duty to use all its influence to make future attorneys worthy of the state of Ohio. The specific tasks included the establishment of appropriate qualifications for admission to the bar, the expulsion of those who were unworthy due to vice or incompetence, and the provision of legal services to the "poor, the unfortunate, the ignorant, those who can not take care of themselves." With regard to the last task, Ranney did not suggest that the legal profession had been remiss; he merely reiterated the lawyer's moral obligation to serve the poor, even if they could not pay his fee. Finally, Ranney returned to a problem that had occupied so much of his time thirty years earlier at the constitutional convention, the law's delays. For cases to take five or six years from commencement in the trial court through final appeals was not merely inconvenient for the parties but sometimes ruinous. No controversy, thought Ranney, should take more than a year to resolve. There were "too much machinery about our system" and too many "technicalities and fictions." In this speech Ranney merely presented the issues for his colleagues' consideration. He would return to them in greater depth shortly.[17]

After Ranney's address, the delegates broke for lunch. They reconvened in the afternoon to adopt a constitution and elect officers. That a group of more than 160 lawyers[18] could agree on a constitution in one afternoon indicates that the instrument had been prepared well in advance. The section setting forth the association's purposes aligned comfortably with Ranney's welcoming speech, and it is not inconceivable that Ranney had a hand in its drafting; but it was modeled on the statement of purposes in the constitution of the recently formed American Bar Association. The organization's goals under the constitution were "to advance the science of jurisprudence, to promote reform in the law, to facilitate the administration of justice, to uphold integrity, honor and courtesy in the legal profession; to encourage thorough liberal legal education, and to cultivate cordial intercourse among the members of the bar."[19]

With the constitution attended to, the meeting turned to the election of officers. A nominating committee recommended a slate headed by Ranney as president. The delegates unanimously endorsed the nominees. The following day, the meeting, by resolution, instructed Ranney and the judicial administration committee to prepare a plan to facilitate the administration of justice in this State" and to report the plan to the association.[20]

Speaking on the resolution, Ranney lambasted the intolerable delays in the administration of justice. He illustrated the point with a case in which he represented widows and children who had interests in a tract of land that they desperately needed to convert to cash. It had taken nearly seven years to get a decision from the supreme court on a demurrer, and now, having lost on that ground, Ranney would have to pursue other defenses. He had no expectation of a speedier resolution the second time around. "I beg you to reflect about how much use will it be to the widows and children or to anybody else by the time we get to a final decision of the controversy."[21]

The problem, as Ranney saw it, lay in the district courts, the intermediate appellate courts against which he had contended so strenuously at the constitutional convention in 1850–51. Those courts were meant to be headed by a supreme court judge, "with his knowledge and weight of character," assisted by judges of the common pleas court. In practice, the district courts consisted solely of common pleas judges, with the result that they came to be seen as nothing more than a "stopping place" on the way to an overburdened supreme court.[22]

At the constitutional convention of 1873–74, the problem of judicial backlogs had sparked much debate. Ranney had objected to the calling of a convention because its proponents had given no reason for not using the cheaper, more convenient method of constitutional amendment, a legislative resolution placed on the ballot. The provision that put the question of a convention before the voters every twenty years, he wrote, "was *not* intended to excite periodically a spirit of discontent" with the constitution "or to foster a very prevalent disposition to pull [it] down," without a clear idea of what would go in its place. At the bar association meeting, Ranney recalled that around the time of the 1873–74 constitutional convention he had suggested to the legislature "one simple, radical amendment of the Constitution" that would have addressed the judicial delays without greatly increasing the number of officeholders or the cost of operating the court system. The intervening years had only confirmed his opinion. The solution: abolish the district courts and add four more judges to the supreme court. The supreme court judges would ride circuit in pairs to decide appeals, and the supreme court would hear in bank those cases it chose to hear. This was essentially the system Ranney had proposed at the 1850–51 convention. He added now that the judges of the supreme court should be brought closer to the people by having them run in separate elections, so that they would not "be put onto the tail of somebody's political ticket, and never heard from again." He also recommended lengthening the term of office to nine years and electing three judges every three years. The current backlog of cases could be disposed of, he thought, by hard work on the part of the present judges, provided they did not stop to write books or treatises.[23]

In addition to urging reorganization of the judicial system, Ranney criticized the practice of hearing equity cases *de novo* on appeal to the district court.[24] Three-quarters of every district court session, complained Ranney, were taken up in hearing witnesses all over again "at interminable length . . . and a large percentage of perjury manufactured in the meantime, and you call that doing justice."[25]

The bar convention adopted the resolution on the judiciary, then adjourned to December 28, 1880, when they would meet again in the statehouse in Columbus. Its business at the adjourned meeting included action on a state constitutional amendment, proposed by the association's judicial administration committee, to hold elections for judges of the supreme court on a date other than the date for the election of other state officers, to add four judges to the supreme court, to abolish district courts and superior courts, and to establish a special commission to handle the supreme court's backlog of cases. The proposal comported with Ranney's ideas for streamlining the business of the courts, and he spoke "at length" in its support. Apparently, the only part of the proposal that encountered resistance was the one to hold the election of supreme court justices on a separate day. Ranney quashed the objection by declaring that under the amendment "[j]udges would then be elected without the help of politicians, I trust in God, for once."[26]

The association adopted the amendment and brought it to the General Assembly, where it quietly died.[27] At the association's second annual meeting in Toledo in 1881, some members wanted to try again, but Ranney opposed further demands on the General Assembly on the grounds that the association had done its duty and the matter was now in legislative hands. The members voted to recommit the proposal to the committee for further consideration. On Ranney's motion, they also recommitted a resolution condemning retrials on appeal, which had received no legislative attention. Given Ranney's interest in both issues, as well as his prestige, the members naturally added Ranney to the committee.[28]

As president of the association, Ranney had the constitutional duty of delivering an address to the lawyers gathered in Toledo. He reprised, at greater length, all the major points of his welcoming address of the previous year. He reiterated his belief that jurisprudence was a science—more precisely, an applied science—"resting upon natural truths and principles." He stressed again the need for a broadly educated bar. Wherever man's enterprise led him, said Ranney, whether out on the oceans, down into mines, or into industry, "questions of competency, care and skill could never be intelligently solved without resorting to the great repositories of natural law." Lawyers therefore had to possess a "comprehensive and systematic knowledge" of at least the general principles of the natural sciences, together with, added Ranney for good measure, an ability to speak and write English correctly. Ranney did not regard such scientific and literary attainments as mere aspirational goals. Knowledge of law, science, and language was essential if attorneys were to be faithful to the trust reposed in them by their clients. The necessary educational qualifications should not only "be *encouraged,* but if need be, absolutely *coerced* as a condition of admission to the profession."[29]

Jurisprudence being, in Ranney's eyes, such an important science, embracing every facet of human life, Ranney believed that every educated person, not just the lawyer, should be familiar with its basic principles. He suggested that law, like every other science, be made a part of the regular college curriculum. If something needed to give way to make room for the study of law, "two dead languages, seldom used, and soon forgotten," were likely candidates. In saying this Ranney was in accord with contemporary academic notables who sought to reform the college curriculum.[30]

But while a general knowledge of jurisprudence was a necessary part of a liberal education, it would not close the gap between laymen and professionals. Professional study would commence after the completion of a general education, and there would be "a much wider space" between the layman and the "properly educated" lawyer than presently existed. Such language sounds surprisingly elitist coming from Ranney, but he had always been a meritocrat. He believed "that in the future, as in all times past," the bar would continue to "draw a majority of its brightest recruits from the humbler classes." In a state just emerging from frontier status, as Ohio had been when Ranney became a lawyer, many members of the bar may indeed have come from humble stations. But where the bar was older and better established, most lawyers probably came from the middle and upper classes. Ranney cavalierly dismissed concerns that his educational proposals would deter "young men of limited means" from becoming lawyers. "[T]here is not the slightest reason to think that a single one of this class would, to save a little time and exertion, desire to obtrude himself upon a profession unprepared to meet its responsibilities or discharge its duties." Ranney himself had risen from poor farm boy to respected attorney, but he had been admitted to the bar without the college degree and advanced professional education that he now seemed to be advocating.[31]

For all his insistence on a better-educated bar, Ranney said nothing about the rising law schools. The sense that preparation for legal practice required formal training in university law departments or law schools spread after the Civil War. By the time Ranney addressed the Ohio State Bar Association in the 1880s, that sense had sunk deep roots among the leaders of the profession and produced a significant and rapidly rising number of programs. Cleveland had a law school from 1857 until 1876, headed for most of that period by John Crowell, Ranney's old political opponent. When Crowell resigned due to poor health, the school folded. Concerned about the lack of a law school in Ohio's most populous area, a group of prominent Cleveland attorneys incorporated the Cleveland Law College in 1882, with Ranney as president of the board of trustees. Three years later the college offered a preliminary series of lectures in the old Cleveland courthouse. Ranney spoke on constitutional law. Buoyed by the success of the experiment, the trustees decided to investigate the feasibility of a permanent organization, but there the project ended.[32]

In May 1891 a dozen judges and lawyers met in the office of Samuel E. Williamson, one of the incorporators of the Cleveland Law College and a trustee of Western Reserve University, to discuss the situation. They unanimously agreed to ask the university to establish a law school, which it did the following year, after Ranney's death. Whether Ranney was at the meeting or otherwise took part in the creation of the school is unknown. But Ranney did contribute to legal education posthumously. For a time in the twentieth century, a joint program of the Johns Hopkins Institute for the Study of Law and the graduate school at Western Reserve University offered a generous scholarship in Ranney's name. In 1931 Ranney's daughter-in-law left a substantial endowment for scholarships at the Western Reserve law school. In 1915 a law school named for Ranney opened in Cleveland. It suspended operations in 1917, reopened in 1921 as the Lake Erie Law School after Ranney's heirs threatened to sue if the school continued to use Ranney's name, and closed for good during the Great Depression.[33]

Ranney devoted the bulk of his 1881 bar association address to education in the science of law, but he also briefly discussed legal reform. The General Assembly had failed to act on the association's recommendations on practice in equity cases in the district court and on reorganizing the judiciary. The lawmakers might have been pardoned for neglecting the latter matter. They had placed constitutional amendments relating to the court system on the ballot in 1877 and 1879, only to see the voters reject both proposals.[34] In 1883 the General Assembly proposed an amendment to abolish the district courts, replace them with circuit courts, and authorize the legislature to increase the number of supreme court justices and to fix their terms at more than five years. Ranney had already gone on record as favoring the elimination of the district courts, expanding the supreme court, and giving supreme court justices longer tenures, but he opposed the amendment. The proposal would allow the General Assembly to create an unspecified number of new offices and, by giving the legislature the power to set the terms and compensation of the judges of the supreme and circuit courts, would destroy the independence of the judiciary.[35]

Nevertheless, Ranney would not have gone public with his opposition had he not caught wind, shortly before election day, of a "conspiracy" on the part of the Democratic and Republican state committees to ensure passage of the amendment. In the absence of an official, state-printed ballot, not yet adopted in Ohio, the party committees had reportedly agreed to print ballots reading "Judiciary Amendment, Yes," but not including an option to vote no. Voters could still strike through the printed language, but that was something many voters, especially those who didn't care much about this particular issue, would not bother to do. In fact, the public did not pay much attention to the measure, overshadowed as it was by more inflammatory amendments relating to prohibition and the liquor traffic. But the shenanigans of the party committees incensed Ranney, who labeled the absence of a "no" option on the ballot "a base fraud and imposition upon the electors and an attempt to change the constitution by a species of jugglery without the free assent of the majority of them." The committee on future amendments of the 1850–51 constitutional convention, recalled its chairman, expected that constitutional amendments would reflect the "mature judgment of a majority of the electors" and not the chicanery of party leaders. Aided by the one-sided ballot language, the court amendment passed overwhelmingly.[36]

Perhaps because of the failures of the 1877 and 1879 constitutional amendments, Ranney, in his 1881 address to the state bar association, did not dwell on the need for reform of the judicial system. Instead, he stressed the need to eliminate the repetition of oral evidence in equity cases that were appealed to the district court. "Our lives are too short, and litigation is too irritating and unpleasant," he declared, "to justify such endurance." Unfortunately, Ohioans had to endure new trials on equity appeals until long after Ranney left the scene. Ranney also put in a plug for codification, lauding France's Napoleonic Code as one of the greatest advancements in the science of jurisprudence and attributing its accomplishment to "the early instruction of French youth in . . . the general principles upon which French jurisprudence is founded."[37]

The other great advance in jurisprudence, said Ranney, had come with the American Revolution, which "emancipated that science from the trammels and defects of the past" and brought about constitutional government. Ranney reaffirmed his attachment to judicial review under the American political system. From being mere forums for the settlement of private disputes or the punishment of crimes established by the legislatures, courts were "placed as sentinels upon the watch-towers of these constitutions to give warning of the approach of danger, and to protect persons and property from all illegal invasions, by giving effect to the spirit and purposes of these instruments, no matter from what quarter such invasions may come."[38]

The founding of the American and Ohio bar associations and similar bodies in other professions, all concerned with enhancing professional education and qualifications to practice, presaged the Progressive program of government conducted, or at least advised, by natural and social scientists and other highly trained specialists. Bar leaders imbued with an admiration for scientific progress believed that lawmakers, like practitioners in other fields, should be educated for their positions. Ranney thought it "absolutely essential" that the makers and administrators of law have "a higher degree of the legal intelligence." Quoting Blackstone, he found it "perfectly amazing that there should be no other state of life, no other occupation, art or science, in which some method of instruction is not looked upon as requisite, except only the science of legislation, the noblest and most difficult of any."[39]

Unfortunately, Ranney grumbled with unconscious irony, America's educated classes were too engrossed in the "eager pursuit of wealth" to pay attention to the laws that alone protected their property. As a result, the performance of great public duties fell to "ignorant and incompetent substitutes." The note of alarm is almost palpable. Ranney, one of the nouveaux riches, sounds like Henry Adams lamenting America's descent into barbarism. With the ignoramuses in charge, said Ranney, "one by one, our great safeguards are either totally lost or seriously impaired." Jury trials in the great cities had been so suffused with ignorance, incompetence, or worse that thoughtful men now wondered whether trial by jury was a blessing or a curse. The press, the nation's great "public teacher," too often took cover behind freedom of the press to "attack private reputations" and sensationalize important court cases to the detriment of justice and public morals. Ranney concluded his remarks on this pessimistic note, although his final words expressed confidence that the bar, at least, would advance its standard ever closer toward "absolute and eternal justice . . . with no one so high as to be above its power, and no one so humble as to be beneath its protecting care."[40]

Ranney was hardly alone in his disenchantment with cherished institutions of liberty. Mark Twain complained that the jury system put "a premium upon ignorance, stupidity and perjury," while legal commentators called the jury "the clown of the law" and lamented that juries decided cases "in accordance with the prejudice and sympathies of comparatively ignorant men." Respectable newspaper publishers protested their rivals' invasions of privacy and sensationalization of lawsuits to feed an insatiable public appetite for scandal. If Ranney seemed to be losing his old Jacksonian faith in the people, it must be remembered that he had never fully trusted the people to begin with. The Ranney of the Jacksonian era had sought not only to protect the rights of the people from a government controlled by a wealthy elite but also to safeguard the property rights of minorities from attacks by majorities. No one could be safely entrusted with power, which was why the best government was the one that governed least.

Democrats of the Gilded Age remained true, at least in their party platforms, to many of their antebellum positions, such as low tariffs, low taxes, and opposition to monopoly. But, in an effort to draw support from workers and farmers who had legislative agendas, they were moving toward an abandonment of the key Jacksonian principle of limited government. In 1879 Ohio Democrats appealed to members of the populist Greenback-Labor Party by including an inflationary monetary plank in their platform and nominating Thomas Ewing Jr. for governor. A breakaway faction of the Greenback-Labor Party then held its own convention, where it adopted a platform that favored a graduated income tax and laws regulating labor, demonstrated great enthusiasm for Ewing, and declined to nominate a candidate of its own. By 1890 Columbus Democrats, led by Allen Thurman, had allied themselves with organized labor, and reform-minded Democrats in other states supported labor movements that demanded federal labor and agricultural legislation. The national Democratic platform of 1892 called for antitrust legislation, federal internal improvements, generous state appropriations for public schools, and state and federal laws to protect railroad and sweatshop workers and to prohibit child labor. Ranney left no record of his thinking on such issues, but he might well have disdained late-nineteenth-century populism as an abandonment of Jacksonian tenets.[41]

The end of Ranney's second term as president of the state bar association brought his public career to a close. Ranney continued to practice law, appearing as counsel of record in an important appellate case as late as 1890,[42] but little else is known of his last years. He was in "feeble health" for some time, but in the late summer and fall of 1891 he seemed to improve and could often be seen out and about. In November, though, he grew weaker and in early December lapsed into unconsciousness. Ranney died on December 6. After a funeral service that was "simple and without ostentation" at the Ranney home, Ranney was interred at Cleveland's Lakeview Cemetery. The *Plain Dealer* called the Episcopal burial service "private," but the attendees included not just family but also ex-president Rutherford B. Hayes, former U.S. senator Henry B. Payne, and a host of current and former judges.[43]

The Ranney name remained current in the Cleveland area for some time. There was the unsuccessful law school, not the happiest memorial to Ranney's illustrious legal career. Two ships named *Rufus P. Ranney* plied the Great Lakes between 1881 and 1961.[44] A more appropriate tribute was a statue of Ranney installed on one side of the entrance to the new Cleveland courthouse in 1912. The figure guarding the other doorpost was, and is, John Marshall. Marshall, who died just as Ranney was coming of age, was a Federalist stalwart and antagonist of Ranney's heroes Jefferson and Jackson. But he was also a champion of judicial review in the federal courts, as Ranney was in the courts of Ohio. To have Marshall and Ranney as companion courthouse sentinels is therefore fitting.

Ranney also remains in close proximity to John D. Rockefeller; both are buried in Cleveland's Lakeview Cemetery. That, too, seems appropriate for a Bourbon Democrat. Although Ranney angered Democratic Party regulars in 1872 by taking a leading role in the Reunion and Reform movement, he never wavered in his Jacksonian faith as long as he stayed politically active. In his last ten or twelve years he turned his attention to other matters: the bar association, judicial reform, higher education. He may have grown weary of politics. Perhaps he foresaw the demise of the old Democratic Party. Just five years after Ranney's death, the Democrats repudiated Grover Cleveland, the "last Jacksonian," and adopted a populist platform, signaling the beginning of the end of the Democratic conservatism that rested on the limited-government ideals of Jefferson and Jackson.[45]

NOTES

Abbreviations

BC *Belmont Chronicle* (St. Clairsville)
CML *Cleveland Morning Leader*
OS *Daily Ohio Statesman* (Columbus)
OSJ *Daily Ohio State Journal* (Columbus)
PD *Daily Plain Dealer* (Cleveland)
SCD *Stark County Democrat* (Canton)
WRC *Western Reserve Chronicle* (Ravenna)

Note regarding case citations: For most of the nineteenth century, the reports of decisions of the Ohio Supreme Court do not give the date on which the court issued its decision but rather the month in which the term of the court began. That month was usually December, which means that the court in most cases issued its decision in the calendar year following the year given in the citation.

Introduction

1. S. E. Williamson, "Memorial of Rufus P. Ranney," in Ohio State Bar Association, *Proceedings of the Annual Meeting of the Association, Held at Put-in-Bay, on July 13, 14 and 15, 1892* (Akron: Werner Ptg. & Lith. Co., 1892), 189; A. G. Riddle, *The Life of Benjamin F. Wade* (Cleveland: Williams, 1888), 105; James Ford Rhodes, *History of the United States from the Compromise of 1850*, vol. 2, *1854–1860* (1892; reprint, New York: Macmillan, 1900), 380–81.

2. John Phillip Reid, "Beneath the Titans," *New York University Law Review* 70 (June 1995): 654; James W. Ely Jr., "Property Rights and Democracy in the American Constitutional Order," in *The Judicial Branch*, ed. Kermit L. Hall and Kevin T. McGuire (New York: Oxford University Press, 2005), 496–98; Leonard W. Levy, *The Law of the Commonwealth and Chief Justice Shaw* (Cambridge, MA: Harvard University Press, 1957), 3–4.

3. Walter A. McDougall, *Throes of Democracy: The American Civil War Era, 1829–1877* (New York: Harper, 2008), 102–3; John Ashworth, *"Agrarians" and "Aristocrats": Party Political Ideology in the United States, 1837–1846* (New York: Cambridge University Press, 1987), 146; Harry L. Watson, *Liberty and Power: The Politics of Jacksonian America*, rev. ed. (New York: Hill & Wang, 2006), 237–43.

4. James D. Richardson, comp., *A Compilation of the Messages and Papers of the Presidents, 1789–1897*, vol. 2 (Washington, DC: Government Printing Office, 1900), 448; Gerald Leonard, *The Invention of Party Politics: Federalism, Popular Sovereignty, and Constitutional Development in Jacksonian Illinois* (Chapel Hill: University of

North Carolina Press, 2002), 35–36; *Chicago Democrat*, 8 July 1835, quoted in Larry D. Kramer, *The People Themselves: Popular Constitutionalism and Judicial Review* (New York: Oxford University Press, 2004), 196; *New York Evening Post*, quoted in Mary P. Ryan, *Civic Wars: Democracy and Public Life in the American City during the Nineteenth Century* (Berkeley: University of California Press, 1997), 112. Ryan cites the *Evening Post* of 2 July 1827, but her text indicates that the quotation is from an editorial published in the spring of 1835.

5. Daniel Walker Howe, *What Hath God Wrought: The Transformation of America, 1815–1848* (New York: Oxford University Press, 2007), 4–5; Gregory S. Alexander, *Commodity and Propriety: Competing Visions of Property in American Legal Thought, 1776–1970* (Chicago: University of Chicago Press, 1997), 101–2.

6. Richardson, *Messages,* 449; Jackson to John Quincy Adams, 26 August 1821, in Andrew Jackson, *Correspondence of Andrew Jackson,* ed. John Spencer Bassett, vol. 3, *1820–1828* (Washington, DC: Carnegie Institution of Washington, 1928), 115; Richardson, *Messages,* 590; Jackson to James Hamilton Jr., 29 June 1828, in Jackson, *Correspondence,* 412; Robert V. Remini, *Andrew Jackson and the Course of American Empire, 1767–1821* (New York: Harper & Row, 1977), 414.

7. *Congressional Globe,* Appendix, 28th Cong., 1st sess., 1844, 13, pt. 2, 461 (John B. Weller); Ashworth, *"Agrarians" and "Aristocrats,"* 18–20; Robert V. Remini, *Andrew Jackson and the Course of American Democracy, 1833–1845* (New York: Harper & Row, 1984), 339, 342; Leonard, *Party Politics,* 177–92.

8. Robert V. Remini, *Andrew Jackson and the Course of American Freedom, 1822–1832* (New York: Harper & Row, 1981), 255–56.

9. Richardson, *Messages,* 452, 509–10.

10. John Ashworth, *The Republic in Crisis, 1848–1861* (New York: Cambridge University Press, 2012), 43.

11. Jackson to James K. Polk, 4 December 1826, quoted in Remini, *Course of Freedom,* 32; Russell Kirk, *John Randolph of Roanoke: A Study in American Politics, with Selected Speeches and Letters* (Chicago: Regnery, 1964), 446, 448; "Mr. Maxcy's Oration," *Examiner, and Journal of Political Economy* 1 (30 October 1833): 102; William Leggett, *Democratick Editorials: Essays in Jacksonian Political Economy,* comp. and ed. Lawrence H. White (Indianapolis: Liberty Press, 1984), 48.

12. H. Fowler, reporter, *Report of the Debates and Proceedings of the Convention for the Revision of the Constitution of the State of Indiana* (Indianapolis: A. H. Brown, 1850), 1:705 (William R. Haddon).

13. J. V. Smith, reporter, *Report of the Debates and Proceedings of the Convention for the Revision of the Constitution of the State of Ohio* (Columbus: S. Medary, 1851), 1:684; Robert M. Cover, *Justice Accused: Antislavery and the Judicial Process* (New Haven, CT: Yale University Press, 1975), 252–56.

14. Clinton Rossiter, *Conservatism in America: The Thankless Persuasion,* 2nd ed., rev. (New York: Vintage, 1962), 5; Russell Kirk, *The Politics of Prudence,* 2nd ed. (Wilmington, DE: ISI Books, 2004), 16. For characterizations of the different parties as conservative, see Patrick Allitt, *The Conservatives: Ideas and Personalities throughout American History* (New Haven, CT: Yale University Press, 2009), 46–66

(Whigs); Clyde N. Wilson, "The Jeffersonian Conservative Tradition," *Modern Age* 14 (Winter 1969–70): 36–48 (Democrats); Adam I. P. Smith, "Conservatism, Transformation, and the War for the Union," in *Reconfiguring the Union: Civil War Transformations,* ed. Iwan W. Morgan and Philip John Davies (New York: Palgrave Macmillan, 2013), 41–58 (Republicans).

15. "The Whig Party, Its Positions, and Duties," *American Review* 2 (December 1845): 548; "The Convention—Reorganization of the Judiciary," *American Review* 2 (November 1845): 474; "Responsibility of the Ballot Box: With an Illustration," *American Review* 4 (November 1846): 445. "Loco-foco" originally referred to a radical faction of New York Democrats, but Whigs used it derisively for Democrats in general.

16. "The Duty of the Democratic Party," *United States Magazine and Democratic Review* 6 (November 1839): 440; "Jefferson and Fox," *United States Magazine and Democratic Review* 27 (September 1850): 196; Jean H. Baker, *Affairs of Party: The Political Culture of Northern Democrats in the Mid-Nineteenth Century* (Ithaca, NY: Cornell University Press, 1983), 181–82; Drew Maciag, *Edmund Burke in America: The Contested Career of the Father of Modern Conservatism* (Ithaca, NY: Cornell University Press, 2013), 58–104.

17. Orestes Brownson, "Introductory Statement," *Boston Quarterly Review* 3 (January 1840): 16; Watson, *Liberty and Power,* 238; Russell Kirk, *The Conservative Mind: From Burke to Eliot,* 7th ed. (Washington, DC: Regnery, 1985), 73. For the argument that Jefferson was a conservative, see Wilson, "Jeffersonian Conservative Tradition."

18. Remini, *Course of Empire,* 33, 94.

19. *Boston Daily Advertiser and Patriot,* 10 October 1832, quoted in Sean Wilentz, *The Rise of American Democracy: Jefferson to Lincoln* (New York: Norton, 2005), 372; Remini, *Course of Democracy,* 125; Rush Welter, *The Mind of America, 1820–1860* (New York: Columbia University Press, 1975), 210.

20. Jackson to Francis Preston Blair, 31 October 1837, quoted in Remini, *Course of Democracy,* 440.

21. "Radicalism," *United States Magazine and Democratic Review* 25 (September 1849): 205, 208.

22. *WRC,* 27 March 1850; Smith, *Report,* 2:622–23; *Weekly OSJ,* 12 July 1859.

23. Daniel Walker Howe, *The Political Culture of the American Whigs* (Chicago: University of Chicago Press, 1979), 70 and chapter 4 generally; Edward Everett, *Orations and Speeches on Various Occasions,* vol. 3 (Boston: Little, Brown, 1870), 3:228–29; "W. A. B.," "Revolution in England," *United States Magazine and Democratic Review* 16 (February 1845): 119; John L. O'Sullivan, "Introduction," *United States Magazine and Democratic Review* 1 (October 1837): 8–9.

24. Robert J. Walker, letter to the Democratic Committee, Pittsburgh, 30 September 1856, published as *An Appeal for the Union: Letter from the Hon. Robert J. Walker* (New York: John F. Trow, 1856), 6, http://hdl.handle.net/2027/umn.31951001786773v; *Weekly Indiana State Sentinel* (Indianapolis), 4 September 1856; Rufus Choate to the Maine Whig State Central Committee, 9 August

1856, in *New York Times,* 15 August 1856; *Cadiz* (Ohio) *Democratic Sentinel,* 1 June 1859.

25. Ranney to Charles E. Rice, 24 September 1890, Charles E. Rice Collection, Ohio Historical Society.

26. Ranney was the editor of the "code department" of the new *Western Law Monthly* in 1859. The department addressed issues involving the Ohio code of civil procedure, which the legislature enacted in 1853. Ranney resigned due to the "pressure of professional and other engagements" in the summer of 1859, when he was running for governor and about to embark on a series of debates around the state against his opponent. "Introductory," *Western Law Monthly* 1 (January 1859): II; "Hon. R. P. Ranney," editorial, *Western Law Monthly* 1 (August 1859): 486.

Chapter 1: Western Reserve Democrat

1. *OSJ,* 3 April 1839; H. L. Trefousse, *Benjamin Franklin Wade: Radical Republican from Ohio* (New York: Twayne, 1963), 34–37, 113.

2. Charles Collard Adams, *Middletown Upper Houses: A History of the North Society of Middletown, Connecticut, from 1650 to 1800, with Genealogical and Biographical Chapters on Early Families and a Full Genealogy of the Ranney Family* (New York: Grafton, 1908), 143, 186, 213–24; Alfred Minot Copeland, ed., *"Our County and Its People": A History of Hampden County, Massachusetts* (N.p.: Century Memorial, 1902), 2:497–500.

3. *History of Portage County, Ohio* (Chicago: Warner, Beers, 1885), 454–55; Adams, *Middletown Upper Houses,* 213; Maurice Joblin, *Cleveland, Past and Present: Its Representative Men . . .* (Cleveland: Fairbanks, Benedict, 1869), 228; S. E. Williamson, "Memorial of Rufus P. Ranney," in Ohio State Bar Association, *Proceedings of the Annual Meeting of the Association, Held at Put-in-Bay, on July 13, 14 and 15, 1892* (Akron: Werner Ptg. & Lith. Co., 1892), 187; Edwin Jay Blandin, "Rufus Percival Ranney," in *Great American Lawyers: The Lives and Influence of Judges and Lawyers Who Have Acquired Permanent National Reputation, and Have Developed the Jurisprudence of the United States: A History of the Legal Profession in America,* ed. William Draper Lewis (Philadelphia: John C. Winston, 1909), 6:408.

4. Williamson, "Memorial," 187.

5. Carroll Cutler, *A History of Western Reserve College, during Its First Half Century, 1826–1876* (Cleveland: Crocker's, 1876), 15–31; Williamson, "Memorial," 187; David French, "Elizur Wright, Jr., and the Emergence of Anti-Colonization Sentiments on the Connecticut Western Reserve," *Ohio History* 85 (Winter 1976): 55–56; Blandin, "Ranney," 409; Brooks Mather Kelley, *Yale: A History* (New Haven, CT: Yale University Press, 1974), 156, 167.

6. *American National Biography,* s.vv. "Giddings, Joshua Reed" and "Wade, Benjamin Franklin"; Joblin, *Cleveland,* 228; Lawrence M. Friedman, *A History of American Law,* 3rd ed. (New York: Simon & Schuster, 2005), 238; Act of 14 February 1824, §§ 1–3, 22 Ohio Laws 374, 374 (1824); A. G. Riddle, *The Life of Benjamin F. Wade* (Cleveland: Williams, 1888), 80; Judge [Alfred G. W.] Carter, *The Old Court House:*

Reminiscences and Anecdotes of the Courts and Bar of Cincinnati (Cincinnati: Peter G. Thomson, 1880), 245–46; Williamson, "Memorial," 188.

7. Frederick T. Wallace, "The Bar Banquets," in *The Bench and Bar of Cleveland,* ed. James Harrison Kennedy and Wilson M. Day (Cleveland: Cleveland Printing & Publishing Co., 1889), 201; [Albert G. Riddle], *Bart Ridgeley: A Story of Northern Ohio* (Boston: Nichols & Hall, 1873), 136–38, 149, 237.

8. [Riddle], *Bart Ridgeley,* 144.

9. Blandin, "Ranney," 409; Riddle, *Wade,* 122–23; Williamson, "Memorial," 188; Franklin Bowditch Dexter, *Biographical Notices of Graduates of Yale College, Including Those Graduated in Classes Later than 1815, Who Are Not Commemorated in the Annual Obituary Records* (New Haven, CT: n.p., 1913), 293; Charles Horatio Gates, *Memorials of the Class of 1835, Harvard University* (Boston: David Clapp & Son, 1886), 100; William W. Williams, *History of Ashtabula County, Ohio, with Illustrations and Biographical Sketches of Its Pioneers and Most Prominent Men* (1878; reprint, Evansville, IN: Unigraphics, 1974), 97, 105; *Portage Sentinel,* 28 July 1847.

10. Riddle, *Wade,* 100–101.

11. Ibid., 121. The cases in which Ranney or his firm appeared were located by a search of the LEXIS legal research database.

12. Lucien C. Warner and Josephine Genung Nichols, comps., *The Descendants of Andrew Warner* (New Haven, CT: Tuttle, Morehouse & Taylor, 1919), 408, 563–64; James Harrison Kennedy, *A History of the City of Cleveland: Biographical Volume* (Cleveland: Imperial Press, 1897), 191–96; Samuel P. Orth, *A History of Cleveland, Ohio* (Chicago: S. J. Clarke, 1910), 2:16–20, 574–77; ibid., 3:538, 1072.

13. *Lancaster Eagle,* 31 July 1862; Williams, *Ashtabula County,* 43, 151–52; Act of 28 February 1843, 41 Ohio Laws (local) 91 (1843); *Ashtabula Sentinel,* 23 September 1843.

14. David M. Gold, *Democracy in Session: A History of the Ohio General Assembly* (Athens: Ohio University Press, 2009), 190–91; *OS,* 10 January 1844, 11 January 1844.

15. Edgar Allen Holt, "Party Politics in Ohio, 1840–1850," pt. 1, *Ohio Archaeological and Historical Quarterly,* 37 (July 1928): 546–47; Michael J. Dubin, *United States Congressional Elections, 1788–1997: The Official Results of the Elections of the 1st through 105th Congresses* (Jefferson, NC: McFarland, 1998), 134–35, 140, 147, 153, 159, 165, 171, 177.

16. Frederick T. Wallace, "Judge Rufus P. Ranney," *Western Reserve Law Journal* 1 (February 1895): 2; *Portage Sentinel,* 2 September 1846, 9 September 1846.

17. *History of Trumbull and Mahoning Counties, with Illustrations and Biographical Sketches* (Cleveland: H. Z. Williams & Bro., 1882), 1:192; *Portage Sentinel,* 23 September 1846; Dubin, *Congressional Elections,* 147.

18. *WRC,* 27 September 1848; *Portage Sentinel,* 6 September 1848.

19. Michael F. Holt, *The Rise and Fall of the American Whig Party: Jacksonian Politics and the Onset of the Civil War* (New York: Oxford University Press, 1999), 338–39; O. C. Gardiner, *The Great Issue: or, The Three Presidential Candidates; Being a Brief Historical Sketch of the Free Soil Question in the United States, from*

the Congresses of 1774 and '87 to the Present Time (New York: Wm. C. Bryant, 1848), 138–40.

20. *Philanthropist* (Cincinnati), 23 July 1842, 3; *History of Trumbull and Mahoning Counties,* 1:447–48; *Portage Sentinel,* 4 October 1848.

21. Holt, *Whig Party,* 310; *WRC,* 27 September 1848; *Portage Sentinel,* 4 October 1848; William H. Seward, *The Works of William Seward,* ed. George E. Baker (New York: Redfield, 1853), 3:295.

22. *Mahoning Index*, reprinted in the *Portage Sentinel,* 4 October 1848; *Portage Sentinel,* 27 September 1848; *WRC,* 4 October 1848.

23. S. Journal, 47th Gen. Assemb. 128 (Ohio 1849); H. Journal, 47th Gen. Assemb. 58–59 (Ohio 1849); "Election Returns, by States, Congressional Districts, and Counties," in *The Whig Almanac and United States Review for 1849* (New York: Greeley & McElrath, 1849), 56.

Chapter 2: The Constitutional Convention: Corporations and Citizens

1. *OS,* 9 August 1867; Jacob G. Ullery, comp., *Men of Vermont: An Illustrated Biographical History of Vermonters and Sons of Vermont* (Brattleboro, VT: Transcript, 1894), 124; *Report of the Select Committee to Investigate the Alleged Credit Mobilier Bribery, Made to the House of Representatives, February 18, 1873* (Washington, DC: Government Printing Office, 1873), x.

2. David M. Gold, *Democracy in Session: A History of the Ohio General Assembly* (Athens: Ohio University Press, 2009), 38; Barbara A. Terzian, "Ohio's Constitutional Conventions and Constitutions," in *The History of Ohio Law,* ed. Michael Les Benedict and John F. Winkler (Athens: Ohio University Press, 2004), 1:50–52.

3. H. Journal, 47th Gen. Assemb., app. 3, 8 (Ohio 1849); S. Journal, 47th Gen. Assemb. 236–37 (1849); *Portage Sentinel,* 6 September 1848.

4. Resolution of 23 March 1849, 47 Ohio Laws (local) 395 (1849); Act of 22 February 1850, 48 Ohio Laws 19 (1850); *WRC,* 27 March 1850.

5. *WRC,* 10 April 1850; Eugene H. Roseboom, *The Civil War Era, 1850–1873,* vol. 4 of *The History of the State of Ohio,* ed. Carl Wittke (Columbus: Ohio State Archaeological & Historical Society, 1944), 130–34; Terzian, "Ohio's Constitutional Conventions," 59–60.

6. J. V. Smith, reporter, *Report of the Debates and Proceedings of the Convention for the Revision of the Constitution of the State of Ohio* (Columbus: S. Medary, 1851), 2:78–79, 622–23.

7. "Responsibility of the Ballot Box; With an Illustration," *American Review* 4 (November 1846): 445.

8. Eric Foner, "Radical Individualism in America: Revolution to Civil War," *Literature of Liberty* 1 (July–September 1978): 5–31; "Radicalism," *United States Magazine and Democratic Review* 3 (October 1838): 105, 106, 111; "Opinions of the Council of Three: Political Bigotry—Conservatism—Radicalism," *American Review* 6 (September 1847): 243, 242.

9. *Bangor Daily Whig and Courier,* 17 August 1836.

10. Marvin Meyers, *The Jacksonian Persuasion: Politics and Belief* (New York: Vintage, 1960), 13, 194; Harry L. Watson, *Liberty and Power: The Politics of Jacksonian America,* rev. ed. (New York: Hill & Wang, 2006), 234, 238; Harry L. Watson, "The Venturous Conservative Reconsidered: Social History and Political Culture in the Market Revolution," *Reviews in American History* 22 (December 1994): 739.

11. The convention gave up the idea of securing the copyright. Smith, *Report,* 1:86. Most references to Smith's *Report* in chapters 2 and 3 are cited parenthetically in the text by volume and page.

12. Gold, *Democracy,* 183–85.

13. Welles, quoted in "Incorporating the Republic: The Corporation in Antebellum Political Culture," *Harvard Law Review* 102 (June 1989): 1900; "Democracy—What Is It?" *United States Review* 2 (July 1853): 11–12.

14. Act of 15 February 1849, § 1, 47 Ohio Laws (local) 12, 12 (1849); Act of 22 March 1849, § 1, 47 Ohio Laws (local) 38, 38 (1849).

15. Compare the remarks of Dorsey and Reemelin in Smith, *Report,* 1:371–73.

16. Harwell Wells, "The Rise of the Close Corporation and the Making of Corporation Law," *Berkeley Business Law Journal* 5 (September 2008): 281.

17. By the time of the convention, the American law of shareholder liability generally held that shareholders were not liable for corporate obligations beyond the amount of their shares unless the corporate charter or a statute expressly imposed greater liability. Phillip I. Blumberg, "Limited Liability and Corporate Groups," *Journal of Corporation Law* 11 (Summer 1986): 587–603.

18. For a discussion of Ranney's amendment and an endorsement of a proposed constitutional amendment to repeal it, see Smith W. Bennett, "Double Liability: Ohio's Destructive Policy," *Public Policy* 9 (25 July 1903): 45–48. The voters approved the repeal amendment in 1903. Steven H. Steinglass and Gino J. Scarselli, *The Ohio State Constitution: A Reference Guide* (Westport, CT: Praeger, 2004), 305–6.

19. Ohio Const. art. I, § 2; Trustees of Dartmouth College v. Woodward, 17 U.S. 518, 675–80, 712 (Story, J., concurring).

20. Ohio Const. art. XIII, § 4.

21. Charles Reemelin, quoting Matthew 6:3, in Stephen E. Maizlish, *The Triumph of Sectionalism: The Transformation of Ohio Politics, 1844–1856* (Kent, OH: Kent State University Press, 1983), 182.

22. Michael F. Holt, *The Rise and Fall of the American Whig Party: Jacksonian Politics and the Onset of the Civil War* (New York: Oxford University Press, 1999), 399–402; Stephen Middleton, *The Black Laws: Race and the Legal Process in Early Ohio* (Athens: Ohio University Press, 2005), 148–53.

23. The published report of the debates refers to remarks made by Ranney on the issue, but the remarks are not printed in the report. Smith, *Report,* 2:18.

24. Ranney would later explain his votes as an effort to leave the question of school segregation to the legislature to adjust "from time to time" in accordance with the "feelings of the white race, as to what was practicable to elevate and enlighten all classes of the population." Ranney to George W. Johnson, 25 August

1860, in *Iron Valley Express* (Jackson Court House, Ohio), reprinted in *McArthur Democrat,* 4 October 1860.

25. Fugitive Slave Act, 9 Stat. 462 (1850); Steven Lubet, *Fugitive Justice: Runaways, Rescuers, and Slavery on Trial* (Cambridge, MA: Harvard University Press, 2010), 42–43.

26. *Mahoning Index,* 1 November 1850, reprinted in *OSJ,* 24 September 1859.

27. *OS,* 14 July 1859.

Chapter 3: The Constitutional Convention: Government

1. John L. O'Sullivan, "Introduction," *United States Magazine and Democratic Review* 1 (October 1837): 3, 6.

2. Ohio Const. art. VII, § 2.

3. Francis J. Amer, "The Growth and Development of the Ohio Judicial System," in *A History of the Courts and Lawyers of Ohio,* ed. Carrington T. Marshall (New York: American Historical Society, 1934), 1:189–90; Act of 15 April 1803, Ch. XIV, §§ 3–4, 1 Ohio Laws 35, 36 (1803); Act of 16 February 1810, Ch. LXXIV, §§ 2, 5–6, 8 Ohio Laws 259, 259 (1810); Ohio Const. of 1802, art. III, § 5.

4. Ohio Const. of 1802, art. III, §§ 2, 10; Act of 17 February 1808, Ch. XII, 6 Ohio Laws 32 (1808).

5. Amer, "Growth," 1:190–92; F. R. Aumann, "The Development of the Judicial System of Ohio," *Ohio Archaeological and Historical Quarterly* 41 (April 1932): 201–3, 205–7; John C. Wright, *Reports of Cases at Law and in Chancery, Decided by the Supreme Court of Ohio, during the Years 1831, 1832, 1833, 1834: Taken from Original Minutes* (Columbus: Isaac N. Whiting, 1835), "Preface" (unpaginated).

6. Act of 4 March 1851, 49 Ohio Laws 21 (1851); H. Journal, 17th Gen. Assemb. 103 (Ohio 1818); H. Journal, 46th Gen. Assemb., app. 45 (Ohio 1848); Aumann, "Development," 203–4, 209.

7. Amer, "Growth," 1:194; Clement L. Vallandigham, *Speeches, Arguments, Addresses, and Letters of Clement L. Vallandigham* (New York: J. Walter, 1864), 82; H. Journal, 46th Gen. Assemb., app. 47 (Ohio 1848); S. Journal, 46th Gen. Assemb. 202 (Ohio 1848); Barbara A. Terzian, "Ohio's Constitutional Conventions and Constitutions," in *The History of Ohio Law,* ed. Michael Les Benedict and John F. Winkler (Athens: Ohio University Press, 2004), 1:50–51; David M. Gold, "Judicial Elections and Judicial Review: Testing the Shugerman Thesis," *Ohio Northern University Law Review* 40 (2013), 45–46.

8. By June 1849 the *Toledo Commercial* had observed that the idea of popular election of judges had "already triumphed." See "Election of Judges by the People," *New Constitution,* 9 June 1849 (reprinting comments from the *Toledo Commercial*), 91.

9. Kirkwood belonged to the judiciary committee minority that wanted the district court to meet in each county in the district every year, but he had gone along with the compromise embodied in the majority report. Smith, *Report,* 1:615.

10. *SCD,* 15 March 1888.

1. S. Journal, 49th Gen. Assemb. 714 (Ohio 1851).

2. Ibid., 768–97.

3. Michael F. Holt, *The Rise and Fall of the American Whig Party: Jacksonian Politics and the Onset of the Civil War* (New York: Oxford University Press, 1999), 399–402; S. Journal, 49th Gen. Assemb. 790, 788 (Ohio 1851).

4. Edgar B. Kinkead, "A Sketch of the Supreme Court of Ohio," pt. 3, *Green Bag* 7 (May 1895): 233. For a defense of Corwin by his nephew, see John A. Corwin to editor, 23 May 1895, in *Green Bag* 7 (July 1895): 355–56.

5. S. Journal, 49th Gen. Assemb. 796 (Ohio 1851); "Hon. Rufus P. Ranney," *Weekly Law Bulletin and Ohio Law Journal* 26 (14 December 1891): 353.

6. H. Journal, 49th Gen. Assemb. 877 (Ohio 1851); S. Journal, 49th Gen. Assemb. 796 (Ohio 1851); *OSJ*, 18 March 1851.

7. *OSJ*, 18 March 1851.

8. Ohio Const. schedule, § 4; *OSJ*, 7 August 1851.

9. Frederick J. Blue, "The Ohio Free Soilers and Problems of Factionalism," *Ohio History* 76, nos. 1–2 (Winter–Spring 1967): 17–32; *National Era*, 28 August 1851; *OS*, 22 August 1851, 26 August 1851.

10. Kinkead, "Sketch," pt. 3, 233–36; S. Winifred Smith, "Thomas W. Bartley," in *Governors of Ohio*, 2nd ed. (Columbus: Ohio Historical Society, 1969), 51.

11. David M. Gold, *Democracy in Session: A History of the Ohio General Assembly* (Athens: Ohio University Press, 2009), 194–97.

12. Ohio Const. art. IV, § 11 (repealed 1883); Act of 19 February 1852, § 2, 50 Ohio Laws 67, 67 (1852); 1 Ohio St. xiv–xv

13. Ohio Const. art. IV, §§ 2 (amended 1883, 1913, 1944, 1968, 1995), 5 (repealed 1883), and 6 (amended 1883, 1913, 1945, 1959; repealed 1968); J. V. Smith, reporter, *Report of the Debates and Proceedings of the Convention for the Revision of the Constitution of the State of Ohio* (Columbus: S. Medary, 1851), 2:382, 669; Act of 23 March 1852, § 1, 50 Ohio Laws 93, 93 (1852). A LEXIS search turned up twelve reported decisions of the district court for Cuyahoga County, all dating from the October 1855 term, in which Ranney wrote an opinion.

14. Charles W. Smith, *Roger B. Taney: Jacksonian Jurist* (Chapel Hill: University of North Carolina Press, 1936); Arthur M. Schlesinger Jr., *The Age of Jackson* (Boston: Little, Brown, 1945), 322–29; Robert E. Mensel, "'Privilege against Public Right': A Reappraisal of the Charles River Bridge Case" *Duquesne Law Review* 33 (Fall 1994): 1–38; Daniel Walker Howe, *What Hath God Wrought: The Transformation of America, 1815–1848* (New York: Oxford University Press, 2007), 441–45.

15. Austin Allen, *Origins of the Dred Scott Case: Jacksonian Jurisprudence and the Supreme Court, 1837–1857* (Athens: University of Georgia Press, 2006), 36–51.

16. Perry Miller, "The Common Law and Codification in Jacksonian America," *Proceedings of the American Philosophical Society* 103 (June 1959): 463–68; Alfred S. Konefsky, "The Legal Profession: From the Revolution to the Civil War," in *The Cambridge History of Law in America*, vol. 2, *The Long Nineteenth Century*

(1789–1920), ed. Michael Grossberg and Christopher Tomlins (New York: Cambridge University Press, 2008), 97–99; Edwin Jay Blandin, "Rufus Percival Ranney," in *Great American Lawyers: The Lives and Influence of Judges and Lawyers Who Have Acquired Permanent National Reputation, and Have Developed the Jurisprudence of the United States: A History of the Legal Profession in America,* ed. William Draper Lewis (Philadelphia: John C. Winston, 1909), 6:427; J. V. Smith, reporter, *Report of the Debates and Proceedings of the Convention for the Revision of the Constitution of the State of Ohio* (Columbus: S. Medary, 1851), 1:557; Cincinnati, Hamilton & Dayton R.R. v. Waterson, 4 Ohio St. 424, 432–33 (Dec. 1854).

17. Ellis and Morton v. Ohio Life Ins. and Trust Co., 4 Ohio St. 628, 646 (Dec. 1855); Work v. State, 2 Ohio St. 296, 302 (1853); Smith, *Report,* 1:290; Waterson, 4 Ohio St. 424; James O. Troup, letter to the editor, in "The Scintilla Rule—A Symposium," *Western Reserve Law Journal* 4 (December 1898): 173; Hamden Lodge No. 517, Independent Order of Odd Fellows v. Ohio Fuel Gas Co., 127 Ohio St. 469 (1934). On the Jacksonian regard for the jury, see Maxwell Bloomfield, "Law vs. Politics: The Self-Image of the American Bar (1830–1860)," *American Journal of Legal History* 12 (October 1968): 306; Caleb Nelson, "A Re-evaluation of Scholarly Explanations for the Rise of the Elective Judiciary in Antebellum America," *American Journal of Legal History* 37 (April 1993), 208–9; Robert D. Rucker, "The Right to Ignore the Law: Constitutional Entitlement versus Judicial Interpretation," *Valparaiso University Law Review* 33 (Spring 1999): 457–59.

18. Little Miami R.R. v. Stevens, 20 Ohio 415 (Dec. 1851).

19. Hard v. Vermont & Canada R.R., 32 Vt. 473 (1860); Isaac F. Redfield, *The Law of Railways,* 4th ed. (Boston: Little, Brown, 1869), 1:521; Gillenwater v. Madison & Indianapolis R.R., 5 Ind. 350 (1854); Moseley v. Chamberlain, 18 Wis. 700 (1861). See also Jerrilyn Marston, "The Creation of a Common Law Rule: The Fellow Servant Rule, 1837–1860," *University of Pennsylvania Law Review* 132 (March 1984): 605–11.

20. *Stevens,* 20 Ohio at 432–35; ibid., 436–38 (Hitchcock, C.J., concurring); ibid., 438–52 (Spalding. J., dissenting).

21. Cleveland, Columbus & Cincinnati R.R. v. Keary, 3 Ohio St. 201, 204–6 (1854).

22. Ibid., 208–10, 217, 213–14. Judge Warden, in a concurring opinion that rejected Shaw's "ingenious invention," said that the master should be liable for all injuries, including those caused by employees on an equal footing with the injured worker. Ibid., 225–27 (Warden, J., concurring).

23. 4 Ohio St. 399, 415, 417 (1854).

24. A few courts recognized *Carman* as standing for strict liability in blasting cases. See Klepsch v. Donald, 4 Wash. 436 (1892); Colton v. Onderdonk, 69 Cal. 155 (1886); Veigel v. Lukenheimer, 9 Ohio Dec. Reprint 48 (Dist. Ct. 1883). In *Carman* Ranney cited an even earlier New York case, *Hay v. Cohoes Co.,* 2 N.Y. 159 (1849). Jed Shugerman challenges the traditional view that most American courts initially rejected the *Rylands* rule, but he too finds that Ohio accepted it only in the 1890s. Jed Handelsman Shugerman, "The Floodgates of Strict Liability: Bursting

Reservoirs and the Adoption of *Fletcher v. Rylands* in the Gilded Age," *Yale Law Journal* 110 (November 2000): 351–52.

25. *Carman,* 4 Ohio St. at 417–18.

26. Gary T. Schwartz, "The Character of Early American Tort Law," *UCLA Law Review* 36 (April 1989): 711–12; Peter Karsten, *Heart versus Head: Judge-Made Law in Nineteenth-Century America* (Chapel Hill: University of North Carolina Press, 1997), 116; Ohio Const. art. VIII, § 4; ibid., art. XIII, §§ 1, 4; Joseph K. Angell and Samuel Ames, *A Treatise on the Law of Private Corporations Aggregate,* 2nd ed. (Boston: Charles C. Little & James Brown, 1843), 328–31; Henderson v. R.R., 17 Tex. 560 (1856); Hopkins v. Atlantic & St. Lawrence R.R., 36 N.J. 9 (1857).

27. Schwartz, "Early American Tort Law," 713.

28. At the constitutional convention, Ranney had argued on behalf of the "men of small capital." See page 28. Other nineteenth-century judges who supported the fellow-servant rule expressed concern about the exposure of small employers to liability. See Karsten, *Heart versus Head,* 119–20.

29. Smith, *Report,* 2:303.

30. Courts quickly developed exceptions to the fellow-servant rule, allowing many plaintiffs to recover damages for their injuries. Karsten, *Heart versus Head,* 122–24.

31. Daniel Walker Howe, *The Political Culture of the American Whigs* (Chicago: University of Chicago Press, 1979), 36; David M. Gold, *An Exemplary Whig: Edward Kent and the Whig Disposition in American Politics and Law* (Lanham, MD: Lexington, 2012), 68; Lewis v. Eutsler, 4 Ohio St. 354, 358 (1854) Duncan v. Duncan, 4 Ohio Dec. Reprint 26 (1855), *rev'd,* 10 Ohio St. 181, 188 (1859).

32. Gishwiler v. Dodez, 4 Ohio St. 615, 617–18, 621–22 (1855). An Ohio statute of 1893 finally gave fathers and mothers equal rights to custody and allowed a child of ten years or older to choose the custodial parent, provided both parents were fit for the responsibility. Act of 14 April 1893, 90 Ohio Laws 186 (1893).

33. United States v. Wiltberger, 18 U.S. 76, 95 (1820); Dana v. State, 2 Ohio St. 91, 92, 97–98 (1853).

34. Greer v. Ohio, 2 Ohio St. 575, 577, 578, 582, 580 (1853).

35. Larry D. Kramer, *The People Themselves: Popular Constitutionalism and Judicial Review* (New York: Oxford University Press, 2004), 200–201. For a similar description of Andrew Jackson's understanding of the relationship between the people and the courts, see Robert V. Remini, *Andrew Jackson and the Course of American Democracy, 1833–1845* (New York: Harper & Row, 1984), 338–40. On departmentalism as a Democratic Party position, see Gerald Leonard, "Party as a 'Political Safeguard of Federalism': Martin Van Buren and the Constitutional Theory of Party Politics," *Rutgers Law Review* 54 (Fall 2001): 262–66; Keith E. Whittington, *Political Foundations of Judicial Supremacy: The Presidency, the Supreme Court, and Constitutional Leadership in U.S. History* (Princeton, NJ: Princeton University Press, 2007), 59–61.

36. Kramer, *People Themselves,* 199–200; Leonard, "Political Safeguard," 257.

37. John L. O'Sullivan, "Introduction," *United States Magazine and Democratic Review* 1 (October 1837): 5–6.

38. Kramer, *People Themselves,* 148–64. Kramer also points to changes in party organization (165–68) and the need for an arbiter to decide otherwise intractable political issues, especially those related to slavery (170–89). On these issues, see also Whittington, *Political Foundations,* 248–55.

39. James A. Henretta, "The Strange Birth of Liberal America: Michael Hoffman and the New York Constitution of 1846," *New York History* 77 (April 1996): 170–71. See also Jed Handelsman Shugerman, *The People's Courts: Pursuing Judicial Independence in America* (Cambridge, MA: Harvard University Press, 2012), arguing that the state constitutional conventions of the mid-nineteenth century had the expansion of judicial review as an explicit aim. For a critical review of Shugerman's thesis, see David M. Gold, "Judicial Elections and Judicial Review: Testing the Shugerman Thesis," *Ohio Northern University Law Review* 40 (2013): 39–85.

40. See, for example, Parker v. Commonwealth, 6 Pa. 507 (1847) (Bell, J.); Griffith v. Comm'rs of Crawford Cnty., 20 Ohio 609 (1851) (Spalding, J.); Madison & Indianapolis R.R. v. Whiteneck, 8 Ind. 201 (1856) (Perkins, J.). Bell and Perkins were Democrats, Spalding a Free Soiler who had recently left the Democratic Party.

41. Smith, *Reports,* 2:216.

42. Cincinnati, Wilmington & Zanesville R.R. v. Clinton Cnty., 1 Ohio St. 77, 81–82 (1852).

43. Donald F. Melhorn Jr., *Lest We Be Marshall'd: Judicial Power and Politics in Ohio, 1806–1812* (Akron: University of Akron Press, 2003), 69; State v. Commercial Bank of Cincinnati, 7 Ohio St. 125 (1835); Smith, *Report,* 1:281.

44. *Cincinnati, Wilmington & Zanesville R.R.,* 1 Ohio St. at 83, 84, 86, 105. The court in this case upheld the statute because it had been enacted under the old constitution.

45. Saul Cornell, "The People's Constitution vs. the Lawyer's Constitution: Popular Constitutionalism and the Original Debate over Originalism," *Yale Journal of Law and the Humanities* 23 (Summer 2011): 295–337; Randy E. Barnett, "Whence Comes Section One? The Abolitionist Origins of the Fourteenth Amendment," *Journal of Legal Analysis* 3 (Spring 2011): 165–263; State *ex rel.* Dirs. of the Eastern & Western School Dists. of Cincinnati v. City of Cincinnati 19 Ohio 178, 197 (1850); Ohio Const. of 1802, art. VIII, § 18; see Bank of State v. Cooper, 10 Tenn. 599 (1831).

46. Hitchcock to son, 10 August 1851, Hitchcock Papers, Box 2, Folder 3, Western Reserve Historical Society.

47. Cass v. Dillon, 2 Ohio St. 607, 612 (1853).

48. Ibid., 627–28 (Ranney, J., dissenting).

49. Ibid., 628. Mid-nineteenth-century decisions holding that a state constitution was a limitation of power rather than, as Ranney maintained, a grant of power, include *Ponder v. Graham,*, 4 Fla. 23 (1851); *State v. Sorrels,* 15 Ark. 664 (1855); *People v. Brown,* 11 Ill. 478 (1850) (Treat, C.J.); *Concord Railroad v. Greeley,* 17 N.H. 47 (1845) (Gilchrist, J.); *Thorpe v. Rutland,* 27 Vt. 140 (1854) (Redfield, C.J.).

50. *Cass,* 2 Ohio St. at 628–29.

51. Ibid., 629–30, 631.

52. Ibid., 634.

53. Ibid. In using the quoted language, Ranney was referring to § 4, limiting the power of the state, but Ranney argued that the state could not evade § 4 by allowing local governments to do what the state itself could not.

54. Ibid., 637, 645. In *Cincinnati, Wilmington & Zanesville R.R.,* 1 Ohio St. 77, Ranney held that when the county held a popular vote and the subscription occurred before September 1, 1851, but the bonds had not been issued before then, the railroad could compel issuance of bonds after September 1. See also Ranney's opinion in *Exchange Bank of Columbus v. Hines,*, 3 Ohio St. 1, 53 (Dec. 1853).

55. *Cass,* 2 Ohio St. at 620–21. Thurman quoted from the part of the constitutional convention debates where Ranney objected to robbing people twice. Smith, *Report,* 2:310. See page 40.

56. Ibid., 2 Ohio St. at 647.

57. Ibid., 646 (emphasis added). See also Ranney's opinion in *Cincinnati, Wilmington & Zanesville R.R.,* 1 Ohio St. at 87 (the constitution's "checks, balances, and safeguards . . . are intended no less for the protection and safety of the minority, than the majority").

58. Redfield, *Railways,* 1:52 (Isaac F. Redfield); People *ex rel.* Detroit & Howell R.R. v. Twp. Bd. of Salem, 20 Mich. 452, 478 (1870) (Thomas M. Cooley); Pine Grove v. Talcott, 86 U.S. 666, 676 (1874) (Noah Swayne).

59. Giesy v. Cincinnati, Wilmington & Zanesville R.R., 4 Ohio St. 308, 324–25 (1854). See also Scovill v. City of Cleveland, 1 Ohio St. 125, 135 (1853).

60. *Giesy,* 4 Ohio St. at 325. See also Cincinnati, Wilmington & Zanesville R.R. v. Comm'rs of Clinton Cnty., 1 Ohio St. 77, 95 (1852); Chagrin Falls & Cleveland Plank-Rd. Co. v. Cane, 2 Ohio St. 419, 427–28 (Dec. 1853).

61. *Cincinnati, Wilmington & Zanesville R.R.,* 1 Ohio St. at 101–2; *Scovill,* 1 Ohio St. at 135; Debolt v. Ohio Life Ins. & Trust Co., 1 Ohio St. 563, 579–81 (1853).

62. *Cincinnati, Wilmington & Zanesville R.R.,* 1 Ohio St. at 94, 95.

63. Ibid., 86.

64. Mays v. City of Cincinnati, 1 Ohio St. 268, 273 (1853); *Ohio Life Ins. & Trust Co.,* 1 Ohio St. at 573, 579; *Cincinnati, Wilmington & Zanesville R.R.,* 1 Ohio St. at 87.

65. William G. Shade, *Banks or No Banks: The Money Issue in Western Politics, 1832–1865* (Detroit: Wayne State University Press, 1972); Smith, *Report,* 2:346, 416.

66. Act of 24 February 1845, § 60, 43 Ohio Laws 24, 48 (1845); Act of 21 March 1851, 49 Ohio Laws 56 (1851); C. C. Huntington, "A History of Banking and Currency in Ohio before the Civil War," *Ohio Archaeological and Historical Quarterly* 24 (July 1915): 420–26, 458–60.

67. Trs. of Dartmouth Coll. v. Woodward, 17 U.S. 518, 626 (1819). The Ohio constitutions had similar clauses, but they did not figure in the bank cases. Ohio Const. of 1802, art. VIII, § 16; Ohio Const. art. II, § 28.

68. See, for example, Peter Hitchcock's majority opinion in *State v. Commercial Bank of Cincinnati,* 7 Ohio 125 (1835).

69. Proprietors of Charles River Bridge v. Proprietors of Warren Bridge, 36 U.S. 420 (1837).

70. Stanley I. Kutler, *Privilege and Creative Destruction: The Charles River Bridge Case* (1971; reprint, Baltimore: Johns Hopkins University Press, 1990), 117–21,

133–54; Allen, *Origins,* 114–15; Herbert J. Hovenkamp, "The Classical Corporation in American Legal Thought," *Georgetown Law Journal* 76 (June 1988), 1612. See also Mensel, "Privilege against Public Right."

71. Bank of Toledo v. Toledo, 1 Ohio St. 622 (1853); Debolt v. Ohio Life Ins. & Trust Co., 1 Ohio St. 563 (1853); Mechanics' & Traders' Branch of the State Bank of Ohio v. Debolt, 1 Ohio St. 591 (1853); Knoup v. Piqua Branch of the State Bank of Ohio, 1 Ohio St. 603 (1853).

72. *Bank of Toledo,* 1 Ohio St. at 703 (Ranney, J., concurring).

73. Ibid., 627 (majority opinion).

74. *Ohio Life Ins. & Trust Co.,* 1 Ohio St. at 572–77. Ranney also suggested that the banks that had organized under the Kelley Law had given the state no consideration for their favored treatment and therefore had no valid contractual claim.

75. Ibid., 577, 579–81.

76. Ibid., 582–83.

77. Ibid., 587.

78. Piqua Branch of the State Bank of Ohio v. Knoop, 57 U.S. 369 (1854); Ohio Life Ins. & Trust Co. v. DeBolt, 57 U.S. 416 (1854); Mechanics'& Traders' Bank v. DeBolt, 59 U.S. 380 (1856); Dodge v. Woolsey, 59 U.S. 331 (1856).

79. *Ohio Life Ins. & Trust Co.,* 57 U.S. at 431–32.

80. Ibid., 432–38.

81. Ibid., 443 (Daniel, J., concurring).

82. Kutler, *Privilege,* 143–44.

83. *Piqua Branch,* 57 U.S. at 380–82, 384, 389.

84. Ibid, 393 (Taney, C.J., concurring), 395, 403–4, 400–401 (Catron, J., dissenting).

85. Ibid., 406–10 (Campbell, J., dissenting).

86. Ross Cnty. Bank v. Lewis, 5 Ohio St. 447 (1856); Matheny v. Golden, 5 Ohio St. 361 (1856); State *ex rel.* Morgan v. Moore, 5 Ohio St. 444 (1856).

87. Allen, *Origins,* 73.

88. Keating v. Spink, 3 Ohio St. 105 (1853).

89. Ibid., 129; Act of 26 February 1845, 5 Stat. 726; "From Judicial Grant to Legislative Power: The Admiralty Clause in the Nineteenth Century," *Harvard Law Review* 67 (May 1954): 1214–37.

90. *Keating,* 3 Ohio St. at 116, 118–19.

91. Ibid., 119–21.

92. Taylor v. Carryl, 61 U.S. 583, 595 (1858) and 601 (Taney, C.J., dissenting).

93. Frederick T. Wallace, *Men and Events of Half a Century* (Cleveland: Evangelical Association, 1882), 82. Wallace's remarks on Ranney first appeared in the *Boston Post* in 1856.

Chapter 5: The Republican Challenge

1. S. Exec. Journal, 33d Cong., 2d sess. 412 (1855); *New York Times,* 13 February 1855; *Toledo Blade,* 14 February 1855; "Editorial Notes," *Magazine of Western History*

12 (June 1890): 218. The *Plain Dealer* disputed reports of a fight within the Ohio congressional delegation over the nomination, saying that the members had "urgently sought" Willson's appointment. *PD*, 19 February 1855.

2. Eugene H. Roseboom, *The Civil War Era, 1850–1873,* vol. 4 of *The History of the State of Ohio,* ed. Carl Wittke (Columbus: Ohio State Archaeological & Historical Society, 1944), 126; David M. Gold, *Democracy in Session: A History of the Ohio General Assembly* (Athens: Ohio University Press, 2009), 194–95.

3. [J.], "The National Anniversary," *Southern Quarterly Review,* n.s., 2 (September 1850): 177–82, 185, 186–87.

4. Hamilton Fish, letter to James A. Hamilton, 12 September 1856, in *Fremont the Conservative Candidate: Correspondence between Hamilton Fish and J. A. Hamilton, etc.* ([New York?]: n.p., [1856?]), 12; Tyler Anbinder, *Nativism and Slavery: The Northern Know Nothings and the Politics of the 1850s* (New York: Oxford University Press, 1992), 221–22; Rufus Choate to the Maine Whig State Central Committee, 9 August 1856, in *New York Times,* 15 August 1856. The "belligerent foreign policy" mentioned by Fish referred generally to the interest of the Pierce administration and slavery expansionists in acquiring Cuba from Spain and more specifically to the Ostend Manifesto, which declared that the United States would be justified in "wresting" Cuba from Spain if Spain refused to sell the island.

5. *OSJ,* 9 January 1856.

6. James H. Goodsell, reporter, *Official Proceedings of the Democratic National Convention, Held in 1864 at Chicago* (Chicago: Times Steam Book & Job Printing, 1864), 39–45; *OS,* 22 June 1856. Both the *Official Proceedings* and the *Ohio Statesman* listed forty-six members of the Ohio delegation, but, according to the official record, Ohio cast only twenty-three votes. Presumably, the other twenty-three members were alternates.

7. Joseph P. Smith, ed., *History of the Republican Party in Ohio* (Chicago: Lewis, 1898), 1:61–62, 65, 67; *Cong. Globe,* 34th Cong., 3d sess. app. 48 (1856); Edgar B. Kinkead, "A Sketch of the Supreme Court of Ohio," pt. 4, *Green Bag* 7 (June 1895): 273–74.

8. *WRC,* 3 December 1856.

9. *OSJ,* 7 January 1857; R. C. Parsons, "Franklin T. Backus," *Magazine of Western History* 3 (November 1885): 8–15; Talcott E. Wing, ed., *History of Monroe County, Michigan* (New York: Munsell, 1890), 312–13; Judiciary Act of 1789, ch. 20, § 35, 1 Stat. 73, 92–93; Ranney to Jeremiah S. Black, 17 April 1857, 8 July 1857, in Frederick S. Calhoun, ed., *Letters Received by the Attorney General, 1809–1870: Northern Law and Order,* reel 16 (Bethesda, MD: University Publications of America, 1998); *Ohio Farmer,* 18 July 1857 (citing the *Akron Beacon*); Ranney, letter, *PD,* 3 August 1857; *PD,* 27 July 1857 (quoting the *Lebanon Democratic Citizen*); Act of 26 February 1853, ch. 80, 10 Stat. 161, 161–62; *PD,* 27 July 1857. Ranney's salary as a state supreme court judge was $1,700. Act of 1 May 1852, § 1, 50 Ohio Laws 221, 221 (1852). As a young lawyer in rural Pennsylvania in 1864, Samuel Dodd netted more than $4,000. Samuel C. T. Dodd, *Memoirs of S. C. T. Dodd Written for His Children and Friends, 1837–1907* (New York: Robert Grier Cooke, 1907), 14.

10. *OSJ,* 7 January 1857 (quoting the *Zanesville Aurora*); *PD,* 28 July 1857; *OSJ,* 25 April 1857; *PD,* 4 May 1857.

11. *PD,* 28 July 1857.

12. *PD,* 27 July 1857, 3 August 1857.

13. *OSJ,* 5 August 1857, 7 August 1857, 6 August 1857; *National Era,* 5 November 1857; Salmon P. Chase, *The Salmon P. Chase Papers,* ed. John Niven, vol. 1, *Journals, 1829–1872* (Kent, OH: Kent State University Press, 1993), 296.

14. Roseboom, *Civil War Era,* 326–28; Scott v. Sandford, 60 U.S. 393 (1857); Anderson v. Poindexter, 6 Ohio St. 622 (1856).

15. B. W. Collins, "Economic Issues in Ohio's Politics during the Recession of 1857–1858," *Ohio History* 89 (Winter 1980): 46–64; Ernest Ludlow Bogart, *Financial History of Ohio* (Urbana-Champaign: University of Illinois, 1912), 154–72; Roseboom, *Civil War Era,* 325.

16. See, for example, Jeffries v. Ankeny, 11 Ohio 372 (1842); William Cheek and Aimee Lee Cheek, *John Mercer Langston and the Fight for Black Freedom, 1829–65* (Urbana: University of Illinois Press, 1989), 283. *Jeffries* was decided under the constitution of 1802, but, as the supreme court later held in *Anderson v. Milliken,* 9 Ohio St. 568 (1859), there was no reason to think that framers of the 1851 constitution intended to change judicial constructions of "white."

17. Gold, *Democracy,* 197–98; Roseboom, *Civil War Era,* 341–42.

18. For detailed accounts of the case, see Jacob R. Shipherd, comp., *History of the Oberlin-Wellington Rescue* (Boston: John P. Jewett, 1859), and Nat Brandt, *The Town That Started the Civil War* (Syracuse, NY: Syracuse University Press, 1990).

19. Shipherd, *Oberlin-Wellington Rescue,* 16, 3.

20. Ibid., 225; *Ex parte* Bushnell, 9 Ohio St. 77 (May 1859); Robert M. Cover, *Justice Accused: Antislavery and the Judicial Process* (New Haven, CT: Yale University Press, 1975), 252–56.

21. John J. Kulewicz, "Reinventing the Governor: A History of Executive Power under Ohio Law," in *The History of Ohio Law,* ed. Michael Les Benedict and John F. Winkler (Athens: Ohio University Press, 2004), 1:147–53.

22. See Larry Gara, *The Liberty Line: The Legend of the Underground Railroad* (1961; reprint, Lexington: University Press of Kentucky, 1996), 127–28; *Cong. Globe,* 36th Cong., 2d sess. 56 (1860).

23. *CML,* 25 May 1859; Paul Finkelman, "Race, Slavery, and Law in Antebellum Ohio," in *The History of Ohio Law,* ed. Michael Les Benedict and John F. Winkler (Athens: Ohio University Press, 2004), 2:771–72.

24. *CML,* 27 May 1859.

25. *Cincinnati Daily Times,* 27 May 1859; *McArthur Democrat,* 9 June 1859; *WRC,* 8 June 1859.

26. *CML,* 28 May 1859.

27. Ibid., 4 June 1859.

28. John S. Still, "William Dennison, Jr.," in *Governors of Ohio,* 2nd ed. (Columbus: Ohio Historical Society, 1969), 76–79; *CML,* 25 May 1859, 4 June 1859.

Chapter 6: The Great Debates

1. Harold Holzer, ed., *The Lincoln-Douglas Debates: The First Complete, Unexpurgated Text* (New York: HarperCollins, 1993), 3, 5–7; Roeliff Brinkerhoff, *Recollections of a Lifetime* (Cincinnati: Robert Clarke, 1900), 36; Charles Eugene Hamlin, *The Life and Times of Hannibal Hamlin* (Cambridge, MA: Riverside, 1899), 73–74.

2. Holzer, *Lincoln-Douglas Debates,* 306, 316, 171, 361.

3. Ibid., 75, 264, 291, 76, 315, 304.

4. Ibid., 263, 108.

5. Ibid., 303, 311, 356.

6. Ibid., 356, 367, 359.

7. Ibid., 213, 318, 289.

8. *OS,* 31 July 1859; *Cincinnati Enquirer,* 28 August 1859; *PD,* 28 July 1859.

9. *PD,* 2 August 1859; *CML,* 6 August 1859; *OSJ,* 21 September 1859.

10. Dennison to Trumbull, 21 July 1859, quoted in Harry V. Jaffa and Robert W. Johannsen, eds., *In the Name of the People: Speeches and Writings of Lincoln and Douglas in the Ohio Campaign of 1859* (Columbus: Ohio State University Press, 1959), 17; Dennison to Giddings, 8 August 1859, Joshua R. Giddings Papers, Ohio History Center.

11. *OSJ,* 21 September 1859.

12. For the complete transcript, see *OSJ,* 8 September 1859.

13. The supreme court struck down the laws in *State* ex rel. *Attorney General v. Kennon,* 7 Ohio St. 546 (1857).

14. *CML,* 16 September 1859; *Tiffin Weekly Tribune,* 22 July 1859.

15. *OSJ,* 6 October 1859

16. *CML,* 16 September 1859; *PD,* 16 September 1859; *OS,* 14 July 1859.

17. *Mahoning Register,* 22 September 1859, in *OSJ,* 16 September 1859; *OSJ,* 19 September 1859, 24 September 1859, 10 September 1859.

18. *PD,* 16 September 1859; *OSJ,* 21 September 1859.

19. *PD,* 19 July 1859; *Cincinnati Enquirer,* 10 September 1859.

20. *PD,* 16 September 1859.

21. *OSJ,* 8 September 1859, 21 September 1859; *CML,* 16 September 1859.

22. *OSJ,* 21 September 1859, 6 October 1859; *CML,* 16 September 1859.

23. *OSJ,* 21 September 1859, 6 October 1859; Jaffa and Johanssen, *In the Name of the People,* 6.

24. *OSJ,* 21 September 1859; *CML,* 16 September 1859; *OSJ,* 6 October 1859. Ranney did not give a rationale for his view. Perhaps he believed that because the validity of an act of Congress and not of a territorial legislature was before the Court, any statements that the Court made regarding the power of territorial legislatures over slavery were obiter dicta. See Don E. Fehrenbacher, *The Dred Scott Case: Its Significance in American Law and Politics* (New York: Oxford University Press, 1978), 379.

25. *Pittsburgh Post,* 14 March 1857, in Paul Finkelman, *Dred Scott v. Sandford: A Brief History with Documents* (Boston: Bedford Books, 1997), 142; Austin Allen,

Origins of the Dred Scott Case: Jacksonian Jurisprudence and the Supreme Court, 1837–1857 (Athens: University of Georgia Press, 2006), 192–93, 216; *Nashville Patriot,* 19 September 1859 (quoting the *Louisville Courier*), 27 September 1859 (quoting the *Jackson Mississippian*).

26. *Cincinnati Enquirer,* 13 July 1859; *OSJ,* 12 September 1859, 10 September 1859; *CML,* 16 September 1859; *OSJ,* 6 October 1859.

27. Daniel J. Ryan, *History of Ohio: The Rise and Progress of an American State* (New York: Century History Co., 1912), 4:144. James Ford Rhodes wrote that "[a]s a speaker and reasoner, Ranney was much superior to Dennison," but whether Rhodes was referring to Ranney's general reputation or his performance in the debates is not clear. James Ford Rhodes, *History of the United States from the Compromise of 1850,* vol. 2, *1854–1860* (1892; reprint, New York: Macmillan, 1900), 381.

28. *PD,* 9 September 1859; *Dayton Daily Empire,* 9 September 1859; *Dayton Gazette,* quoted in *OSJ,* 10 September 1859; *PD,* 8 September 1859; *OSJ,* 21 September 1859; *PD,* 16 September 1859; Theodore J. Huesemann, "A Study of the Rhetoric in the Dennison-Ranney Debate at Tiffin, Ohio, 1859, Together with a Study of Audience Adaptation of Major Issues in the Remaining Debates, and Including the Text of the Tiffin Debate" (M.A. thesis, Ohio State University, 1949), 75 (quoting the *Newark North American* and *CML*). Huesemann provides additional newspaper comments at pages 72–79. He generally does not state the party with which each newspaper was associated, but all of the papers that gave Ranney the edge were Democratic and all of the papers that thought Dennison was superior were Republican.

29. *OS,* 3 August 1859, 13 September 1859; *PD,* 15 September 1859; *OSJ,* 21 September 1859.

30. Jaffa and Johannsen, *In the Name of the People,* 12–13, 200–30; *Mount Vernon Democratic Banner,* 27 September 1859; *OSJ,* 10 September 1859, 16 September 1859, 23 September 1859; *PD,* 13 September 1859, 8 September 1859.

31. *PD,* 10 October 1859; *OSJ,* 4 November 1859; George H. Porter, *Ohio Politics during the Civil War Period* (New York: Columbia University, 1911), map following page 26.

32. Kenneth M. Stampp, *America in 1857: A Nation on the Brink* (New York: Oxford University Press, 1990), viii; Allen C. Guelzo, *Fateful Lightning: A New History of the Civil War and Reconstruction* (New York: Oxford University Press, 2012), 119–21.

33. Guelzo, *Fateful Lightning,* 119; *CML,* 16 September 1859; *OSJ,* 21 September 1859.

Chapter 7: Constitution and Union

1. Sean Wilentz, *The Rise of American Democracy: Jefferson to Lincoln* (New York: Norton, 2005), 773; Jean H. Baker, *Affairs of Party: The Political Culture of Northern Democrats in the Mid-Nineteenth Century* (Ithaca, NY: Cornell University Press, 1983), 152.

2. H. Journal, 55th Gen. Assemb., 2d sess. 363–64 (Ohio 1863).

3. Joel H. Silbey, *A Respectable Minority: The Democratic Party in the Civil War Era, 1860–1868* (New York: Norton, 1977), 41–49; Eric J. Cardinal, "The Ohio Democracy and the Crisis of Disunion, 1860–1861," *Ohio History* 86 (Winter 1977): 33–38.

4. Robert F. Paine to Edward Bates, 11 September 1861, 26 September 1861, in Frederick S. Calhoun, ed., *Letters Received by the Attorney General, 1809–1870: Northern Law and Order*, reel 16 (Bethesda, MD: University Publications of America, 1998).

5. *Cleveland Daily Herald,* reprinted in *BC,* 24 October 1861; *CML,* 9 October 1861, 18 October 1861, 14 November 1861; *BC,* 24 October 1861; Catherine M. Tarrant, "To 'insure domestic Tranquility': Congress and the Law of Seditious Conspiracy, 1859–1861," *American Journal of Legal History* 15 (April 1971): 118–19, 121–22. For a summary of the Court and Christian cases, see Frank L. Klement, *Dark Lanterns: Secret Political Societies, Conspiracies, and Treason Trials in the Civil War* (Baton Rouge: Louisiana State University Press, 1984), 14–16. Klement erroneously calls the proceedings a trial, as did some of the newspapers. See Stephen E. Towne, *Surveillance and Spies in the Civil War: Exposing Confederate Conspiracies in America's Heartland* (Athens: Ohio University Press, 2015), 28–32, for a discussion of related cases.

6. *OSJ,* 7 July 1862.

7. *OS,* 26 July 1862, 7 July 1862; *PD,* 7 July 1862.

8. *OS,* 26 July 1862; *Lancaster Eagle,* 31 July 1862.

9. *Cincinnati Gazette* and *Cincinnati Enquirer,* quoted in *OS,* 6 July 1862; *OSJ,* 7 July 1862; *OS,* 22 July 1862, 26 July 1862.

10. *Lancaster Gazette,* 24 July 1862, 31 July 1862; *Lancaster Eagle,* 31 July 1862.

11. *Cincinnati Commercial,* 25 July 1862; George H. Porter, *Ohio Politics during the Civil War Period* (New York: Columbia University, 1911), 143; *Lancaster Eagle,* 10 July 1862, 24 July 1862.

12. *Cincinnati Enquirer,* 10 August 1862; *OSJ,* 16 August 1862. A Democratic paper quoted Ranney as saying that if "this enormous expense is made, and the blood flows, to undermine that glorious old fabric [of government], then every drop of blood that is shed is but infusing poison into the body politic; and every dollar that is contributed goes to forge the chains of yourselves and your children." *OS,* 26 July 1862.

13. R. C. Parsons, "Franklin T. Backus," *Magazine of Western History* 3 (November 1885): 11–12; S. E. Williamson, "Memorial of Rufus P. Ranney," in Ohio State Bar Association, *Proceedings of the Annual Meeting of the Association, Held at Put-in-Bay, on July 13, 14 and 15, 1892* (Akron: Werner Ptg. & Lith. Co., 1892), 188.

14. *OSJ,* 19 August 1862; *The History of Darke County, Ohio . . .* (Chicago: W. H. Beers, 1880), 524–25; *Lancaster Eagle,* 28 August 1862, 4 September 1862, 11 September 1862.

15. Joseph P. Smith, ed., *History of the Republican Party in Ohio* (Chicago: Lewis, 1898), 1:150.

16. Eugene H. Roseboom, *The Civil War Era, 1850–1873,* vol. 4 of *The History of the State of Ohio,* ed. Carl Wittke (Columbus: Ohio State Archaeological & Historical Society, 1944), 408–10.

17. Frank L. Klement, *The Limits of Dissent: Clement L. Vallandigham and the Civil War* (Lexington: University Press of Kentucky, 1970), 146–89.

18. Ibid., 22–23, 229–56; Roseboom, *Civil War Era,* 419–23.

19. *PD,* 21 February 1865.

20. Comm'rs of Knox Cnty. v. Nichols, 14 Ohio St. 260, 268–69 (1863).

21. John E. Pixton Jr., "Faith vs. Economics: The Marietta and Cincinnati Railroad, 1845–1883," *Ohio Historical Quarterly* 66 (January 1957): 1–10; Atkinson v. Marietta & Cincinnati R.R., 15 Ohio St. 21 (1864), 33–34; H. Journal, 54th Gen. Assemb., 1st sess. 288 (Ohio 1860). The protesters also claimed that the act deprived individual stockholders of their property without due process, created a new corporation with the rights but not the liabilities of the old corporation, and granted authority to political subdivisions to become stockholders in the new corporation.

22. *Atkinson,* 15 Ohio St. at 36–38; David M. Gold, *Democracy in Session: A History of the Ohio General Assembly* (Athens: Ohio University Press, 2009), 218–21.

23. Cincinnati & Spring Grove Avenue Street Ry. v. Inc. Vill. of Cumminsville, 14 Ohio St. 523 (1863).

24. Crawford v. Vill. of Delaware, 7 Ohio St. 459 (1857); Robert Brauneis, "The First Constitutional Tort: The Remedial Revolution in Nineteenth-Century State Just Compensation Law," *Vanderbilt Law Review* 52 (January 1999): 89n141.

25. *Cumminsville,* 14 Ohio St. at 544–45, 547, 550. Cases similar to *Cumminsville* arose throughout the country, with no consensus as to the right of property owners to compensation when street railroads blocked access to their lots. For a discussion and favorable comment on the Ohio doctrine, see *Hobart v. Milwaukee City R.R.,* 27 Wis. 194 (1870). On Ohio's exceptionalism, see W. H. Whittaker, "Street Railways and Their Relation to Highways," *American Law Review* 15 (June 1881): 390–404.

26. J. V. Smith, reporter, *Report of the Debates and Proceedings of the Convention for the Revision of the Constitution of the State of Ohio* (Columbus: S. Medary, 1851), 2:631–32, 2:194, 1:397.

27. Ibid., 2:247.

28. Ibid., 1:290. Edwin Jay Blandin called Ranney the "author" of the clause. Edwin Jay Blandin, "Rufus Percival Ranney," in *Great American Lawyers: The Lives and Influence of Judges and Lawyers Who Have Acquired Permanent National Reputation, and Have Developed the Jurisprudence of the United States: A History of the Legal Profession in America,* ed. William Draper Lewis (Philadelphia: John C. Winston, 1909), 6:419; Williamson, "Memorial," 191. The eminent domain provision originally appeared in the report of the committee on the legislative department. It was this report that Ranney successfully moved in the committee of the whole to amend. In the constitution as finally adopted, the eminent domain section is in the bill of rights.

29. Smith, *Report,* 2:178–79.

30. James v. Pruden, 14 Ohio St. 252, 253–54 (1863).

31. Ibid., 257–59.

32. For a discussion of the laws authorizing Ohio's soldiers to vote and their effect on elections, see Josiah Henry Benton. *Voting in the Field: A Forgotten Chapter of the Civil War* (Boston: privately printed, 1915), 73–79.

33. Lehman v. McBride, 15 Ohio St. 573, 592, 599 (1863).

34. Kenneth J. Winkle, *The Politics of Community: Migration and Politics in Antebellum Ohio* (New York: Cambridge University Press, 1988), 48–54.

35. Jeffries v. Ankeny, 11 Ohio 372 (1842); William Cheek and Aimee Lee Cheek, *John Mercer Langston and the Fight for Black Freedom, 1829–65* (Urbana: University of Illinois Press, 1989), 283; Kenneth J. Winkle, "Ohio's Informal Polling Place: Nineteenth-Century Suffrage in Theory and Practice," in *The Pursuit of Public Power: Political Culture in Ohio, 1787–1861,* ed. Jeffrey P. Brown and Andrew R. L. Cayton (Kent, OH: Kent State University Press, 1994), 180–81.

36. Winkle, *Politics,* 60–70; Act of 20 March 1841, § 2, 39 Ohio Laws 13, 14 (1841); Gold, *Democracy,* 68–70.

37. Smith, *Report,* 2:8–9.

38. Ibid., 2:10; Winkle, *Politics,* 82–83.

39. Smith, *Report,* 2:9–10; Ohio Const. art. V, § 1 (amended 1923, 1957, 1971, 1976, 1977).

40. Lehman v. McBride, 15 Ohio St. 573, 652, 616–18 (1863) (Ranney, J., dissenting).

41. Ibid., 625, 630, 629, 649.

42. Ibid., 633 (referring to Ohio Const. art. V, § 1).

43. Ibid., 628, 646–47, 650, 651–52.

44. Ibid., 632–33. Ranney also objected to the 1863 act on the grounds that it represented an attempt to exercise extraterritorial sovereignty, when in fact no state could enact a law to operate outside the state's borders. *Lehman,* 15 Ohio St. at 636–45.

45. Winkle, *Politics,* 68.

Chapter 8: Conserving Democracy

1. George H. Porter, *Ohio Politics during the Civil War Period* (New York: Columbia University, 1911), 178–79n2, 193–94; Frank L. Klement, *The Limits of Dissent: Clement L. Vallandigham and the Civil War* (Lexington: University Press of Kentucky, 1970), 246, 266–68; *OS,* 24 March 1864.

2. *Dayton Daily Empire,* 17 June 1864; *PD,* 27 August 1864; James H. Goodsell, reporter, *Official Proceedings of the Democratic National Convention, Held in 1864 at Chicago* (Chicago: Times Steam Book & Job Printing, 1864), 16, 63, 64; George Wakeman, reporter, *Official Proceedings of the National Democratic Convention, Held at New York, July 4–9, 1868* (Boston: Rockwell & Rollins, 1868), 9. Vallandigham, defeated for delegate-at-large, attended the Chicago convention as a representative of his congressional district and played a major role.

3. *CML,* 11 August 1863; *Hancock Jeffersonian* (Findlay), 4 September 1863; *Lancaster Gazette,* 29 October 1863; Frank L. Klement, *The Copperheads in the Middle West* (Chicago: University of Chicago Press, 1960), 76, 83. A more recent study uses

the terms Copperhead, Peace Democrat, and conservative Democrat interchangeably. Jennifer L. Weber, *Copperheads: The Rise and Fall of Lincoln's Opponents in the North* (New York: Oxford University Press, 2006).

4. Ranney to Cox, 14 September 1864, Cox Papers, Brown University Library; *CML,* 19 April 1864; *WRC,* 28 September 1864; *CML,* 12 September 1864; *PD,* 8 November 1864.

5. *CML,* 12 September 1864; *Urbana Union,* 26 October 1864; Klement, *Vallandigham,* 234–35.

6. *OS,* 22 February 1865; *PD,* 25 August 1865.

7. On the National Union movement and convention, see Eric L. McKitrick, *Andrew Johnson and Reconstruction* (Chicago: University of Chicago Press, 1960), 394–420; Thomas Wagstaff, "The Arm-in-Arm Convention," *Civil War History* 14 (June 1968): 101–19.

8. *PD,* 11 July 1866, 23 July 1866.

9. Ibid., 23 July 1866.

10. Reginald C. McGrane, *William Allen: A Study in Western Democracy* (Columbus: Ohio State Archaeological and Historical Society, 1925), 176–78; *Cincinnati Commercial,* 16 July 1866; Klement, *Vallandigham,* 299; *New York Times,* 16 August 1866.

11. *OS,* 15 August 1866, 16 August 1866; *New York Times,* 16 August 1866; *Proceedings of the National Union Convention, Held at Philadelphia, August 14, 1866* (Washington, DC: National Union Executive Committee, 1866), 8.

12. *PD,* 23 July 1866; Mathew Carey Jr., comp., *The Democratic Speaker's Hand-Book: Containing Every Thing Necessary for the Defense of the National Democracy in the Coming Presidential Campaign, and for the Assault of the Radical Enemies of the Country and Its Constitution* (Cincinnati: Miami Printing & Publishing Co., 1868), 177.

13. *OS,* 2 August 1867, 7 August 1867, 17 August 1867, 6 September 1867.

14. *OS,* 9 August 1867; Rufus P. Ranney, *Speech of Hon. Rufus P. Ranney, Delivered at Mansfield, Ohio, Aug. 6, 1867* (Columbus: The Crisis, 1867).

15. Jack Maskell, *Expulsion, Censure, Reprimand, and Fine: Legislative Discipline in the House of Representatives* (Washington, DC: Congressional Research Service, 2016), http://www.fas.org/sgp/crs/misc/RL31382.pdf, 4n20; United States Senate, "Expulsion and Censure," http://www.senate.gov/artandhistory/history/common/briefing/Expulsion_Censure.htm (accessed 28 July 2013).

16. Senator Charles Sumner, who in March 1867 introduced a bill "guarantying a republican form of government by securing the elective franchise to colored citizens," wrote that "[n]othing can be more certain than that Kentucky, at this time, is without a republican form of government." S. Journal, 40th Cong., 1st sess. 96 (1867); *Cincinnati Commercial,* 31 May 1867 (quoting a letter to General James S. Brisbin). With regard to Delaware and Maryland, see John A. Munroe, *History of Delaware,* 5th ed. (Newark: University of Delaware Press, 2006), 148; William Starr Myers, *The Self-Reconstruction of Maryland, 1864–1867* (Baltimore: Johns Hopkins University Press, 1909), 127–30. For the resolutions calling for the inquiries, see H. Journal, 40th Cong., 1st sess. 211–12, 244 (1867).

17. Ben H. Severance, *Tennessee's Radical Army: The State Guard and Its Role in Reconstruction, 1867–1869* (Knoxville: University of Tennessee Press, 2005), 61–144.

18. *Ex parte* Milligan, 71 U.S. 2 (1866); Charles Warren, *The Supreme Court in United States History* (Boston: Little, Brown, 1922), 3:149–69.

19. *OS,* 7 October 1867.

20. David M. Gold, *Democracy in Session: A History of the Ohio General Assembly* (Athens: Ohio University Press, 2009), 202.

21. *CML,* 30 October 1860, 24 January 1863; *Vinton Record* (McArthur), 22 August 1867; J. V. Smith, reporter, *Report of the Debates and Proceedings of the Convention for the Revision of the Constitution of the State of Ohio* (Columbus: S. Medary, 1851), 2:597–605.

22. Ranney to George W. Johnson, 25 August 1860, in *Iron Valley Express* (Jackson Court House), reprinted in *McArthur Democrat,* 4 October 1860.

23. John P. Green, *Fact Stranger than Fiction: Seventy-Five Years of a Busy Life, with Reminiscences of Many Great and Good Men and Women* (Cleveland: Riehl, 1920), 161–62.

24. *Urbana Union,* 15 January 1868, 7 July 1869; Samuel P. Orth, *A History of Cleveland, Ohio* (Chicago: S. J. Clarke, 1910), 1:285; Office of the Clerk, U.S. House of Representatives, *Biographical Directory of the United States Congress, 1774–Present,* http://bioguide.congress.gov, s.v. "Rice, Americus Vespucius"; *OS,* 8 July 1869; *OS,* 12 August 1869.

25. James F. Faran to Allen G. Thurman, 26 May 1876, Allen G. Thurman Papers, Ohio History Center; *OSJ,* 27 September 1871; *Cincinnati Commoner,* reprinted in *BC,* 15 July 1869.

Chapter 9: Conservative Reform in the Gilded Age

1. Robert H. Wiebe, *The Search for Order, 1877–1920* (New York: Hill & Wang, 1967), 4–5; Eric J. Cardinal, "The Ohio Democracy and the Crisis of Disunion, 1860–1861," *Ohio History* 86 (Winter 1977): 40, 20.

2. Clinton Rossiter, *Conservatism in America: The Thankless Persuasion,* 2nd ed., rev. (New York: Vintage, 1962), 130; Charles Ledyard Norton, *Political Americanisms: A Glossary of Terms and Phrases Current at Different Periods in American Politics* (New York: Longmans, Green, 1890), 20–21; Jennifer Coates, "Bourbons," in *Encyclopedia of the Reconstruction Era,* ed. Richard Zuczek (Westport, CT: Greenwood, 2006), 1:98–99; Horace Samuel Merrill, *Bourbon Democracy of the Middle West, 1865–1896* (Baton Rouge: Louisiana State University Press, 1953), vii–viii; Morton Keller, *America's Three Regimes: A New Political History* (New York: Oxford University Press, 2007), 149.

3. J. G. Carlisle, "The Recent Election," *North American Review* 151 (December 1890): 642, 649; S. S. Cox, "Lessons of the New York City Election: III. The Democratic View," *North American Review* 143 (December 1886): 577, 582.

4. See, for example, James A. Henretta, "The Strange Birth of Liberal America: Michael Hoffman and the New York Constitution of 1846," *New York History* 77 (April 1996): 164. In *The Anti-Rent Era in New York Law and Politics, 1839–1865* (Chapel

Hill: University of North Carolina Press, 2001), Charles W. McCurdy explains how the limited-government constitutionalism of radical Democrats, intended to protect the majority from the abuse of governmental power for the benefit of the privileged few, kept radicals from aiding a popular movement against feudal privilege.

5. Alan Sykes, *The Rise and Fall of British Liberalism, 1776–1988* (London: Longman, 1997), 73; Thomas S. Barclay, *The Liberal Republican Movement in Missouri, 1865–1870* (Columbia: State Historical Society of Missouri, 1926), 162, 247–48, 248n89. In Maine in 1854 the supporters of a Democratic Party faction opposed to the state's stringent prohibition law called themselves Liberals or Liberal Democrats and ran their own candidates in that year's elections. Neal Dow, *The Reminiscences of Neal Dow: Recollections of Eighty Years* (Portland, ME: Evening Express, 1898), 503–6; Richard R. Wescott, *New Men, New Issues: The Formation of the Republican Party in Maine* (Portland: Maine Historical Society, 1986), 116, 121.

6. Andrew L. Slap, *The Doom of Reconstruction: The Liberal Republicans in the Civil War Era* (New York: Fordham University Press, 2006), 142.

7. Ibid, xx. The former Democrats were Jacob Brinkerhoff, Roeliff Brinkerhoff, Murat Halstead, George Hoadly, Donn Piatt, and John Stallo. The lone ex-Whig was Jacob D. Cox.

8. *PD,* 11 September 1871, 15 September 1871, 16 September 1871, 28 September 1871, 11 October 1871, 13 October 1871; *Cleveland Daily Leader,* 11 September 1871, 18 September 1871, 25 September 1871, 4 October 1871; *WRC,* 20 September 1871.

9. Earle Dudley Ross, *The Liberal Republican Movement* (New York: Henry Holt, 1919), 70–76, 104; Slap, *Doom of Reconstruction,* 131; *Cincinnati Commercial,* 3 May 1872. The correspondent for the *Ohio State Journal* reported that four hundred to five hundred delegates eventually showed up on the first day of the convention but that on the second day, with public attention focused on the Liberal Republican convention, attendance dropped to perhaps one hundred. *OSJ,* 3 May 1872.

10. *Cincinnati Commercial,* 3 May 1872. Ranney had gone south during the winter in an attempt to improve his health. *WRC,* 27 December 1871.

11. Ross, *Liberal Republican Movement,* 93–96, 104–5; J. M. H. Frederick, comp., *National Party Platforms of the United States, Presidential Candidates, Electoral and Popular Votes* (Akron: Werner, 1896), 39–40; *PD,* 6 May 1872.

12. *PD,* 6 May 1872.

13. Roeliff Brinkerhoff, *Recollections of a Lifetime* (Cincinnati: Robert Clarke, 1900), 218–19; *PD,* 4 May 1872; Ross, *Liberal Republican Movement,* 105.

14. *Cincinnati Commercial,* 28 June 1872, 1 July 1872.

15. Ibid., 16 November 18; *SCD,* 3 July 1873; Ross, *Liberal Republican Movement,* 200.

16. Reginald C. McGrane, *William Allen: A Study in Western Democracy* (Columbus: Ohio State Archaeological and Historical Society, 1925), 194–96; *Cincinnati Commercial,* 31 July 1873; *OSJ,* 7 August 1873.

17. *OSJ,* 6 August 1873; *Cincinnati Commercial,* 7 August 1873.

18. *Cincinnati Commercial,* 17 June 1875, 18 June 1875.

19. Ward M. McAfee, *Religion, Race, and Reconstruction: The Public School in the Politics of the 1870s* (Albany: State University of New York Press, 1998), 177–81;

Cincinnati Gazette, reprinted in *BC*, 17 June 1875; Ohio Const. art. VI, § 2 ("no religious or other sect or sects shall ever have any exclusive right to, or control of, any part of the school funds of this State"). Republican newspapers charged Ranney with hypocrisy on the school funding issue, noting that he had voted against the report of the committee on education at the 1850–51 constitutional convention. *BC*, 26 August 1875 (quoting the *Dayton Journal*), 16 September 1875. Ranney did vote against the committee's second report, but probably for the same reason that he objected to the committee's initial report: that it was too vague. J. V. Smith, reporter, *Report of the Debates and Proceedings of the Convention for the Revision of the Constitution of the State of Ohio* (Columbus: S. Medary, 1851), 2:16, 711.

20. Forrest William Clonts, "The Political Campaign of 1875 in Ohio," *Ohio Archaeological and Historical Quarterly* 31 (January 1922): 69–72. A Republican paper observed that Ranney and some other leading Democrats "declare themselves uncompromisingly opposed to the financial plank in the Democratic platform." *BC*, 2 September 1875.

21. *PD*, 18 June 1875; *SCD*, 24 June 1875; *OSJ*, 18 June 1875; *Cincinnati Commercial*, 18 June 1875, 19 June 1875.

22. *SCD*, 25 May 1875; *New York Times*, 23 June 1876; *OSJ*, 27 June 1876, 29 June 1876; *PD*, 27 June 1876.

23. *PD*, 12 May 1876, 22 June 1876, 26 August 1876, 2 September 1876.

24. Thomas S. Mach, *"Gentleman George" Hunt Pendleton: Party Politics and Ideological Identity in Nineteenth-Century America* (Kent, OH: Kent State University Press, 2007), 161–62.

25. *PD*, 5 October 1880, 23 July 1880. Democratic candidate Samuel J. Tilden appeared to have won both the popular and electoral votes in the 1876 presidential election, but fraud and violence in three southern states plus a dispute over the qualifications of an elector in Oregon led to the establishment of a special federal electoral commission to determine the outcomes in those states. The commission, with an 8–7 Republican majority, gave the electoral victory to Republican candidate Rutherford B. Hayes. During the controversy, in a letter that was published as a pamphlet, Ranney refuted Republican arguments that Congress could not question the election certificates it received from state returning boards and that the president of the U.S. Senate, not Congress as a whole (including the Democrat-majority House), had the duty to count the votes of presidential electors. Ranney denounced the fraud committed by the Republican-controlled returning boards in the three southern states, but he ignored the intimidation of Republican voters by Democrats in those states. R. P. Ranney, *The Proper Method of Counting the Electoral Vote* (New York: D. Appleton, 1877).

26. *PD*, 5 October 1880; *CML*, 5 October 1880.

27. *CML*, 29 September 1880.

Chapter 10: Corporate Lawyer

1. Act of 10 March 1851, 49 Ohio Laws 444 (1851). The act creating the Franklin & Warren lists Rufus L. Ranney of Trumbull County as an incorporator. As

reproduced in the annual report of the Ohio railroad commissioner for 1870, the act says Rufus P. Ranney. George B. Wright, *Annual Report of the Commissioner of Railroads and Telegraphs, for the Year 1870,* vol. 1 (Columbus: Nevins & Myers, 1870), 560.

2. Giesy v. Cincinnati, Wilmington & Zanesville R.R., 4 Ohio St. 308, 324–25 (1854); Bureau of Railway Economics, *Railway Economics: A Collective Catalogue of Books in Fourteen American Libraries* (Chicago: University of Chicago Press, 1912), 201; Henry V. Poor, *Manual of the Railroads of the United States, for 1868–69. . . .* (New York: H. V. & H. W. Poor, 1868), 235; S. Journal, 57th Gen. Assemb., app. 180 (Ohio 1867) (Reemelin indicating in a letter to a special committee, dated December 21, 1866, that he was a director of the Cincinnati & Zanesville and president of the Miami Coal Company); Charles Reemelin, *Treatise on Politics As a Science* (Cincinnati: Robert Clarke, 1875), 29.

3. Edward Hungerford, *Men of Erie: A Story of Human Effort* (New York: Random House, 1946), 182, 180; Wright, *Annual Report,* 1:548, 554; Allan Nevins, *Study in Power: John D. Rockefeller, Industrialist and Philanthropist* (New York: Charles Scribner's Sons, 1953), 1:22–24, 37–38, 83; P. Barry, *Over the Atlantic and Great Western Railway* (London: Sampson Low, Son, & Marston, 1866), 139–40.

4. *OS,* 22 February 1865; *Memorial Record of the County of Cuyahoga and City of Cleveland, Ohio* (Chicago: Lewis, 1894), 218–24; *WRC,* 25 July 1855.

5. *Memorial Record,* 222; Wright, *Annual Report,* 1:554–55; *Bradshaw's Railway Manual, Shareholders' Guide, and Official Directory for 1881* (London: W. J. Adams & Sons, 1881), 507; *History of Trumbull and Mahoning Counties, with Illustrations and Biographical Sketches* (Cleveland: H. Z. Williams & Bro., 1882), 1:195.

6. *Forty-fourth Annual Report of the President and Directors to the Stockholders of the Cleveland & Pittsburgh Railroad Company* (Cleveland: J. B. Savage, 1892), 13–14; *Bradshaw's Railway Manual,* 507, 511; McHenry v. New York, P. & O. R.R., 25 F. 65 (Cir. Ct. W.D. Pa. 1885); McHenry v. New York, P. & O. R.R., 25 F. 114 (Cir. Ct. W.D. Pa. 1885); United States Rolling Stock Co. v. Atl. & Great W. R.R., 34 Ohio St. 450 (1878); Matter of United States Rolling Stock Co., 55 How. Pr. 286 (N.Y. Sup. Ct. 1878); State v. Vanderbilt, 37 Ohio St. 590 (1882); *Ohio Law Journal* 2 (23 February 1882): 363; *BC,* 2 September 1886.

7. J. H. Kennedy, "The Bar of Ohio," pt. 1, "Henry Clay Ranney," *Magazine of Western History* 4 (October 1886): 823; Ohio State Bar Association, *Proceedings of the Thirty-Fifth Annual Session of the Association Held at Cedar Point, Ohio, July, 7, 8, and 9, 1914* (Cleveland: Evangelical Press, 1914), 182; Samuel P. Orth, *A History of Cleveland, Ohio* (Chicago: S. J. Clarke, 1910), 2:574. At some point former judge Henry McKinney teamed up with the Ranneys. Accounts vary as to the years in which the different partners joined and left the firm.

8. W. R. Rose, "Noted Criminal and Other Cases," in *The Bench and Bar of Cleveland,* ed. James Harrison Kennedy and Wilson M. Day (Cleveland: Cleveland Printing & Publishing Co., 1889), 103; *Ashtabula Weekly Telegraph,* 24 December 1870; J. V. Smith, reporter, *Report of the Debates and Proceedings of the Convention for the Revision of the Constitution of the State of Ohio* (Columbus: S. Medary, 1851),

1:716–17. The extent of Ranney's participation in the proceedings over the decade-long life of the case is unknown, but he did make the closing argument at the end of the second, seventeen-day trial. *PD,* 17 December 1870.

9. *New York Times,* 29 May 1884; Butzman v. Whitbeck, 42 Ohio St. 223 (1884). Ranney and other prominent attorneys had vetted the Scott Law before it passed and pronounced it constitutional, and the Ohio Supreme Court initially upheld it. *Pittsburgh Commercial Gazette,* 31 October 1884; State *ex rel.* v. Frame, 39 Ohio St. 399 (1883). However, the court overruled that decision in *Butzman.* For a discussion as to whether the Scott Law was a true antiliquor bill or a "brewers' bill," see [Walter W. Spooner], ed., *The Cyclopædia of Temperance and Prohibition: A Reference Book of Facts, Statistics, and General Information on All Phases of the Drink Question, the Temperance Movement and the Prohibition Agitation* (New York: Funk & Wagnalls, 1891), 106–7.

10. See, for example, Bowen v. Bowen, 34 Ohio St. 164 (1877) (right of a widow to take under both an antenuptial agreement and a will); Hickock v. Hine, 23 Ohio St. 523 (1872) (navigable rivers as public highways).

11. Comm'rs of Geauga Cnty. v. Ranney, 13 Ohio St. 388 (1862); J. O. Converse et al., "Chardon," in *Pioneer and General History of Geauga County, with Sketches of Some of the Pioneers and Prominent Men* (n.p.: Historical Society of Geauga County, 1880), 308; Rose, "Noted Cases," 101–2; John Stark Bellamy II, *Women Behaving Badly: True Tales of Cleveland's Most Ferocious Female Killers* (Cleveland: Gray & Co., 2005), 175; *In re* Victor, 31 Ohio St. 206 (1877).

12. *SCD,* 4 July 1878, 25 July 1878, 1 August 1878, 12 September 1878, 26 September 1878, 8 May 1879. Fessler was sentenced to prison but pardoned in 1881. Ibid., 27 October 1881.

13. Edwin Jay Blandin, "Rufus Percival Ranney," in *Great American Lawyers: The Lives and Influence of Judges and Lawyers Who Have Acquired Permanent National Reputation, and Have Developed the Jurisprudence of the United States: A History of the Legal Profession in America,* ed. William Draper Lewis (Philadelphia: John C. Winston, 1909), 6:413–14; Harvey Rice, *Sketches of Western Life* (Boston: Lee & Shepard, 1887), 126.

14. Nevins, *Rockefeller,* 1:314; *Painesville Telegraph,* 26 March 1885; *New-York Tribune,* 21 March 1885. While on a river excursion in Florida with Ranney and two other prominent Ohioans, Kerr fell overboard and drowned. Ranney had the melancholy task of telegraphing the circumstances of Kerr's death. *PD,* 23 March 1885.

15. Phillip I. Blumberg, "Limited Liability and Corporate Groups," *Journal of Corporation Law* 11 (Summer 1986): 605–7. In *Railway Company v. Iron Company,* 46 Ohio St. 44 (1888), the Ohio Supreme Court expressly adopted the general American rule that one corporation could not purchase the stock of another. The court based its holding on the principle that corporations have only those powers granted or implied by the statutes under which they were organized. In support of that principle, the court cited Ranney's opinion in *Straus v. Eagle Insurance Company,* 5 Ohio St. 59 (1855).

16. Alfred D. Chandler Jr., *The Visible Hand: The Managerial Revolution in American Business* (Cambridge, MA: Harvard University Press, 1977), 316–19; Nevins, *Rockefeller,* 1:382–84.

17. Nevins, *Rockefeller,* 1:382–84.

18. Taylor v. Rockefeller, 23 F. Cas. 792 (Cir. Ct. W.D. Pa. 1878). Nevins discusses Rockefeller's legal challenges in Pennsylvania in *Rockefeller,* 1:304–22, where he states that Rockefeller wanted Ranney to "take complete charge" of pending criminal charges and Rockefeller's possible extradition (1:314).

19. Nevins, *Rockefeller,* 1:385. The 1879 trust agreement, executed on April 8, is reproduced in William S. Stevens, ed., *Industrial Combinations and Trusts* (New York: Macmillan, 1922), 14–17.

20. Alfred S. Eichner, *The Emergence of Oligopoly: Sugar Refining as a Case Study* (Baltimore: Johns Hopkins University Press, 1969), 16. In *State* ex rel. *Attorney General v. Standard Oil Company,* 49 Ohio St. 137 (1892), the Ohio Supreme Court found the Standard Oil trust to be an illegal monopoly. But by that time, under Dodd's trust scheme, separate corporations had been set up in different states, with the stock still being held in trust, and New Jersey had passed a law authorizing corporations to hold stock in other corporations and to own property in other states. After the Ohio decision, Standard Oil of New Jersey became "the dominant corporation in the Standard Oil empire." John Steele Gordon, "The Other Half of Standard Oil," *The American,* 29 October 2008, http://www.aei.org/publication/the-other-half-of-standard-oil/.

21. Nevins, *Rockefeller,* 1:384–87 (quotation at 1:385).

22. "Majority and Minority Reports of the Committee Appointed to Investigate the Cornering of Grain and Other Articles," Senate doc. no. 45, in *Documents of the Senate of the State of New York: One Hundred and Sixth Session, 1883,* vol. 5 (Albany: Weed, Parsons, 1883), 635–63 (testimony of Henry M. Flagler, 27 December 1882); Henry R. Seager and Charles A. Gulick Jr., *Trust and Corporation Problems* (New York: Harper & Bros., 1929), 50n1. Ida Tarbell knew nothing about the 1879 trust when she published her history of Standard Oil in 1904. Ida M. Tarbell, *The History of the Standard Oil Company* (New York: McClure, Phillips, 1904), 2:135. The original trust agreement was published in the documents of the antitrust suit. See *In the Circuit Court of the United States for the Eastern Division of the Eastern Judicial District of Missouri: United States of America, Petitioner, v. Standard Oil Company of New Jersey et al., Defendants,* vol. 19, *Defendants' Exhibits* (Washington, DC: Government Printing Office, 1909), 618–20.

23. Nevins does not document this characterization of Ranney, but his papers include summaries and copies of correspondence indicating the high regard in which Rockefeller and other Standard Oil attorneys held Ranney, some difficulty getting Ranney to give Standard Oil his "earnest attention," Ranney's illness in 1880, and Ranney's reluctance to go east on Standard Oil business (but not an aversion to travel in general). George H. Vilas to Rockefeller, 3 April 1878; Rockefeller and Flagler to Ranney, 8 April 1878, Letterbook 4, no. 93 (summary); Oliver H. Payne to Rockefeller, 23 March 1881, Letterfile 10, no. 112 (summary); Payne to Rockefeller,

26 April 1880, Letterfile 8, no. 30 (summary); Payne [?] to Rockefeller, 14 March 1879; all in Series 3, Box 126, Allan Nevins Papers, Rare Book and Manuscript Library, Columbia University Library. I am grateful to Anya Berg for researching the Nevins Papers on my behalf.

24. Nevins, *Rockefeller,* 1:389–93. The Standard Oil trust became the model for other industrial trusts in the 1880s. The trusts succumbed to legal challenges in the late 1880s and early 1890s, but the term "trust" caught on and came to be applied to all kinds of industrial combinations.

25. Nevins, *Rockefeller,* 1:439n7; Samuel C. T. Dodd, *Memoirs of S. C. T. Dodd Written for His Children and Friends, 1837–1907* (New York: Robert Grier Cooke, 1907), 30.

26. James H. Goodsell, reporter, *Official Proceedings of the Democratic National Convention, Held in 1864 at Chicago* (Chicago: Times Steam Book & Job Printing, 1864), 16, 63, 64; *BC,* 7 September 1876; *WRC,* 27 December 1871; Frederick T. Wallace, *Men and Events of Half a Century* (Cleveland: Evangelical Association, 1882), 3, 51; Payne to Rockefeller, 23 March 1881 (summary), Series 3, Box 126, Letterfile 10, no. 112, Nevins Papers; Commonwealth v. Standard Oil Co., 101 Pa. 119 (1882).

27. Gregory Mark, "On Limited Liability: A Speculative Essay on Evolution and Justification," in *Transformations in American Legal History: Essays in Honor of Professor Morton J. Horwitz,* ed. Daniel W. Hamilton and Alfred L. Brophy (Cambridge, MA: Harvard Law School, 2009), 181.

28. *Debates of the Convention to Amend the Constitution of Pennsylvania: Convened at Harrisburg, November 12, 1872; Adjourned, November 27, to Meet at Philadelphia, January 7, 1873* (Harrisburg, PA: Benjamin Singerly, 1873), 3:522–23, 4:581–82, 6:22–23, 7:765–66, 8:261–62.

29. Paul Kens, "*Lochner v. New York:* Tradition or Change in Constitutional Law?" *New York University Journal of Law and Liberty* 1 (2005): 418; Vernon L. Parrington, *The Beginnings of Critical Realism in America, 1860–1920,* vol. 3 of *Main Currents in American Thought* (New York: Harcourt, Brace & World, 1930), 118; Chester McArthur Destler, *American Radicalism, 1865–1901: Essays and Documents* (1946; reprint, New York: Octagon, 1963), 222; Michael Kazin, *The Populist Persuasion: An American History,* rev. ed. (Ithaca, NY: Cornell University Press, 1998), 32; Paul Kens, *Justice Stephen Field: Shaping Liberty from the Gold Rush to the Gilded Age* (Lawrence: University Press of Kansas, 1997), 267, 270–71.

30. Clinton Rossiter coined the term "laissez-faire conservatism" as a label for what he saw as the pseudo-Jeffersonian philosophy of pro-business conservatives in the late nineteenth century. Clinton Rossiter, *Conservatism in America: The Thankless Persuasion,* 2nd ed., rev. (New York: Vintage, 1962), 131. Bray Hammond linked Jacksonian and postbellum limited-government thought unflatteringly, calling "the age of Jackson a festival of *laisser faire* prelusive to the age of Grant and the robber barons." *Banks and Politics in America from the Revolution to the Civil War* (Princeton, NJ: Princeton University Press, 1957), 328. That the "blunt pragmatism of the business community" really represented conservatism is a proposition that even some

scholars who put it forth as such, including Rossiter, accept only grudgingly. See, for example, Rossiter, *Conservatism,* 130–31; John G. Sproat, *"The Best Men": Liberal Reformers in the Gilded Age* (New York: Oxford University Press, 1968), 5.

31. William Leggett, *A Collection of the Political Writings of William Leggett,* ed. Theodore Sedgwick Jr. (New York: Taylor & Dodd, 1840), 1:259; H. Fowler, reporter, *Report of the Debates and Proceedings of the Convention for the Revision of the Constitution of the State of Indiana* (Indianapolis: A. H. Brown, 1850), 1:645–46. On the prevalence of small-government, laissez-faire ideas at the state constitutional conventions of the mid-nineteenth century, see David M. Gold, *The Great Tea Party in the Old Northwest: State Constitutional Conventions, 1847–1851* (New Orleans: Quid Pro, 2015).

32. Smith, *Report,* 1:248.

33. Michael Les Benedict, "Laissez-Faire and Liberty: A Re-Evaluation of the Meaning and Origins of Laissez-Faire Constitutionalism," *Law and History Review* 3 (Fall 1985): 293–331.

34. Hall v. State, 20 Ohio 7, 15 (1851).

35. Ibid., 9–11, 15, 17. Ranney also showed a concern for small businessmen when he insisted that the credits required to be taxed under the constitution's uniform rule of taxation were the net amount of a taxpayer's credits, not the gross amount. The effect of the court's decision to the contrary, he thought, was to shift the burden of taxation from banks and from individuals without debts to individuals less able to afford to pay, especially entrepreneurs who depended on their own credit and extended credit to their customers. Exchange Bank of Columbus v. Hines, 3 Ohio St. 1, 66 (1853) (Ranney, J., dissenting). The supreme court eventually vindicated Ranney's position, although not without an ironic twist along the way. In *Payne v. Watterson,* 37 Ohio St. 121 (1881), Ranney represented Henry B. Payne, who, in listing his property for taxation, had tried to deduct his indebtedness of nearly $31,000 from the value of his corporate bonds. At the time Payne harbored realistic presidential aspirations and was hardly a small businessman. In 1884 the General Assembly would send him to the U.S. Senate amid allegations that Standard Oil and its treasurer, Payne's son, had purchased his election. The supreme court ruled against Payne, but, on the question of deducting debts from credits, conceded that the General Assembly had "not acquiesced" in the *Hines* decision. In fact the holding had become a dead letter as tax collectors gave up trying to enforce the statute. Through a combination of executive inaction, legislative action, and judicial acquiescence, the majority holding in *Hines* was "effectively, though not expressly, overruled." Hess v. Columbus Life Ins. Co., 116 Ohio St. 416, 423 (1927).

36. Sidney Fine, *Laissez Faire and the General-Welfare State: A Study of Conflict in American Thought, 1865–1901* (Ann Arbor: University of Michigan Press, 1956), 134 (quoting Cooley's opinion in *People* ex rel. *Detroit & Howell R.R. v. Township Bd. of Salem,* 20 Mich. 452 [1870]); Benjamin R. Twiss, *Lawyers and the Constitution: How Laissez Faire Came to the Supreme Court* (Princeton, NJ: Princeton University Press, 1942), 18; Alan Jones, "Thomas M. Cooley and 'Laissez-Faire Constitutionalism': A Reconsideration," *Journal of American History* 53 (March 1967): 751–71.

37. *In re* Jacobs, 98 N.Y. 98 (1885); Twiss, *Lawyers,* 99–100; Clyde E. Jacobs, *Law Writers and the Courts: The Influence of Thomas M. Cooley, Christopher G. Tiedeman, and John F. Dillon upon American Constitutional Law* (1954; reprint, New York: Da Capo, 1973), 51; William E. Forbath, *Law and the Shaping of the American Labor Movement* (Cambridge, MA: Harvard University Press, 1991), 39; William M. Wiecek, *The Lost World of Classical Legal Thought: Law and Ideology in America, 1886–1937* (New York: Oxford University Press, 1998), 127; Fine, *Laissez Faire,* 136.

38. Eileen Boris, *Home to Work: Motherhood and the Politics of Industrial Homework in the United States* (New York: Cambridge University Press, 1994), 42; Felice Batlan, "A Reevaluation of the New York Court of Appeals: The Home, the Market, and Labor, 1885–1905," *Law and Social Inquiry* 27 (Summer 2002): 516; *In re* Jacobs, 98 N.Y. at 114. Boris and Batlan expand the context of the New York statute and *Jacobs* beyond the realm of law. As Batlan writes, it is "impossible and indeed simplistic to argue that the legislation was simply about protecting the worker and that the court's decision to strike down the legislation was merely an exercise in laissez-faire judicial activism. Rather, the legislation was about a complex interplay among unions, child labor, female labor, homework, factory work, the home, and the male breadwinner." "Reevaluation," 518. Forbath notes that the unions "championed the law to halt the transformation of their craft into a sweated trade." *American Labor Movement,* 41n17. The statement is no doubt true, but it is also consistent with the goal of driving homeworkers out of independent business and into factories—if they could find jobs. See James W. Ely Jr., "'To Pursue any Lawful Trade or Avocation': The Evolution of Unenumerated Economic Rights in the Nineteenth Century," *University of Pennsylvania Journal of Constitutional Law* 8 (September 2006): 938–43.

39. Forbath, *American Labor Movement,* 40; *Herkimer County Democrat,* 16 March 1848; Robert Earl, "Excessive Legislation," *Albany Law Journal* 57 (22 January 1898): 58. Forbath suggests that *Jacobs* was rooted in the free-labor ideology that rose together with the Republican Party. *American Labor Movement,* 40. Earl was a lifelong Democrat who grew up in the Age of Jackson and as a young newspaper publisher in 1848–50 gave no hint of devotion to free labor. In fact, while he opposed slavery, he denounced Democrats who bolted for the Free Soilers, whose free-labor ideas the Republicans would, in a few years, absorb. A college classmate who published a rival paper lamented that his old friend, in taking over "a somewhat notorious journal of the conservative school," had gone over to the dark side. Excerpt from *Jefferson County Democrat,* reprinted in *Herkimer County Democrat,* 30 March 1848. But Earl's "conservatism" consisted chiefly of his opposition to the Barnburner wing of the New York Democratic Party, which had split with the regular Democrats over the extension of slavery and allied itself with the Free Soil movement. See Robert Earl, "Gleanings from the Mohawk Courier and the Herkimer Democrat, and Some Interesting Facts of Local as Well as of General Interest, 1846–1850," in *Papers Read before the Herkimer County Historical Society during the Years 1899, 1900, 1901, to July 1, 1902,* vol. 2, comp. Arthur T. Smith (Herkimer, NY: Citizen, 1902), 424. Earl regarded the Barnburners as traitors who would accomplish nothing but

the triumph of the Whigs. From a statement of principles in Earl's first issue of the *Democrat* and his subsequent endorsement of Democratic principles assembled from the national platforms of 1840, 1844, and 1848, Earl seems to have been a standard-issue, strict-constructionist, small-government Jacksonian. *Herkimer County Democrat,* 16 March 1848, 22 June 1848, 6 September 1848.

Chapter 11: Elder Statesman

1. Eugene F. Provenzo Jr., *Culture as Curriculum: Education and the International Expositions (1876–1904)* (New York: Peter Lang, 2012), 3–4.

2. Ohio State Board of Agriculture, *Thirtieth Annual Report of the Ohio State Board of Agriculture, with an Abstract of the Proceedings of the County Agricultural Societies, to the General Assembly of Ohio, for the Year 1875* (Columbus: Nevins & Myers, 1876), 114–16.

3. Ohio State Board of Centennial Managers, *Final Report of the Ohio State Board of Centennial Managers to the General Assembly of the State of Ohio* (Columbus: Nevins & Meyers, 1877), 11–21.

4. Ibid., 5; Act of 28 February 1843, 41 Ohio Laws (local) 91 (1843); Act of 23 March 1850, 48 Ohio Laws (local) 640 (1850); Joseph G. Butler Jr., *History of Youngstown and the Mahoning Valley, Ohio* (Chicago: American Historical Society, 1921), 1:442–43; C. H. Cramer, *Case Institute of Technology: A Centennial History, 1880–1980* (Cleveland: Case Western Reserve University, 1980), 10. Ranney was also a life member of the Western Reserve and Northern Ohio Historical Society and chaired its finance committee. Charles Whittlesey, "Sixth Annual Meeting—Report of the President," Tract 21 (Cleveland: Western Reserve and Northern Ohio Historical Society, May 1874), 3; "Societies and Their Proceedings," *New-England Historical and Genealogical Register* 41 (October 1887): 418; "Editorial Notes," *Magazine of Western History* 6 (September 1887): 512.

5. Samuel P. Orth, *A History of Cleveland, Ohio* (Chicago: S. J. Clarke, 1910), 1:570–76; Cramer, *Case Institute,* 9–10, 268; C. H. Cramer, *Case Western Reserve University: A History, 1826–1976* (Boston: Little, Brown, 1976), 5–9, 202–3; Christian Smith, "Introduction: Rethinking the Secularization of American Public Life," in *The Secular Revolution: Power, Interests, and Conflict in the Secularization of American Public Life,* ed. Christian Smith (Berkeley: University of California Press, 2003), 74–78.

6. Cramer, *Case Institute,* 19–20; Cramer, *Case Western Reserve,* 377–78n.

7. Ohio State Bar Association, *Proceedings of Adjourned Meeting of the Association, Held at the City of Columbus on the 28th and 29th of December, 1880, and of the Annual Meeting of the Association held at the City of Toledo, on the 20th and 21st days of July, 1881* (Columbus: Lord & Bowman, 1881), 90–93.

8. Gerard W. Gawalt, *The Promise of Power: The Emergence of the Legal Profession in Massachusetts, 1760–1840* (Westport, CT: Greenwood, 1979), 179–84; Maxwell Bloomfield, "William Sampson and the Codifiers: The Roots of American Legal Reform, 1820–1830," *American Journal of Legal History* 11 (July 1967): 234–52;

Frederick Robinson, *An Oration Delivered before the Trades Union of Boston and Vicinity, on Fort Hill, Boston, on the Fifty-eighth Anniversary of American Independence* (Boston: Charles Douglas, 1834), 12–17.

9. J. V. Smith, reporter, *Report of the Debates and Proceedings of the Convention for the Revision of the Constitution of the State of Ohio* (Columbus: S. Medary, 1851), 1:557.

10. In 1880 two years of apprenticeship, a certificate of good character, and an examination by two judges still sufficed for admission to the bar, but by then the aspiring attorney could substitute graduation from a law school or the law department of a college for the apprenticeship. The graduate still had to undergo an examination by a committee of lawyers appointed by the local district court. Ohio Rev. Stat. §§ 558–61 (1880).

11. Lawrence M. Friedman, *A History of American Law,* 3rd ed. (New York: Simon & Schuster, 2005), 495–96.

12. William R. Van Aken, *Buckeye Barristers: A Centennial History of the Ohio State Bar Association* (Columbus: Ohio State Bar Association, 1980), 4; C. W. Heaton, "The Cleveland Bar Association," in *The Bench and Bar of Cleveland,* ed. James Harrison Kennedy and Wilson M. Day (Cleveland: Cleveland Printing & Publishing Co., 1889), 77.

13. American Bar Association, *Report of the Second Annual Meeting of the American Bar Association Held at Saratoga Springs, New York, August 20th and 21st, 1879* (Philadelphia: E. C. Markley & Son, 1879), 8; Jerold S. Auerbach, *Unequal Justice: Lawyers and Social Change in Modern America* (New York: Oxford University Press, 1976), 63–64; James Willard Hurst, *The Growth of American Law: The Law Makers* (Boston: Little, Brown, 1950), 287–88; "Annual Meeting of the State Bar Association of Ohio," *Weekly Cincinnati Law Bulletin* 6 (1 August 1881), 429, 433, 438; Frederick T. Wallace, "The Bar Banquets," in *The Bench and Bar of Cleveland,* ed. James Harrison Kennedy and Wilson M. Day (Cleveland: Cleveland Printing & Publishing Co., 1889), 196–201.

14. Van Aken, *Buckeye Barristers,* 6; Ohio State Bar Association, *Report of the Convention, Held at Cleveland, July 8th and 9th, 1880, for the Purpose of Forming a State Bar Association* (Cleveland: Home Companion Publishing Co., 1880), 3, 36, 39–40.

15. E. L. Campbell, *The Science of Law According to the American Theory of Government* (Jersey City, NJ: Frederick D. Linn, 1887), 6; Howard Schweber, "The 'Science' of Legal Science: The Model of the Natural Sciences in Nineteenth-Century American Legal Education," *Law and History Review* 17 (Fall 1999): 421–66; Friedman, *American Law,* 467–69; Robert Stevens, *Law School: Legal Education in America from the 1850s to the 1980s* (Chapel Hill: University of North Carolina Press, 1983), 35–37, 51–55; Ohio State Bar Association, *Report of the Convention,* 53.

16. Ohio State Bar Association, *Report of the Convention,* 37–39.

17. Ibid., 40–44.

18. Although more than four hundred lawyers showed up for the meeting, only 164 were accredited delegates of local bar associations. The convention also granted delegate privileges to all judges present. Van Aken, *Buckeye Barristers,* 13.

19. Ibid., 14; Ohio State Bar Association, *Report of the Convention,* 10.

20. Van Aken, *Buckeye Barristers,* 14–17.

21. Ohio State Bar Association, *Report of the Convention,* 64–65.

22. Ibid., 66.

23. *PD,* 18 July 1871; Ohio State Bar Association, *Report of the Convention,* 66–70.

24. Technically, the right to a new trial of the facts as well as the law applied not in equity (chancery) cases, but in cases in which the appellant had not had a right to trial by jury. While that rule precluded trials *de novo* in some equity cases, it meant that most if not all of the cases that did get retried on appeal were equitable in nature. Silas A. Harris, *Appellate Courts and Appellate Procedure in Ohio* (Baltimore: Johns Hopkins University Press, 1933), 144–45.

25. Ohio State Bar Association, *Report of the Convention,* 71.

26. Ohio State Bar Association, *Proceedings of Adjourned Meeting,* 13–17.

27. A special committee, including Ranney, composed a memorial to the General Assembly in support of the amendment. The memorial is at ibid., 32–44. Introduced as S.J.R. 77, the amendment was referred to, but not reported out by, the senate judiciary committee.

28. Ibid., 30, 45–47.

29. Ibid., 80, 83–84, 86.

30. Ibid., 99–102; Charles W. Eliot, "What Is a Liberal Education?" *Century Illustrated Magazine* 28 (June 1884): 203–12; William G. Sumner, "Our Colleges before the Country," *Princeton Review* 13 (March 1884): 139.

31. Ohio State Bar Association, *Proceedings of Adjourned Meeting,* 101, 97; Friedman, *American Law,* 228–29; Hurst, *Growth,* 254.

32. Stevens, *Law School,* 20–28, 73–84; Henry Wade Rogers, "Legal Education in the United States," *American Law School Review* 1 (Fall 1902): 14; Orth, *History of Cleveland,* 1:265; Kennedy and Day, *Bench and Bar,* 120–22; Stanley A. Samad, *A History of Legal Education in Ohio* (Akron: [University of Akron], 1972) (bound typescript), 180–81.

33. C. H. Cramer, *The Law School at Case Western Reserve University: A History, 1892–1977* (Cleveland: The Law School at Case Western Reserve University, 1977), 19, 51–52, 121–22; "Lake Erie School of Law," in *The Encyclopedia of Cleveland History,* ed. John J. Grabowski, http://ech.case.edu/cgi/article.pl?id=LESOL (last modified 18 July 1997).

34. For the text of the proposed amendments, see H.J.R. 97, 62d Gen. Assemb., 74 Ohio Laws 533 (1877) and *SCD,* 25 September 1879. For the votes on the amendments, see J. H. Newman, ed., *Organic Law of Ohio and Proposed Amendments or Helps to Constitution Makers* (Columbus: F. J. Heer, 1913), 172–73.

35. H.J.R. 73, 65th Gen. Assemb., 80 Ohio Laws 382 (1883); *PD,* 6 October 1883.

36. *PD,* 6 October 1883; Newman, *Organic Law,* 176.

37. Ohio State Bar Association, *Proceedings of Adjourned Meeting,* 95, 104, 106; William J. Lee, "Appellate Jurisdiction of the Courts of Appeals in Ohio," *Ohio State Law Journal* 9 (Winter 1948): 157–64.

38. Ohio State Bar Association, *Proceedings of Adjourned Meeting,* 106–7.

39. Stevens, *Law School,* 134–36; Auerbach, *Unequal Justice;* Ohio State Bar Association, *Proceedings of Adjourned Meeting,* 109.

40. Ohio State Bar Association, *Proceedings of Adjourned Meeting,* 109–12.

41. *SCD,* 5 June 1879; *Spirit of Democracy* (Woodsfield), 1 July 1879; Michael Pierce, *Striking with the Ballot: Ohio Labor and the Populist Party* (DeKalb: Northern Illinois University Press, 2010), 119–21; Michael Kazin, *A Godly Hero: The Life of William Jennings Bryan* (New York: Knopf, 2006), 20–22; *New-York Tribune,* 23 June 1892.

42. State *ex rel.* Hadden v. East Cleveland R.R., 3 Ohio Cir. Dec. 471 (8th Cir. 1891), *aff'd without report,* 27 Wkly. L. Bull. & Ohio L.J. 64 (Ohio 1892).

43. *PD,* 7 December 1891, 9 December 1891.

44. Great Lakes Vessels Online Index, Historical Collections of the Great Lakes, Bowling Green State University, http://greatlakes.bgsu.edu/vessel/search (accessed 23 August 2015).

45. Charles W. Calhoun, *From Bloody Shirt to Full Dinner Pail: The Transformation of Politics and Governance in the Gilded Age* (New York: Hill & Wang, 2010), 97; Kazin, *Godly Hero,* 55–56; Edward Stanwood, "The Democratic Predicament," *Atlantic Monthly* 95 (February 1905): 145.

BIBLIOGRAPHY

Manuscript Collections

Samuel Sullivan Cox Papers, Brown University (microfilm at Ohio Historical Society)
Joshua R. Giddings Papers, Ohio Historical Society
Peter Hitchcock Family Papers, Western Reserve Historical Society
Allen Nevins Papers, Rare Book and Manuscript Library, Columbia University Library
Charles E. Rice Collection, Ohio Historical Society
Allen G. Thurman Papers, Ohio Historical Society

Books, Articles, and Theses

Adams, Charles Collard. *Middletown Upper Houses: A History of the North Society of Middletown, Connecticut, from 1650 to 1800, with Genealogical and Biographical Chapters on Early Families and a Full Genealogy of the Ranney Family.* New York: Grafton, 1908.
Alexander, Gregory S. *Commodity and Propriety: Competing Visions of Property in American Legal Thought, 1776–1970.* Chicago: University of Chicago Press, 1997.
Allen, Austin. *Origins of the Dred Scott Case: Jacksonian Jurisprudence and the Supreme Court, 1837–1857.* Athens: University of Georgia Press, 2006.
Allitt, Patrick. *The Conservatives: Ideas and Personalities throughout American History.* New Haven, CT: Yale University Press, 2009.
Amer, Francis J. "The Growth and Development of the Ohio Judicial System." In *A History of the Courts and Lawyers of Ohio,* edited by Carrington T. Marshall, 1:181–216. New York: American Historical Society, 1934.
American Bar Association. *Report of the Second Annual Meeting of the American Bar Association Held at Saratoga Springs, New York, August 20th and 21st, 1879.* Philadelphia: E. C. Markley & Son, 1879.
Anbinder, Tyler. *Nativism and Slavery: The Northern Know Nothings and the Politics of the 1850s.* New York: Oxford University Press, 1992.
Angell, Joseph K., and Samuel Ames. *A Treatise on the Law of Private Corporations Aggregate.* 2nd ed. Boston: Charles C. Little & James Brown, 1843.
"Annual Meeting of the State Bar Association of Ohio." *Weekly Cincinnati Law Bulletin* 6 (1 August 1881): 429–38.
Ashworth, John. *"Agrarians" and "Aristocrats": Party Political Ideology in the United States, 1837–1846.* New York: Cambridge University Press, 1987.

———. *The Republic in Crisis, 1848–1861.* New York: Cambridge University Press, 2012.

Auerbach, Jerold S. *Unequal Justice: Lawyers and Social Change in Modern America.* New York: Oxford University Press, 1976.

Aumann, F. R. "The Development of the Judicial System of Ohio." *Ohio Archaeological and Historical Quarterly* 41 (April 1932): 195–236.

Baker, Jean H. *Affairs of Party: The Political Culture of Northern Democrats in the Mid-Nineteenth Century.* Ithaca, NY: Cornell University Press, 1983.

Barclay, Thomas S. *The Liberal Republican Movement in Missouri, 1865–1870.* Columbia: State Historical Society of Missouri, 1926.

Barnett, Randy E. "Whence Comes Section One? The Abolitionist Origins of the Fourteenth Amendment." *Journal of Legal Analysis* 3 (Spring 2011): 165–263.

Barry, P. *Over the Atlantic and Great Western Railway.* London: Sampson Low, Son, & Marston, 1866.

Batlan, Felice. "A Reevaluation of the New York Court of Appeals: The Home, the Market, and Labor, 1885–1905." *Law and Social Inquiry* 27 (Summer 2002): 489–528.

Bellamy, John Stark, II. *Women Behaving Badly: True Tales of Cleveland's Most Ferocious Female Killers.* Cleveland: Gray, 2005.

Benedict, Michael Les. "Laissez-Faire and Liberty: A Re-Evaluation of the Meaning and Origins of Laissez-Faire Constitutionalism." *Law and History Review* 3 (Fall 1985): 293–331.

Bennett, Smith W. "Double Liability: Ohio's Destructive Policy." *Public Policy* 9 (25 July 1903): 45–48.

Benton, Josiah Henry. *Voting in the Field: A Forgotten Chapter of the Civil War.* Boston: privately printed, 1915.

Blandin, Edwin Jay. "Rufus Percival Ranney." In *Great American Lawyers: The Lives and Influence of Judges and Lawyers Who Have Acquired Permanent National Reputation, and Have Developed the Jurisprudence of the United States: A History of the Legal Profession in America,* edited by William Draper Lewis, 6:405–51. Philadelphia: John C. Winston, 1909.

Bloomfield, Maxwell. "Law vs. Politics: The Self-Image of the American Bar (1830–1860)." *American Journal of Legal History* 12 (October 1968): 306–23.

———. "William Sampson and the Codifiers: The Roots of American Legal Reform, 1820–1830." *American Journal of Legal History* 11 (July 1967): 234–52.

Blue, Frederick J. "The Ohio Free Soilers and Problems of Factionalism." *Ohio History* 76, nos. 1–2 (Winter–Spring 1967): 17–32.

Blumberg, Phillip I. "Limited Liability and Corporate Groups." *Journal of Corporation Law* 11 (Summer 1986): 573–631.

Bogart, Ernest Ludlow. *Financial History of Ohio.* Urbana-Champaign: University of Illinois, 1912.

Boris, Eileen. *Home to Work: Motherhood and the Politics of Industrial Homework in the United States.* New York: Cambridge University Press, 1994.

Bradshaw's Railway Manual, Shareholders' Guide, and Official Directory for 1881. London: W. J. Adams & Sons, 1881.
Brandt, Nat. *The Town That Started the Civil War.* Syracuse, NY: Syracuse University Press, 1990.
Brauneis, Robert. "The First Constitutional Tort: The Remedial Revolution in Nineteenth-Century State Just Compensation Law." *Vanderbilt Law Review* 52 (January 1999): 57–141.
Brinkerhoff, Roeliff. *Recollections of a Lifetime.* Cincinnati: Robert Clarke, 1900.
Brownson, Orestes. "Introductory Statement." *Boston Quarterly Review* 3 (January 1840): 1–20.
Bureau of Railway Economics. *Railway Economics: A Collective Catalogue of Books in Fourteen American Libraries.* Chicago: University of Chicago Press, 1912.
Butler, Joseph G., Jr. *History of Youngstown and the Mahoning Valley, Ohio.* Vol. 1. Chicago: American Historical Society, 1921.
Calhoun, Charles W. *From Bloody Shirt to Full Dinner Pail: The Transformation of Politics and Governance in the Gilded Age.* New York: Hill & Wang, 2010.
Calhoun, Frederick S., ed. *Letters Received by the Attorney General, 1809–1870: Northern Law and Order.* Reel 16. Bethesda, MD: University Publications of America, 1998.
Campbell, E. L. *The Science of Law According to the American Theory of Government.* Jersey City, NJ: Frederick D. Linn, 1887.
Cardinal, Eric J. "The Ohio Democracy and the Crisis of Disunion, 1860–1861." *Ohio History* 86 (Winter 1977): 19–40.
Carey, Matthew, Jr., comp. *The Democratic Speaker's Hand-Book: Containing Every Thing Necessary for the Defense of the National Democracy in the Coming Presidential Campaign, and for the Assault of the Radical Enemies of the Country and Its Constitution.* Cincinnati: Miami Printing & Publishing Co., 1868.
Carlisle, J. G. "The Recent Election." *North American Review* 151 (December 1890): 641–49.
Carter, Judge [Alfred G. W.]. *The Old Court House: Reminiscences and Anecdotes of the Courts and Bar of Cincinnati.* Cincinnati: Peter G. Thomson, 1880.
Chandler, Alfred D., Jr. *The Visible Hand: The Managerial Revolution in American Business.* Cambridge, MA: Harvard University Press, 1977.
Chase, Salmon P. *The Salmon P. Chase Papers.* Edited by John Niven. Vol. 1. *Journals, 1829–1872.* Kent, OH: Kent State University Press, 1993.
Cheek, William, and Aimee Lee Cheek. *John Mercer Langston and the Fight for Black Freedom, 1829–65.* Urbana: University of Illinois Press, 1989.
Clonts, Forrest William. "The Political Campaign of 1875 in Ohio." *Ohio Archaeological and Historical Quarterly* 31 (January 1922): 38–97.
Coates, Jennifer. "Bourbons." In *Encyclopedia of the Reconstruction Era,* edited by Richard Zuczek, 1:98–100. Westport, CT: Greenwood, 2006.
Collins, B. W. "Economic Issues in Ohio's Politics during the Recession of 1857–1858." *Ohio History* 89 (Winter 1980): 46–64.

"The Convention—Reorganization of the Judiciary." *American Review* 2 (November 1845): 474–93.
Converse, J. O., et al. "Chardon." In *Pioneer and General History of Geauga County, with Sketches of Some of the Pioneers and Prominent Men,* 277–359. N.p.: Historical Society of Geauga County, 1880.
Copeland, Alfred Minot, ed. *"Our County and Its People": A History of Hampden County, Massachusetts.* Vol. 2. N.p.: Century Memorial, 1902.
Cornell, Saul. "The People's Constitution vs. the Lawyer's Constitution: Popular Constitutionalism and the Original Debate over Originalism." *Yale Journal of Law and the Humanities* 23 (Summer 2011): 295–337.
Cover, Robert M. *Justice Accused: Antislavery and the Judicial Process.* New Haven, CT: Yale University Press, 1975.
Cox, S. S. "Lessons of the New York City Election: III. The Democratic View." *North American Review* 143 (December 1886): 576–85.
Cramer, C. H. *Case Institute of Technology: A Centennial History, 1880–1980.* Cleveland: Case Western Reserve University, 1980.
———. *Case Western Reserve University: A History, 1826–1976.* Boston: Little, Brown, 1976.
———. *The Law School at Case Western Reserve University: A History, 1892–1977.* Cleveland: The Law School at Case Western Reserve University, 1977.
Cutler, Carroll. *A History of Western Reserve College, during Its First Half Century, 1826–1876.* Cleveland: Crocker's, 1876.
Debates of the Convention to Amend the Constitution of Pennsylvania: Convened at Harrisburg, November 12, 1872; Adjourned, November 27, to Meet at Philadelphia, January 7, 1873. 9 vols. Harrisburg, PA: Benjamin Singerly, 1873.
"Democracy—What Is It?" *United States Review* 2 (July 1853): 1–28.
Destler, Chester McArthur. *American Radicalism, 1865–1901: Essays and Documents.* 1946. Reprint, New York: Octagon, 1963.
Dexter, Franklin Bowditch. *Biographical Notices of Graduates of Yale College, Including Those Graduated in Classes Later than 1815, Who Are Not Commemorated in the Annual Obituary Records.* New Haven, CT: n.p., 1913.
Dodd, Samuel C. T. *Memoirs of S. C. T. Dodd Written for His Children and Friends, 1837–1907.* New York: Robert Grier Cooke, 1907.
Dow, Neal. *The Reminiscences of Neal Dow: Recollections of Eighty Years.* Portland, ME: Evening Express, 1898.
Dubin, Michael J. *United States Congressional Elections, 1788–1997: The Official Results of the Elections of the 1st through 105th Congresses.* Jefferson, NC: McFarland, 1998.
"The Duty of the Democratic Party." *United States Magazine and Democratic Review* 6 (November 1839): 437–41.
Earl, Robert. "Excessive Legislation." *Albany Law Journal* 57 (22 January 1898): 58–62.
———. "Gleanings from the Mohawk Courier and the Herkimer Democrat, and Some Interesting Facts of Local as Well as of General Interest, 1846–1850." In

Papers Read before the Herkimer County Historical Society during the Years 1899, 1900, 1901, to July 1, 1902, compiled by Arthur T. Smith, 2:420–29. Herkimer, NY: Citizen, 1902.

"Editorial Notes." *Magazine of Western History* 12 (June 1890): 218.

"Editorial Notes." *Magazine of Western History* 6 (September 1887): 512–13.

Eichner, Alfred S. *The Emergence of Oligopoly: Sugar Refining as a Case Study.* Baltimore: Johns Hopkins University Press, 1969.

"Election Returns, by States, Congressional Districts, and Counties." In *The Whig Almanac and United States Review for 1849*, 48–59. New York: Greeley & McElrath, 1849.

Eliot, Charles W. "What Is a Liberal Education?" *Century Illustrated Magazine* 28 (June 1884): 203–12.

Ely, James W., Jr. "Property Rights and Democracy in the American Constitutional Order." In *The Judicial Branch*, edited by Kermit L. Hall and Kevin T. McGuire, 487–513. New York: Oxford University Press, 2005.

———. "'To Pursue any Lawful Trade or Avocation': The Evolution of Unenumerated Economic Rights in the Nineteenth Century." *University of Pennsylvania Journal of Constitutional Law* 8 (September 2006): 917–55.

Everett, Edward. *Orations and Speeches on Various Occasions.* Vol. 3. Boston: Little, Brown, 1870.

Fehrenbacher, Don E. *The Dred Scott Case: Its Significance in American Law and Politics.* New York: Oxford University Press, 1978.

Fine, Sidney. *Laissez Faire and the General-Welfare State: A Study of Conflict in American Thought, 1865–1901.* Ann Arbor: University of Michigan Press, 1956.

Finkelman, Paul. *Dred Scott v. Sandford: A Brief History with Documents.* Boston: Bedford, 1997.

———. "Race, Slavery, and Law in Antebellum Ohio." In *The History of Ohio Law*, edited by Michael Les Benedict and John F. Winkler, 2:748–81. Athens: Ohio University Press, 2004.

Fish, Hamilton. Letter to James A. Hamilton, 12 September 1856. In *Fremont the Conservative Candidate: Correspondence between Hamilton Fish and J. A. Hamilton, etc.*, 1–12. [New York?]: n.p., [1856?]. https://books.google.com/books?id=GZ5cAAAAcAAJ.

Foner, Eric. "Radical Individualism in America: Revolution to Civil War." *Literature of Liberty* 1 (July–September 1978): 5–31.

Forbath, William E. *Law and the Shaping of the American Labor Movement.* Cambridge, MA: Harvard University Press, 1991.

Forty-fourth Annual Report of the President and Directors to the Stockholders of the Cleveland & Pittsburgh Railroad Company. Cleveland: J. B. Savage, 1892.

Fowler, H., reporter. *Report of the Debates and Proceedings of the Convention for the Revision of the Constitution of the State of Indiana.* 2 vols. Indianapolis: A. H. Brown, 1850.

Frederick, J. M. H., comp. *National Party Platforms of the United States, Presidential Candidates, Electoral and Popular Votes.* Akron: Werner, 1896.

French, David . "Elizur Wright, Jr., and the Emergence of Anti-Colonization Sentiments on the Connecticut Western Reserve." *Ohio History* 85 (Winter 1976): 49–66.

Friedman, Lawrence M. *A History of American Law.* 3rd ed. New York: Simon & Schuster, 2005.

"From Judicial Grant to Legislative Power: The Admiralty Clause in the Nineteenth Century." *Harvard Law Review* 67 (May 1954): 1214–37.

Gara, Larry. *The Liberty Line: The Legend of the Underground Railroad.* 1961. Reprint, Lexington: University Press of Kentucky, 1996.

Gardiner, O. C. *The Great Issue: or, The Three Presidential Candidates; Being a Brief Historical Sketch of the Free Soil Question in the United States, from the Congresses of 1774 and '87 to the Present Time.* New York: Wm. C. Bryant, 1848.

Gates, Charles Horatio. *Memorials of the Class of 1835, Harvard University.* Boston: David Clapp & Son, 1886.

Gawalt, Gerard W. *The Promise of Power: The Emergence of the Legal Profession in Massachusetts, 1760–1840.* Westport, CT: Greenwood, 1979.

Gold, David M. *Democracy in Session: A History of the Ohio General Assembly.* Athens: Ohio University Press, 2009.

———. *An Exemplary Whig: Edward Kent and the Whig Disposition in American Politics and Law.* Lanham, MD: Lexington, 2012.

———. *The Great Tea Party in the Old Northwest: State Constitutional Conventions, 1847–1851.* New Orleans: Quid Pro, 2015.

———. "Judicial Elections and Judicial Review: Testing the Shugerman Thesis." *Ohio Northern University Law Review* 40 (2013): 39–85.

Goodsell, James H., reporter. *Official Proceedings of the Democratic National Convention, Held in 1864 at Chicago.* Chicago: Times Steam Book & Job Printing, 1864.

Gordon, John Steele. "The Other Half of Standard Oil." *The American,* 29 October 2008. http://www.aei.org/publication/the-other-half-of-standard-oil/.

"Great Lakes Vessels Online Index." Historical Collections of the Great Lakes, Center for Archival Collections, Bowling Green State University. http://greatlakes.bgsu.edu/vessel/search.

Green, John P. *Fact Stranger than Fiction: Seventy-Five Years of a Busy Life, with Reminiscences of Many Great and Good Men and Women.* Cleveland: Riehl, 1920.

Guelzo, Allen C. *Fateful Lightning: A New History of the Civil War and Reconstruction.* New York: Oxford University Press, 2012.

Hamlin, Charles Eugene. *The Life and Times of Hannibal Hamlin.* Cambridge, MA: Riverside, 1899.

Hammond, Bray. *Banks and Politics in America from the Revolution to the Civil War.* Princeton, NJ: Princeton University Press, 1957.

Harris, Silas A. *Appellate Courts and Appellate Procedure in Ohio.* Baltimore: Johns Hopkins University Press, 1933.

Heaton, C. W. "The Cleveland Bar Association." In *The Bench and Bar of Cleveland,* edited by James Harrison Kennedy and Wilson M. Day, 77–80. Cleveland: Cleveland Printing & Publishing Co., 1889.

Henretta, James A. "The Strange Birth of Liberal America: Michael Hoffman and the New York Constitution of 1846." *New York History* 77 (April 1996): 151–76.
The History of Darke County, Ohio. . . . Chicago: W. H. Beers, 1880.
History of Portage County, Ohio. Chicago: Warner, Beers, 1885.
History of Trumbull and Mahoning Counties, with Illustrations and Biographical Sketches. 2 vols. Cleveland: H. Z. Williams & Bro., 1882.
Holt, Edgar Allen. "Party Politics in Ohio, 1840–1850." Pt. 1. *Ohio Archaeological and Historical Quarterly* 37 (July 1928): 439–591.
Holt, Michael F. *The Rise and Fall of the American Whig Party: Jacksonian Politics and the Onset of the Civil War.* New York: Oxford University Press, 1999.
Holzer, Harold, ed. *The Lincoln-Douglas Debates: The First Complete, Unexpurgated Text.* New York: HarperCollins, 1993.
"Hon. R. P. Ranney." Editorial. *Western Law Monthly* 1 (August 1859): 486.
"Hon. Rufus P. Ranney." *Weekly Law Bulletin and Ohio Law Journal* 26 (14 December 1891): 353–56.
Horwitz, Morton J. *The Transformation of American Law, 1780–1860.* Cambridge, MA: Harvard University Press, 1977.
Hovenkamp, Herbert J. "The Classical Corporation in American Legal Thought." *Georgetown Law Journal* 76 (June 1988): 1593–1689.
Howe, Daniel Walker. *The Political Culture of the American Whigs.* Chicago: University of Chicago Press, 1979.
———. *What Hath God Wrought: The Transformation of America, 1815–1848.* New York: Oxford University Press, 2007.
Huesemann Theodore J. "A Study of the Rhetoric in the Dennison-Ranney Debate at Tiffin, Ohio, 1859, Together with a Study of Audience Adaptation of Major Issues in the Remaining Debates, and Including the Text of the Tiffin Debate." M.A. thesis, Ohio State University, 1949.
Hungerford, Edward. *Men of Erie: A Story of Human Effort.* New York: Random House, 1946.
Huntington, C. C. "A History of Banking and Currency in Ohio before the Civil War." *Ohio Archaeological and Historical Quarterly* 24 (July 1915): 235–539.
Hurst, James Willard. *The Growth of American Law: The Law Makers.* Boston: Little, Brown, 1950.
In the Circuit Court of the United States for the Eastern Division of the Eastern Judicial District of Missouri: United States of America, Petitioner, v. Standard Oil Company of New Jersey et al., Defendants. Vol. 19, *Defendants' Exhibits.* Washington, DC: Government Printing Office, 1909.
"Incorporating the Republic: The Corporation in Antebellum Political Culture." *Harvard Law Review* 102 (June 1989): 1883–1903.
"Introductory." *Western Law Monthly* 1 (January 1859): I–IV.
J. "The National Anniversary." *Southern Quarterly Review*, n.s., 2 (September 1850): 170–91.
Jackson, Andrew. *Correspondence of Andrew Jackson.* Edited by John Spencer Bassett. Vol. 3, *1820–1828.* Washington, DC: Carnegie Institution of Washington, 1928.

Jacobs, Clyde E. *Law Writers and the Courts: The Influence of Thomas M. Cooley, Christopher G. Tiedeman, and John F. Dillon upon American Constitutional Law.* 1954. Reprint, New York: Da Capo, 1973.

Jaffa, Harry V., and Robert W. Johannsen, eds. *In the Name of the People: Speeches and Writings of Lincoln and Douglas in the Ohio Campaign of 1859.* Columbus: Ohio State University Press, 1959.

"Jefferson and Fox." *United States Magazine and Democratic Review* 27 (September 1850): 193–204.

Joblin, Maurice. *Cleveland, Past and Present: Its Representative Men. . . .* Cleveland: Fairbanks, Benedict, 1869.

Jones, Alan. "Thomas M. Cooley and 'Laissez-Faire Constitutionalism': A Reconsideration." *Journal of American History* 53 (March 1967): 751–71.

Karsten, Peter. *Heart versus Head: Judge-Made Law in Nineteenth-Century America.* Chapel Hill: University of North Carolina Press, 1997.

Kazin, Michael. *A Godly Hero: The Life of William Jennings Bryan.* New York: Knopf, 2006.

———. *The Populist Persuasion: An American History.* Rev. ed. Ithaca, NY: Cornell University Press, 1998.

Keller, Morton. *America's Three Regimes: A New Political History.* New York: Oxford University Press, 2007.

Kelley, Brooks Mather. *Yale: A History.* New Haven, CT: Yale University Press, 1974.

Kennedy, J. H. "The Bar of Ohio." Pt. 1, "Henry Clay Ranney." *Magazine of Western History* 4 (October 1886): 822–25.

Kennedy, James Harrison. *A History of the City of Cleveland: Biographical Volume.* Cleveland: Imperial Press, 1897.

Kennedy, James Harrison, and Wilson M. Day. *The Bench and Bar of Cleveland.* Cleveland: Cleveland Printing & Publishing Co., 1889.

Kens, Paul. *Justice Stephen Field: Shaping Liberty from the Gold Rush to the Gilded Age.* Lawrence: University Press of Kansas, 1997.

———. "*Lochner v. New York:* Tradition or Change in Constitutional Law?" *New York University Journal of Law and Liberty* 1 (2005): 404–31.

Kinkead, Edgar B. "A Sketch of the Supreme Court of Ohio." Pt. 3, *Green Bag* 7 (May 1895): 225–38, and pt. 4, *Green Bag* 7 (June 1895): 273–94.

Kirk, Russell. *The Conservative Mind: From Burke to Eliot.* 7th ed. Washington, DC: Regnery, 1985.

———. *John Randolph of Roanoke: A Study in American Politics, with Selected Speeches and Letters.* Chicago: Regnery, 1964.

———. *The Politics of Prudence.* 2nd ed. Wilmington, DE: ISI Books, 2004.

Klement, Frank L. *The Copperheads in the Middle West.* Chicago: University of Chicago Press, 1960.

———. *Dark Lanterns: Secret Political Societies, Conspiracies, and Treason Trials in the Civil War.* Baton Rouge: Louisiana State University Press, 1984.

———. *The Limits of Dissent: Clement L. Vallandigham and the Civil War.* Lexington: University Press of Kentucky, 1970.

Konefsky, Alfred S. "The Legal Profession: From the Revolution to the Civil War." In *The Cambridge History of Law in America*, vol. 2, *The Long Nineteenth Century (1789–1920)*, edited by Michael Grossberg and Christopher Tomlins, 68–105. New York: Cambridge University Press, 2008.

Kramer, Larry D. *The People Themselves: Popular Constitutionalism and Judicial Review.* New York: Oxford University Press, 2004.

Kulewicz, John J. "Reinventing the Governor: A History of Executive Power under Ohio Law." In *The History of Ohio Law*, edited by Michael Les Benedict and John F. Winkler, 1:139–210. Athens: Ohio University Press, 2004.

Kutler, Stanley I. *Privilege and Creative Destruction: The Charles River Bridge Case.* 1971. Reprint, Baltimore: Johns Hopkins University Press, 1990.

"Lake Erie School of Law." In *The Encyclopedia of Cleveland History*, edited by John J. Grabowski. Case Western Reserve University and the Western Reserve Historical Society. Last modified 18 July 1997. http://ech.case.edu/cgi/article.pl?id=LESOL.

Lee, William J. "Appellate Jurisdiction of the Courts of Appeals in Ohio." *Ohio State Law Journal* 9 (Winter 1948): 157–64.

Leggett, William. *A Collection of the Political Writings of William Leggett.* Edited by Theodore Sedgwick Jr. Vol. 1. New York: Taylor & Dodd, 1840.

———. *Democratick Editorials: Essays in Jacksonian Political Economy.* Compiled and edited by Lawrence H. White. Indianapolis: Liberty Press, 1984.

Leonard, Gerald. *The Invention of Party Politics: Federalism, Popular Sovereignty, and Constitutional Development in Jacksonian Illinois.* Chapel Hill: University of North Carolina Press, 2002.

———. "Party as a 'Political Safeguard of Federalism': Martin Van Buren and the Constitutional Theory of Party Politics." *Rutgers Law Review* 54 (Fall 2001): 221–81.

Levy, Leonard W. *The Law of the Commonwealth and Chief Justice Shaw.* Cambridge, MA: Harvard University Press, 1957.

Lubet, Steven. *Fugitive Justice: Runaways, Rescuers, and Slavery on Trial.* Cambridge, MA: Harvard University Press, 2010.

Mach, Thomas S. *"Gentleman George" Hunt Pendleton: Party Politics and Ideological Identity in Nineteenth-Century America.* Kent, OH: Kent State University Press, 2007.

Maciag, Drew. *Edmund Burke in America: The Contested Career of the Father of Modern Conservatism.* Ithaca, NY: Cornell University Press, 2013.

Maizlish, Stephen E. *The Triumph of Sectionalism: The Transformation of Ohio Politics, 1844–1856.* Kent, OH: Kent State University Press, 1983.

"Majority and Minority Reports of the Committee Appointed to Investigate the Cornering of Grain and Other Articles." Senate doc. no. 45. In *Documents of the Senate of the State of New York: One Hundred and Sixth Session, 1883.* Vol. 5. Albany: Weed, Parsons, 1883.

Mark, Gregory. "On Limited Liability: A Speculative Essay on Evolution and Justification." In *Transformations in American Legal History: Essays in Honor of*

Professor Morton J. Horwitz, edited by Daniel W. Hamilton and Alfred L. Brophy, 1:169–84. Cambridge, MA: Harvard Law School, 2009.

Marston, Jerrilyn. "The Creation of a Common Law Rule: The Fellow Servant Rule, 1837–1860." *University of Pennsylvania Law Review* 132 (March 1984): 579–620.

Maskell, Jack. *Expulsion, Censure, Reprimand, and Fine: Legislative Discipline in the House of Representatives.* Washington, DC: Congressional Research Service, 2016. http://www.fas.org/sgp/crs/misc/RL31382.pdf.

Maxcy, Virgil. "Mr. Maxcy's Oration." *Examiner, and Journal of Political Economy* 1 (30 October 1833): 99–104.

McAfee, Ward M. *Religion, Race, and Reconstruction: The Public School in the Politics of the 1870s.* Albany: State University of New York Press, 1998.

McCurdy, Charles W. *The Anti-Rent Era in New York Law and Politics, 1839–1865.* Chapel Hill: University of North Carolina Press, 2001.

McDougall, Walter A. *Throes of Democracy: The American Civil War Era, 1829–1877.* New York: Harper, 2008.

McGrane, Reginald C. *William Allen: A Study in Western Democracy.* Columbus: Ohio State Archaeological and Historical Society, 1925.

McKitrick, Eric L. *Andrew Johnson and Reconstruction.* Chicago: University of Chicago Press, 1960.

Melhorn, Donald F., Jr. *Lest We Be Marshall'd: Judicial Power and Politics in Ohio, 1806–1812.* Akron: University of Akron Press, 2003.

Memorial Record of the County of Cuyahoga and City of Cleveland, Ohio. Chicago: Lewis, 1894.

Mensel, Robert E. "'Privilege against Public Right': A Reappraisal of the Charles River Bridge Case." *Duquesne Law Review* 33 (Fall 1994): 1–38.

Merrill, Horace Samuel. *Bourbon Democracy of the Middle West, 1865–1896.* Baton Rouge: Louisiana State University Press, 1953.

Meyers, Marvin. *The Jacksonian Persuasion: Politics and Belief.* New York: Vintage, 1960.

Middleton, Stephen. *The Black Laws: Race and the Legal Process in Early Ohio.* Athens: Ohio University Press, 2005.

Miller, Perry. "The Common Law and Codification in Jacksonian America." *Proceedings of the American Philosophical Society* 103 (June 1959): 463–68.

Muller, Jerry Z., ed. *Conservatism: An Anthology of Social and Political Thought from David Hume to the Present.* Princeton, NJ: Princeton University Press, 1997.

Munroe, John A. *History of Delaware.* 5th ed. Newark: University of Delaware Press, 2006.

Myers, William Starr. *The Self-Reconstruction of Maryland, 1864–1867.* Baltimore: Johns Hopkins University Press, 1909.

Nelson, Caleb. "A Re-evaluation of Scholarly Explanations for the Rise of the Elective Judiciary in Antebellum America." *American Journal of Legal History* 37 (April 1993): 190–224.

Nevins, Allan. *Study in Power: John D. Rockefeller, Industrialist and Philanthropist.* 2 vols. New York: Charles Scribner's Sons, 1953.

Newman, J. H., ed. *Organic Law of Ohio and Proposed Amendments or Helps to Constitution Makers.* Columbus: F. J. Heer, 1913.

Norton, Charles Ledyard. *Political Americanisms: A Glossary of Terms and Phrases Current at Different Periods in American Politics.* New York: Longmans, Green, 1890.

Office of the Clerk, U.S. House of Representatives. *Biographical Directory of the United States Congress, 1774–Present.* http://bioguide.congress.gov.

Ohio State Bar Association. *Proceedings of Adjourned Meeting of the Association, Held at the City of Columbus on the 28th and 29th of December, 1880, and of the Annual Meeting of the Association held at the City of Toledo, on the 20th and 21st days of July, 1881.* Columbus: Lord & Bowman, 1881.

———. *Report of the Convention, Held at Cleveland, July 8th and 9th, 1880, for the Purpose of Forming a State Bar Association.* Cleveland: Home Companion Publishing Co., 1880.

———. *Proceedings of the Thirty-Fifth Annual Session of the Association Held at Cedar Point, Ohio, July 7, 8, and 9, 1914.* Cleveland: Evangelical Press, 1914.

Ohio State Board of Agriculture. *Thirtieth Annual Report of the Ohio State Board of Agriculture, with an Abstract of the Proceedings of the County Agricultural Societies, to the General Assembly of Ohio, for the Year 1875.* Columbus: Nevins & Myers, 1876.

Ohio State Board of Centennial Managers. *Final Report of the Ohio State Board of Centennial Managers to the General Assembly of the State of Ohio.* Columbus: Nevins & Meyers, 1877.

"Opinions of the Council of Three: Political Bigotry—Conservatism—Radicalism." *American Review* 6 (September 1847): 242–45.

Orth, Samuel P. *A History of Cleveland, Ohio.* 3 vols. Chicago: S. J. Clarke, 1910.

O'Sullivan, John L. "Introduction." *United States Magazine and Democratic Review* 1 (October 1837): 1–15.

Parrington, Vernon L. *The Beginnings of Critical Realism in America, 1860–1920,* vol. 3 of *Main Currents in American Thought.* New York: Harcourt, Brace & World, 1930.

Parsons, R. C. "Franklin T. Backus." *Magazine of Western History* 3 (November 1885): 8–15.

Pierce, Michael. *Striking with the Ballot: Ohio Labor and the Populist Party.* DeKalb: Northern Illinois University Press, 2010.

Pixton, John E., Jr. "Faith vs. Economics: The Marietta and Cincinnati Railroad, 1845–1883." *Ohio Historical Quarterly* 66 (January 1957): 1–10.

Poor, Henry V. *Manual of the Railroads of the United States, for 1868–69. . . .* New York: H. V. & H. W. Poor, 1868.

Porter, George H. *Ohio Politics during the Civil War Period.* New York: Columbia University, 1911.

Proceedings of the National Union Convention, Held at Philadelphia, August 14, 1866. Washington, DC: National Union Executive Committee, 1866.

Provenzo, Eugene F., Jr. *Culture as Curriculum: Education and the International Expositions (1876–1904).* New York: Peter Lang, 2012.
"Radicalism." *United States Magazine and Democratic Review* 3 (October 1838): 99–111.
"Radicalism." *United States Magazine and Democratic Review* 25 (September 1849): 204–8.
Ranney, Rufus P. *The Proper Method of Counting the Electoral Vote.* New York: D. Appleton, 1877.
———. *Speech of Hon. Rufus P. Ranney, Delivered at Mansfield, Ohio, Aug. 6, 1867.* Columbus: The Crisis, 1867.
Redfield, Isaac F. *The Law of Railways.* 4th ed. Vol. 1. Boston: Little, Brown, 1869.
Reemelin, Charles. *Treatise on Politics As a Science.* Cincinnati: Robert Clarke, 1875.
Reid, John Phillip. "Beneath the Titans." *New York University Law Review* 70 (June 1995): 653–76.
Remini, Robert V. *Andrew Jackson and the Course of American Democracy, 1833–1845.* New York: Harper & Row, 1984.
———. *Andrew Jackson and the Course of American Empire, 1767–1821.* New York: Harper & Row, 1977.
———. *Andrew Jackson and the Course of American Freedom, 1822–1832.* New York: Harper & Row, 1981.
Report of the Select Committee to Investigate the Alleged Credit Mobilier Bribery, Made to the House of Representatives, February 18, 1873. Washington, DC: Government Printing Office, 1873.
"Responsibility of the Ballot Box: With an Illustration." *American Review* 4 (November 1846): 435–46.
Rhodes, James Ford. *History of the United States from the Compromise of 1850.* Vol. 2, *1854–1860.* 1892. Reprint, New York: Macmillan, 1900.
Rice, Harvey. *Sketches of Western Life.* Boston: Lee & Shepard, 1887.
Richardson, James D., comp. *A Compilation of the Messages and Papers of the Presidents, 1789–1897.* Vol. 2. Washington, DC: Government Printing Office, 1900.
[Riddle, Albert G.]. *Bart Ridgeley: A Story of Northern Ohio.* Boston: Nichols & Hall, 1873.
Riddle, A. G. *The Life of Benjamin F. Wade.* Cleveland: Williams, 1888.
Robinson, Frederick. *An Oration Delivered before the Trades Union of Boston and Vicinity, on Fort Hill, Boston, on the Fifty-eighth Anniversary of American Independence.* Boston: Charles Douglas, 1834.
Rogers, Henry Wade. "Legal Education in the United States." *American Law School Review* 1 (Fall 1902): 13–16.
Rose, W. R. "Noted Criminal and Other Cases." In *The Bench and Bar of Cleveland,* edited by James Harrison Kennedy and Wilson M. Day, 93–113. Cleveland: Cleveland Printing & Publishing Co., 1889.
Roseboom, Eugene H. *The Civil War Era, 1850–1873.* Vol. 4 of *The History of the State of Ohio,* edited by Carl Wittke. Columbus: Ohio State Archaeological & Historical Society, 1944.

Ross, Earle Dudley. *The Liberal Republican Movement.* New York: Henry Holt, 1919.
Rossiter, Clinton. *Conservatism in America: The Thankless Persuasion.* 2nd ed., rev. New York: Vintage, 1962.
Rucker, Robert D. "The Right to Ignore the Law: Constitutional Entitlement versus Judicial Interpretation." *Valparaiso University Law Review* 33 (Spring 1999): 449–83.
Ryan, Daniel J. *History of Ohio: The Rise and Progress of an American State.* Vol. 4. New York: Century History Co., 1912.
Ryan, Mary P. *Civic Wars: Democracy and Public Life in the American City during the Nineteenth Century.* Berkeley: University of California Press, 1997.
Samad, Stanley A. *A History of Legal Education in Ohio.* Akron: [University of Akron], 1972. Bound typescript.
Schlesinger, Arthur M., Jr. *The Age of Jackson.* Boston: Little, Brown, 1945.
Schwartz, Gary T. "The Character of Early American Tort Law." *UCLA Law Review* 36 (April 1989): 641–718.
Schweber, Howard. "The 'Science' of Legal Science: The Model of the Natural Sciences in Nineteenth-Century American Legal Education." *Law and History Review* 17 (Fall 1999): 421–66.
Seager, Henry R., and Charles A. Gulick Jr. *Trust and Corporation Problems.* New York: Harper & Bros., 1929.
Severance, Ben H. *Tennessee's Radical Army: The State Guard and Its Role in Reconstruction, 1867–1869.* Knoxville: University of Tennessee Press, 2005.
Seward, William H. *The Works of William H. Seward.* Edited by George E. Baker. Vol. 3. New York: Redfield, 1853.
Shade, William G. *Banks or No Banks: The Money Issue in Western Politics, 1832–1865.* Detroit: Wayne State University Press, 1972.
Shipherd, Jacob R., comp. *History of the Oberlin-Wellington Rescue.* Boston: John P. Jewett, 1859.
Shugerman, Jed Handelsman. "The Floodgates of Strict Liability: Bursting Reservoirs and the Adoption of *Fletcher v. Rylands* in the Gilded Age." *Yale Law Journal* 110 (November 2000): 333–77.
———. *The People's Courts: Pursuing Judicial Independence in America.* Cambridge, MA: Harvard University Press, 2012.
Silbey, Joel H. *A Respectable Minority: The Democratic Party in the Civil War Era, 1860–1868.* New York: Norton, 1977.
Slap, Andrew L. *The Doom of Reconstruction: The Liberal Republicans in the Civil War Era.* New York: Fordham University Press, 2006.
Smith, Adam I. P. "Conservatism, Transformation, and the War for the Union." In *Reconfiguring the Union: Civil War Transformations,* edited by Iwan W. Morgan and Philip John Davies, 41–58. New York: Palgrave Macmillan, 2013.
Smith, Charles W. *Roger B. Taney: Jacksonian Jurist.* Chapel Hill: University of North Carolina Press, 1936.
Smith, Christian. "Introduction: Rethinking the Secularization of American Public Life." In *The Secular Revolution: Power, Interests, and Conflict in the*

Secularization of American Public Life, edited by Christian Smith, 1–96. Berkeley: University of California Press, 2003.

Smith, J. V., reporter. *Report of the Debates and Proceedings of the Convention for the Revision of the Constitution of the State of Ohio.* 2 vols. Columbus: S. Medary, 1851.

Smith, Joseph P., ed. *History of the Republican Party in Ohio.* 2 vols. Chicago: Lewis, 1898.

Smith, S. Winifred. "Thomas W. Bartley." In *Governors of Ohio,* 2nd ed., 50–52. Columbus: Ohio Historical Society, 1969.

"Societies and Their Proceedings." *New-England Historical and Genealogical Register* 41 (October 1887): 415–18.

[Spooner, Walter W.], ed. *The Cyclopædia of Temperance and Prohibition: A Reference Book of Facts, Statistics, and General Information on All Phases of the Drink Question, the Temperance Movement and the Prohibition Agitation.* New York: Funk & Wagnalls, 1891.

Sproat, John G. *"The Best Men": Liberal Reformers in the Gilded Age.* New York: Oxford University Press, 1968.

Stampp, Kenneth M. *America in 1857: A Nation on the Brink.* New York: Oxford University Press, 1990.

Stanwood, Edward. "The Democratic Predicament." *Atlantic Monthly* 95 (February 1905): 145–54.

Steinglass, Steven H., and Gino J. Scarselli. *The Ohio State Constitution: A Reference Guide.* Westport, CT: Praeger, 2004.

Stevens, Robert. *Law School: Legal Education in America from the 1850s to the 1980s.* Chapel Hill: University of North Carolina Press, 1983.

Stevens, William S., ed. *Industrial Combinations and Trusts.* New York: Macmillan, 1922.

Still, John S. "William Dennison, Jr." In *Governors of Ohio,* 2nd ed., 76–79. Columbus: Ohio Historical Society, 1969.

Sumner, William G. "Our Colleges before the Country." *Princeton Review* 13 (March 1884): 127–40.

Sykes, Alan. *The Rise and Fall of British Liberalism, 1776–1988.* London: Longman, 1997.

Tarbell, Ida M. *The History of the Standard Oil Company.* 2 vols. New York: McClure, Phillips, 1904.

Tarrant, Catherine M. "To 'insure domestic Tranquility': Congress and the Law of Seditious Conspiracy, 1859–1861." *American Journal of Legal History* 15 (April 1971): 107–23.

Terzian, Barbara A. "Ohio's Constitutional Conventions and Constitutions." In *The History of Ohio Law,* edited by Michael Les Benedict and John F. Winkler, 1:40–87. Athens: Ohio University Press, 2004.

Towne, Stephen E. *Surveillance and Spies in the Civil War: Exposing Confederate Conspiracies in America's Heartland.* Athens: Ohio University Press, 2015.

Trefousse, H. L. *Benjamin Franklin Wade: Radical Republican from Ohio.* New York: Twayne, 1963.

Troup, James O. Letter to the editor. In "The Scintilla Rule—A Symposium." *Western Reserve Law Journal* 4 (December 1898): 169–75.

Twiss, Benjamin R. *Lawyers and the Constitution: How Laissez Faire Came to the Supreme Court.* Princeton, NJ: Princeton University Press, 1942.

Ullery, Jacob G., comp. *Men of Vermont: An Illustrated Biographical History of Vermonters and Sons of Vermont.* Brattleboro, VT: Transcript, 1894.

United States Senate. "Expulsion and Censure." Accessed 28 July 2013. http://www.senate.gov/artandhistory/history/common/briefing/Expulsion_Censure.htm.

Vallandigham, Clement L. *Speeches, Arguments, Addresses, and Letters of Clement L. Vallandigham.* New York: J. Walter, 1864.

Van Aken, William R. *Buckeye Barristers: A Centennial History of the Ohio State Bar Association.* Columbus: Ohio State Bar Association, 1980.

W. A. B. "Revolution in England." *United States Magazine and Democratic Review* 16 (February 1845): 112–120.

Wagstaff, Thomas. "The Arm-in-Arm Convention." *Civil War History* 14 (June 1968): 101–19.

Wakeman, George, reporter. *Official Proceedings of the National Democratic Convention, Held at New York, July 4–9, 1868.* Boston: Rockwell & Rollins, 1868.

Walker, Robert J. *An Appeal for the Union: Letter from the Hon. Robert J. Walker.* New York: John F. Trow, 1856. http://hdl.handle.net/2027/umn.31951001786773v.

Wallace, Frederick T. "The Bar Banquets." In *The Bench and Bar of Cleveland,* edited by James Harrison Kennedy and Wilson M. Day, 176–241. Cleveland: Cleveland Printing & Publishing Co., 1889.

———. "Judge Rufus P. Ranney." *Western Reserve Law Journal* 1 (February 1895): 1–4.

———. *Men and Events of Half a Century.* Cleveland: Evangelical Association, 1882.

Warner, Lucien C., and Josephine Genung Nichols, comps. *The Descendants of Andrew Warner.* New Haven, CT: Tuttle, Morehouse & Taylor, 1919.

Warren, Charles. *The Supreme Court in United States History.* Vol. 3. Boston: Little, Brown, 1922.

Watson, Harry L. *Liberty and Power: The Politics of Jacksonian America.* Rev. ed. New York: Hill & Wang, 2006.

———. "The Venturous Conservative Reconsidered: Social History and Political Culture in the Market Revolution." *Reviews in American History* 22 (December 1994): 732–40.

Weber, Jennifer L. *Copperheads: The Rise and Fall of Lincoln's Opponents in the North.* New York: Oxford University Press, 2006.

Wells, Harwell. "The Rise of the Close Corporation and the Making of Corporation Law." *Berkeley Business Law Journal* 5 (September 2008): 263–316.

Welter, Rush. *The Mind of America, 1820–1860.* New York: Columbia University Press, 1975.

Wescott, Richard R. *New Men, New Issues: The Formation of the Republican Party in Maine.* Portland: Maine Historical Society, 1986.

"The Whig Party, Its Positions, and Duties." *American Review* 2 (December 1845): 547–60.

Whittaker, W. H. "Street Railways and Their Relation to Highways." *American Law Review* 15 (June 1881): 390–404.

Whittington, Keith E. *Political Foundations of Judicial Supremacy: The Presidency, the Supreme Court, and Constitutional Leadership in U.S. History.* Princeton, NJ: Princeton University Press, 2007.

Whittlesey, Charles. "Sixth Annual Meeting—Report of the President." Tract 21. Cleveland: Western Reserve and Northern Ohio Historical Society (May 1874).

Wiebe, Robert H. *The Search for Order, 1877–1920.* New York: Hill & Wang, 1967.

Wiecek, William M. *The Lost World of Classical Legal Thought: Law and Ideology in America, 1886–1937.* New York: Oxford University Press, 1998.

Wilentz, Sean. *The Rise of American Democracy: Jefferson to Lincoln.* New York: Norton, 2005.

Williams, William W. *History of Ashtabula County, Ohio, with Illustrations and Biographical Sketches of Its Pioneers and Most Prominent Men.* 1878. Reprint, Evansville, IN: Unigraphics, 1974.

Williamson, S. E. "Memorial of Rufus P. Ranney." In Ohio State Bar Association, *Proceedings of the Annual Meeting of the Association, Held at Put-in-Bay, on July 13, 14 and 15, 1892.* Akron: Werner Ptg. & Lith. Co., 1892.

Wilson, Clyde N. "The Jeffersonian Conservative Tradition." *Modern Age* 14 (Winter 1969–70): 36–48.

Wing, Talcott E., ed. *History of Monroe County, Michigan.* New York: Munsell, 1890.

Winkle, Kenneth J. "Ohio's Informal Polling Place: Nineteenth-Century Suffrage in Theory and Practice." In *The Pursuit of Public Power: Political Culture in Ohio, 1787–1861,* edited by Jeffrey P. Brown and Andrew R. L. Cayton, 169–184. Kent, OH: Kent State University Press, 1994.

———. *The Politics of Community: Migration and Politics in Antebellum Ohio.* New York: Cambridge University Press, 1988.

Wright, George B. *Annual Report of the Commissioner of Railroads and Telegraphs, for the Year 1870.* Vol. 1. Columbus: Nevins & Myers, 1870.

Wright, John C. *Reports of Cases at Law and in Chancery, Decided by the Supreme Court of Ohio, during the Years 1831, 1832, 1833, 1834: Taken from Original Minutes.* Columbus: Isaac N. Whiting, 1835.

INDEX

Lightning Source UK Ltd.
Milton Keynes UK
UKHW040528190123
415347UK00036B/33

9 780821 422342